Playing on the Edge

Playing on the Edge

Sadomasochism, Risk, and Intimacy

Staci Newmahr

Indiana University Press
Bloomington and Indianapolis

This book is a publication of

Indiana University Press
601 North Morton Street
Bloomington, Indiana 47404-3797 USA

iupress.indiana.edu

Telephone orders 800-842-6796
Fax orders 812-855-7931
Orders by e-mail iuporder@indiana.edu

♾ The paper used in this publication meets the minimum requirements of the American National Standard for Information Sciences—Permanence of Paper for Printed Library Materials, ANSI Z39.48-1992.

Manufactured in the United States of America

Library of Congress Cataloging-in-Publication Data

Newmahr, Staci.
Playing on the edge : sadomasochism, risk, and intimacy / Staci Newmahr.
p. cm.
Includes bibliographical references and index.
ISBN 978-0-253-35597-3 (cloth : alk. paper) — ISBN 978-0-253-22285-5 (pbk. : alk. paper)
1. Sadomasochism. 2. Sexual dominance and submission. 3. Sadomasochists—Case studies.
I. Title.
HQ79.N49 2011
306.77'5—dc22
2010035371

1 2 3 4 5 16 15 14 13 12 11

Portions of earlier versions of this work have appeared in *Journal of Contemporary Ethnography* 37 (2008), *Symbolic Interaction* 33 (3) (2010), and *Qualitative Sociology* 33 (3), (2010). All works were written by Staci Newmahr and reprinted with permission of Sage Publications, University of California Press, and Springer, respectively.

For my mother, Irene,
who taught me to be comfortable with risk,
for Riordan,
whom I hope to teach the same,
and for Paul,
for whom there simply are no words great enough.

Contents

Acknowledgments

Many open-minded and generous people took a leap on this project with me, or for me. I appreciate their adventurousness and their confidence.

I am ineffably grateful to Judy Tanur, my mentor and friend. Her encouragement and support energized this project from the moment of its inception over a decade ago until the last word was written. My thinking and my writing have benefited tremendously from her steadfast commitments to theoretical precision and methodological rigor.

Aisha Khan's unflinching support for this project was a source of inspiration and sustenance from the very beginning. Our conversations about the scene were always exciting and intellectually catalytic. I thank her for her brilliant and contagious energy, and for helping me to trust myself.

I thank Javier Auyero, for breathing life into ethnography in our department, for tirelessly reading draft after draft of my work, and for never pulling his punches. I appreciate also the efforts of Naomi Rosenthal, in finding entry points into this project, in challenging me to think differently, and in letting me know what I was up against. I owe thanks also to Erich Goode, Marc Olshan, and Bob Zussman, all of whom helped hone my thinking in the early stages of this project.

My colleagues at Buffalo State College have been supportive from the moment I arrived there. Gerhard Falk and Tom Weinberg encouraged me and regularly expressed confidence in the book. Virginia Grabiner read excerpts and provided me with helpful responses, and Cheryl Albers graciously provided valuable feedback on a tricky chapter in the final hour. Finally, I am deeply indebted to Allen Shelton for his close and keen readings of pieces of this work, for inspiring me anew in each and every conversation, and for his significant emotional and intellectual support as the book came into being.

Three readers for Indiana University Press offered me wonderfully thoughtful and constructive reviews. Patricia Adler, Leon Anderson, and Katherine Frank provided enthusiastic and meaningful support and made insightful contributions to this work. I owe special thanks to Katherine Frank, whose own work helped me think this one possible, and whose incisive feedback has made it much, much stronger than it would have been otherwise. I would also like to thank Rebecca Tolen and Peter Froehlich at Indiana University Press for their support.

Fieldwork is often an emotionally intense experience, and this project brought with it particular intensities. Over the past ten years I relied heavily on my friends, all of whom shouldered the burdens I placed on them with grace and astounding generosity. They engaged with me in countless conversations about the concepts in this book, about the scene, and about my play and my responses to it. They helped in dozens of incredibly valuable practical ways as well. I cannot overstate the ways in which these relationships sustained me while I was working on this book. Among these are Regina Alandy, Katherine Cherbas, Natasha Khost, and Jaquelyn Lacovara (who may have forgotten her multi-leveled role in this project, but I have not). I thank my brother, Todd Newmahr, for his enthusiasm for my work, and for always being there when I needed him.

For their time, attention, and candid feedback on various pieces of this work, I would also like to thank Martin Barron, Tarek Elnicklawy, Sue Ferziger, Michelle Fox, Paul Fuller, Crystal Galloway, John Galloway, Tor Gunston, Mary Link Habib, Jacob Heller, Kerri Kennedy, Tobin Kramer, Jason Kress, Beth Kress, Jason Lampert, Jon Lehrer, Meitar "Maymay" Moscovitz, Paul Park, Asaf Ronen, Jason Salomone, Natasha Schreib, and Robin Wetherbee.

I suspect that most ethnographers would agree on the futility of trying to express the depth of appreciation for the collaborative relationship that is ethnographic research. I am profoundly indebted to the members of the SM community in Caeden. I thank each one of them for their welcome, their trust, and their intensity.

This work is in part the result of the generosity of the twenty members of the community who spent so many hours talking with me, sharing the stories of their lives, their thoughts and fears, and their answers to my seemingly endless questions. I cannot thank them enough for their openness and their time.

To those who trusted me enough to play, risk, and trust with me—most especially Bo, Dov, Jason, and Mike—I am deeply grateful. Without them, this book would not exist; my journey would not have been what it was and I would not be who I have become.

My partner, Paul Kress, lived and breathed this project alongside me. An inclusive list of his contributions to this project would require a chapter on its own. I thank him for the self-confidence and generosity of spirit that rendered my pursuit of this project possible in the first place. I thank him for his patience with near-constant conversation about my work for such a very, very long time, for reading each draft of everything so thoughtfully, and for his superb skill in complicating questions and in clarifying muddiness. I thank him also for his unwavering encouragement of this project and of me, for his rock-solid optimism and his spirit of adventure.

There are two other people whom I cannot adequately thank, for their positively brilliant insights, provocative questions, loyal friendship, and the fortification that only hearty laughter can provide. It is impossible to extricate my thinking from theirs; this book was, in too many ways to count and ways impossible for anyone else to understand, also written by Mike and Maymay.

Playing on the Edge

Introduction

The warehouses on the street had been closed for hours. Taxis thumped down the pothole-plagued city block. Rap music blasted from a nearby nightclub. I locked my Club onto the steering wheel of my car, double-checked the parking sign, and headed down the street. The pavement glittered under my boots, embedded glass reflecting the reassuring lamplight in this downtown district. Halfway down the block, I stopped at a brick wall. I parted the dirty clear plastic vertical blinds that obscured the threshold, and walked inside. A tall, thin, disheveled man was perched on a stool just inside the unlabeled doorway. He nodded at me as I entered.

The walls were gray concrete. Black stage lights lined the floor of the dark hallway. High along one wall, swirly, high-school girl handwriting welcomed me to "The Playground" in enthusiastic romantic loops. The bass of techno music lent rhythm to the muffled sound of party chatter below. I walked down the winding stairway at the end of the hall. Lorraine sat at the window before the heavy steel entrance to the club. Recognizing me, she smiled warmly and said, "Free for the lady."

I opened the door. The smell of chocolate and freshly made waffles invited me inside. As soon as I entered the room, Jacob saw me from across the soda-fountain counter and waved.

"Dakota!" he called to me.

I waved and headed over to him, past the old-fashioned stools that lined the counter, dropping my bag in a booth along the way. He gave me a hefty hug hello. I climbed onto the sparkly red vinyl seat that threatened to spin out from under me as I tried to sit down. Across from us, handwritten signs offered us milkshakes, Belgian waffles, and nachos.

Jacob looked at me with a solemn expression on his rather large and jowly face. He has kind, intelligent eyes that often sparkle with mischief, but tonight he said seriously, "Dakota, do you know why Jesus died on the cross?"

Surprised, I started to stammer out an answer. "Well . . . sure, I guess . . . I mean, the story goes . . ."

Jacob grinned. "He forgot his safeword."

I laughed and playfully punched him in the arm. The club was noisy, filled with the sounds of chatter and hitting. Slaps, groans, grunts, and screams punctuated the music.

Someone came up behind us, put his hand on the back of my neck, and said hello. I recognized Russ's voice and turned to greet him. Russ is in his mid-forties, a tall, heavy man with a brown goatee. His dark straight hair hung freely down to his waist tonight. He wore black jeans, a black long-sleeved shirt and black sneakers. He looked good in the black light; he was always one of the few people at the club who was not shrouded in a blanket of glowing white lint.

Russ told me that there had been a newbie meeting tonight and some of the newbies had come to the club for the outing afterward. I gestured toward two people I hadn't seen before, and he confirmed: Joey, a muscular, young guy with a buzz cut, who looked very much out of place here, and a barely twenty-something woman who was calling herself Goddess Indigo.

I laughed. "Straight out of the chatrooms, huh?"

"Yeah, AOL probably. I tell ya . . ." Russ trailed off, shaking his head in vague irritation.

I excused myself and headed past the soda counter and the row of diner-style booths that lined the opposite wall. In the main room, Schuyler was perched in a bondage chair along the right wall. She sat spread-eagled, one leg on each plank, bunching up the hem of her jeans so that she could shackle her own ankle to one of the cuffs.

"I can reach, I told you!" she laughed at Liam, who was giggling beside her.

I stopped and cocked my head at the two of them. Schuyler kept laughing, and Liam threw his arms around me in a hug and lifted me several inches off of the ground. We chatted for a few minutes, and then I walked up the stairs on the opposite side of the room. The chocolatey waffle smell faded into stale smoke and too much perfume as I stepped onto the balcony. Upstairs, I found myself directly facing the naked buttocks of a skinny elderly man. He was draped over the lap of a very large redheaded woman wearing a corset shirt and jeans. I did not know either of them. I glanced at the black bistro tables scattered about the balcony. No one else was there.

The music changed, to alternative New-Agey rock . . . B-tribe maybe. I wandered back downstairs to check out the back room. It smelled of fresh smoke and old sweat. Yellowish light glowed from the naked bulbs that dotted the concrete walls. As I rounded the corner into the back room, I heard someone say my name. I turned, and saw that it was Ernie. At over six feet tall and relatively fit, with an Irish, blue-collar savvy all over his face, Ernie likely struck an imposing figure outside the club. At the moment, he was locked inside a human-sized birdcage, clad in white cotton briefs, his arms hanging limply at his side. We chatted for a few minutes before I wandered back to the other room.

Trey had arrived, carrying a black leather toy bag that looked big enough to carry a large dog. Nearly forty, Trey is a big guy, tall and broad—an unkempt man with glasses and a frizzy graying ponytail. Trey was talking to Sam, who, at nineteen, was likely the youngest person there. He is slight of build, with milk-white skin and a head full of impossibly curly red hair. I walked over to say hello. After hugs, we moved to a booth and sat beside Jill.

In what seemed like record time, Trey managed to steer the conversation toward the topic of rope. I asked how I might tie my shoelaces so that they won't come undone every two blocks. Needing no additional inspiration, Trey extracted rope from his bag and asked for my wrists. Not particularly liking the idea of rope around my wrists, but curious about the hoopla about it, I obliged and extended my arms across the table.

He wrapped my wrists, explaining to Jill and Sam what he was doing at each step. As he worked, the impromptu demo grew more involved. He wrapped it underneath my thighs and around my back. Someone asked if I was able to stand. I slid out of the booth, with my arms bound across my torso. At least two people asked whether my nose itched.

I lifted my arms and scratched my suddenly itchy nose. Trey interpreted this as either a challenge or an invitation. He ramped up the bondage. Within about a minute, my arms were immobilized and my long hair was caught in its clip between the rope and my neck. Jill noticed and tried to help, but had trouble with it. Patrice joined the effort, and I shook my hair loose. Almost immediately, Trey grabbed it, very close to my scalp, and tugged me toward the stage. Someone laughed and called, "Have fun!"

Once on the stage, we were even more of a spectacle. I had made no secret of the fact that the particular appeal of bondage still eluded me. The onlookers shared their amusement at my predicament loudly and to raucous laughter. At some point, James, the owner of the club, joined the comedy act; he turned off the lights, announced that the club was closing, and ordered everyone out immediately. More raucous laughter.

About an hour and several positions later, I grew uncomfortable. My joints were vaguely achy. My limbs felt antsy to move. And I was bored. I told Trey I'd had enough, and he untied me quickly and easily. By then, the club was actually closing and the buzz began about who was going where to eat. Russ walked by and announced that he wasn't going out, so I hugged him good-bye. He sauntered toward the door. I leaned over to get my bag. When I stood up and turned around, I found myself face-to-chest with Joey from the newbie meeting.

Startled, I took a step back, but the booth was behind me.

Standing much too close to me, Joey said, "I liked your scene. It's good to meet people who think deviant."

I blinked at him, at a loss for words. He asked me whether I was leaving.

I heard Russ's voice before I could answer. Striding toward us, he called, "Hey, Dakota, you taking that ride?"

Puzzled, I glanced at him, and he winked. I nodded and bid Joey good-night. Russ stepped behind me as I walked away from Joey, who never returned to the club.

The National SM Community

Prior to 1971, the SM community ("the scene") in the United States was underground, and mainly gay. Heterosexual people with interest in SM likely either pursued it privately or didn't pursue it. In 1971, the first SM organization (The Eulenspiegel Society, or TES) in the country was founded in New York City, and the heterosexual SM scene was born. Three years later, the pansexual Society of Janus was founded in San Francisco. The two remain the oldest and largest SM organizations in the United States.

Founded by a heterosexual man, TES paved the way for the public pansexual SM scene in terms of both consciousness and practice. Nonetheless, the public SM scene remained male for over a decade, during which time organizations such as TES[1] functioned largely as support groups and sources of SM education.

On the East Coast during the seventies, there were two distinct SM communities—the gay male leather scene and the pansexual scene. The lesbian public SM community first took root on the West Coast when SAMOIS was formed by former Janus members in 1978. New York followed with its own lesbian SM scene in 1981.

By the end of the 1980s, women of all orientations had become more visible in the heterosexual SM scenes on both coasts. Advertisements were appearing in local papers with discreet references to SM activities, and women were obtaining information about safe places to pursue SM through phone sex lines and word of mouth. The arrival of the Internet, however, changed things significantly. For the first time, information about SM was accessible even to people who were reluctant to enter a public space and declare themselves curious. In particular, straight women and college students, underrepresented in earlier incarnations of the leather scene, now had easy access to SM organizations. Across the United States and Europe today, the Internet facilitates the cultivation and perpetuation of SM communities.

Yet to date, very few people have undertaken ethnographic research in real-life pansexual SM communities. Some recent work on SM focuses on self-report psychological profiles (Donnelly and Fraser 1998; Sandnabba, Santtila, and Nordling 1999; Nordling et al. 2006). Other contemporary qualitative studies of SM-related matters draw respondents from websites and chat rooms (Cross and Matheson 2006; Langdridge and Butt 2004; Taylor 1997), in which SM "participants" may never have engaged in SM at all. This book is based on ethnographic research (and I use "ethnographic" in the way that it has historically been used in anthropology, to mean immersive, long-term, multi-sited, full participant observation) in a pansexual SM community.

The Caeden SM Community

The SM participants in this study are not merely a group of individuals who engage in SM activities, or "play."[2] In the loud, large, and bustling northeastern metropolis of Caeden,[3] "the scene" is a community unto itself. It is also connected cross-nationally to other SM scenes, reflecting a larger, national sense of community among SM participants in the United States.

Community life in the Caeden scene revolves around participation in at least one, but usually multiple, sites and venues for SM play, socialization, information-sharing, and activism. In 2002, there were at least five different SM-related formal organizations, three public play spaces, three private dungeons in which play parties were held, several informal SM-related social organizations, and a vast number of Internet discussion lists. Events included informational lectures, demonstrations and workshops, public play parties, privately hosted play parties, social lunches and dinners, organizational planning meetings, and activist fundraising benefits, as well as multi-day events that included most of these things. It is not uncommon for participants to spend nearly all of their free time in the scene in one capacity or another. This level of involvement—and the crash-burn-resurrect cycle that almost necessarily accompanies it—is the norm among core members of the community.

Within the wide array of related activities, though, the community is built around SM play interaction. Many SM participants in Caeden cannot play comfortably at home. Most are not homeowners, and many have roommates or live with family members where auditory and visual privacy is difficult to ensure. Many kinds of play require adequate space and equipment. SM clubs provide a safe and private venue for SM play. They also serve as a site of community building and sustenance.

The city of Caeden was home to two SM clubs when I began my fieldwork. One closed just after I entered the scene, leaving the other (The Playground) as the main public play space for the Caeden community. It therefore functioned as one of the primary community spaces. Between 2002 and 2006, three other SM clubs opened in the Caeden area. Despite community support and attendance, each closed within a year. The Playground had been in existence for nearly two decades. Its reputation was as a "friendly" place; the owner obeyed local public-sex ordinances and generally ran things smoothly. Women, particularly college-aged women, generally said they were more comfortable at The Playground than any other club that had come and gone in recent years.

The community mainly comprises people who are affiliated with one of two major SM organizations. One of these (Horizons) is larger, older, and less heterosexually oriented than the other (Erotic Power Players, or EPP). Membership in either organization grants insider status to would-be visitors and thus, to an important extent, sets one apart from the unknown and potentially unsafe. This is a particularly central function and objective in Horizons; the organization sponsors regular safety classes and novice meetings, and is generally viewed as the foundation of the scene. There are members of the scene who are unaffiliated, but it is difficult to become a well-established regular without forming at least social connections with members of an organization.

The size of the SM scene in Caeden varies over time and according to the definition of the scene. During my time in the field, I counted nearly two hundred people whom I saw frequently and I knew by name, and approximately another fifty whom I never met but recognized. The official membership in Horizons fluctuated between about six hundred and eight hundred people while I was a member, but most of these people were not regularly visible in the public community (which is also wider than Horizons). Among core members of the Caeden scene—for example, those who hold elected positions in the organizations or who teach SM-related classes—turnover is fairly low; when I last checked (2008), roughly sixty people who regularly participate in local organizations and events had also been involved when I joined in 2002.

Both Horizons and EPP were open to people nationwide; hence participants from other communities were often members. Additionally, because most SM organizations across the nation recognize other memberships in their benefits (such as discounted admission to events and meetings), a portion of the Horizons membership list were out-of-town memberships.

The Caeden SM Scene as Community

The esoteric knowledge of SM, including vocabulary, technique, safety issues, and national SM-community celebrities, connects SM scenes across the country. At the local level, important community ties are rooted in familiarity with Caeden scene, such as the reputations of members of the local scene and local SM history and politics. This shared knowledge overlaps with shared space. Knowledge of local play spaces is intertwined with shared experiences in those spaces, and the memories that emerge from participation in local events over time contributes further to the sense of cohesiveness. A group identity is created in the Caeden scene that stands apart from, for example, the San Francisco scene or the Denver scene.

Despite the increasing visibility of SM activity in popular culture (Weinberg and Magill 1995; Weiss 2006a), SM participants are unified further by the perception of a common enemy, given the marginal status of SM and the reality that public SM remains a mostly underground activity. In 2000, a police raid of a private party in Attleboro, Massachusetts, resulted in arrests on assault charges, despite the fact that no alleged victims pressed charges. In Caeden, under a particularly conservative mayor, The Playground was twice closed by fire marshals claiming violations of paperwork regulations. A major SM organization based in the Washington, D.C., area was forced to cancel its annual national event because the residents of the city—and the tourists who flock to the city—viewed it as an assault on the "family values" that had apparently, prior to the booking of this event, prevailed there. SM participants continue to fear damage to their personal and professional reputations, and the loss of the custody of their children, should their activities become public knowledge (see also Klein and Moser 2006).

If a community is a structure of social relations that produces collective action (Calhoun 1980), Caeden can be understood as a community on other levels as well. First, although the scene is not uniformly activist in intent, there is a vital and vocal activist contingent among its members. The ties between the Caeden scene and the National Coalition for Sexual Freedom[4] are strong, and the impact of the members of Caeden in the national leather scene is significant. The Caeden community, through discourse, interaction, and shared space, gives voice to the political activism and hence constitutes a structure of social relations that produces collective action in the conventional sense. Secondly, beyond the overt activism of the community, membership in it—and indeed engagement in play itself—can be understood as collective action, given its marginal position and the sexual-political context in which its members understand it.

Apart from these unifying characteristics of the SM community in Caeden, though, other experiences of outsiderness connect the members of this community to one another. Prior to entering the SM scene, and often before identifying an SM interest, many people in Caeden lived on social fringes for reasons that would seem to exist entirely independently of their SM interests. These sources of marginality are strikingly common in Caeden; SM identity is linked to marginality more broadly. This overarching marginal identity shapes the role of the SM community in the lives of its members, as well as the meanings they make of SM itself.

Play

Though the community holds meanings for its members that extend past SM itself, it is also built around the facilitation of, education about, and participation in SM interactions. These vary in kind, practice, and meaning. Nevertheless, play generally adheres to a particular structure, utilizes particular symbols, navigates and negotiates aspects of gender and power ideologies, and illuminates various social scripts.

In an SM context, "play" is a complex word. It references recreation and leisure and evokes a romantic sense of innocence and freedom from encumbrances. This romanticism resonates strongly for SM participants, many of whose lives outside the community reflect a worldview devoid of perceptions of obligations that govern more conventional lifestyles. From relentless adherence to unconventional career paths and work hours to the ubiquity of catastrophically messy living environments, the members of this community actively privilege leisure. Yet play is not a simple pursuit. It requires a significant amount of education, both formal and informal. It is exhausting, often physically, emotionally, and psychologically. Play encompasses a wide range of leisure activities and intimate interactions. It is a hobby and a lifestyle rife with political, social, and sexual implications. Community members often liken SM to extreme sports such as skydiving and rock climbing.

On one level, the discursive connections between SM and theater provide access to the ideological (and emotional) defense that SM is somehow not quite real. (SM interactions, for example, are also called "scenes.") On another level, for many people in this community, the fantasy element connects SM to other fantasy interests, such as science fiction novels, films, and role-playing adventure games. From this perspective, SM is more easily understood as an all-encompassing lifestyle that represents liberation from the oppressive plight of the everyman and nurtures identities of marginality. This community is built around play, and it is through play that community identities are constructed, sustained, and nurtured.

Backdrop

Sometime circa 1994, I was taking part in an animated discussion that was, on some level, the inspiration for this book. I was an undergraduate, talking with one of my favorite sociology professors. She had long been tolerant (remarkably so, in retrospect) of my "anti-feminist" proclamations. Long before Rush Limbaugh and his "femi-Nazi" slurs, feminists all over the country were finding that the term, and the movement, was alienating the first generation of women poised to profit most easily from its legacy. Women in my generation were, for the first time in history, dangerously inclined to take previous feminist strides for granted, and thus among the first to view second-wave feminism as anti-feminist. I had proudly identified as "anti-feminist" one time too many for my professor. She was out of patience, and she set me straight. I was, she argued, a feminist—just the kind that would soon become widely known as third-wave.

In graduate school, still struggling to make sense of my gender politics in the context of broader feminist thought, I discovered *Against Sadomasochism* (Rian 1982), and afterward, the book that had inspired it: the lesbian/feminist celebration of SM, *Coming to Power* (SAMOIS 1981). Reading these for the first time fifteen years after they had been written, I wondered if their moment had ended: Was this even happening anymore? Had it been a concern only within the lesbian community? Were only lesbians doing this? Even if only lesbians were engaging in SM in 1981, I figured straight and bisexual women were doing it by the late nineties. If feminist theorists were so passionate about the role of the patriarchy in lesbian bedrooms, what did they think about women who were doing it with *men*? That seemed like a reasonable thing to study if we were concerned about eroticizing male dominance. If there were women out there doing this now, who were they? Were they drug addicts? Did they live the lives of victims? Were they prisoners of false consciousness?

I wanted more insight into the topic, but few people had actually studied SM as it happens and where it happens, or as Robert Zussman phrases it, "people in places" (2004). When I began this project, more than two decades had elapsed since the few pioneering participant observation studies of actual SM communities. Most of this literature focused on gay leathermen (Weinberg 1978; Weinberg and Falk 1980; Kamel 1980), with the exception of Charles Moser's retrospective account of SM interactions at a play party twenty-five years earlier (Moser 1998). Gini Graham Scott's research (1983) confirmed for me that some semblance of sadomasochism was happening outside gay and lesbian communities. It focused on women "dominating" men; clearly there were straight women (and men) out there who were eroticizing female dominance. If straight women were "submitting" to men somewhere, I wondered whether anyone would even admit it.

When a member of my graduate school cohort introduced me to the World Wide Web, I began searching in earnest. Leafing through *Against Sadomasochism,* I typed words into the search engine. *Sadomasochism heterosexual. Power exchange straight. Sado-masochism women. Sadism women* . . . I found myself fervently hoping that the department did not monitor our computer activity. Finally, I found a discussion list for "submissive women and dominant men." After a lengthy debate about research ethics with my colleague, I joined the list and lurked.

The women on the list seemed articulate and educated. They seemed to hold professional positions. Most interestingly to me, they identified as feminists. They discussed whether, or how, it was possible to reconcile submission with feminism. They debated whether the attempt to make such a reconciliation was in itself feminist or anti-feminist.

I wondered whether these were discursive strategies, unsupported by their everyday lives. I wondered whether any of this was even happening in their lives; perhaps this was merely a discussion-list fantasyland. I wondered whether they were all really men. As a pilot study, I conducted a content analysis of (ostensibly) women's posts on the list. The ubiquitous term "power exchange" stymied me; no one was able to explain what, exactly, that was, and how it happened. Subsequently, I became interested in what I suspected was a tension between community discourses about interpersonal power, and how power "worked" in SM play. Because this was a national list, though, there was no site to investigate. Besides, I was skeptical about whether the people on this list actually participated in the lifestyle they claimed as theirs. Armed with my increasing proficiency on the Web, I learned more about the real-life SM community, and I began to consider an ethnographic project.

There were several SM organizations near enough for me to undertake ethnographic research. Joining any one of them seemed simple; I would need to pay dues and attend functions. Assembling a dissertation committee could be a bit of a challenge, I quickly realized; one faculty member whom I had thought might be interested was willing to consider it only "as long as I don't have to look at pictures."

My institutional review board approval was unproblematic, at least beyond what it would have been for any ethnographer going into any field. Research at my institution involved a good deal of medical research, and the process reflected this. I was approaching my fieldwork as an ethnographer; I intended to immerse myself in the subculture and see what came out of it. I had no way of knowing the size of the community or how long I would be there before I was comfortable conducting interviews, or what my questions were going to be. I did not know what I would do or not do in the field; I could only assure them that I would not have sex with minors, medicate anyone, or keep bodily fluids in my refrigerator. Ultimately, the fact that I would be researching sadomasochism appeared less troublesome than the fact that I could not easily predict how many people would be in my "sample" or how many people I was going to "interview."

As I prepared for my fieldwork, I grew increasingly concerned about safety in the field, for no reason other than the stigma of SM and my own ignorance. I purchased my first cell phone. I considered carrying pepper spray. I had little idea what, or whom, I might encounter in a pansexual urban SM scene.

In July 2002, my partner accompanied me to the corner across from the site of my first meeting at an SM organization—"just in case." My heart pounded as we neared the street I would need to cross to get to the building. As long as they hadn't yet seen me, I reasoned, I could change my mind. As we drew close, though, a mob of people stood outside the building. They were all wearing black. I glanced at my watch and wondered why they were all outside. I looked at the crowd more closely. There were maybe twenty-five people or so. Other than the prevalence of black clothing, they looked, in truth, nothing like I had expected.

The scene looked confused. A chubby middle-aged man was on his cell phone, pacing back and forth from the door of the building to the curb and waving his hands in the air in what looked like frustration. Some people leaned against cars chatting, and some stood in small circles and smoked cigarettes. Some were laughing. The meeting should have begun, but they all remained outside.

We watched for about ten more minutes. Suddenly, the group erupted in loud applause. The catalyst seemed to be another man hurrying down the street, his shaggy long blonde hair flapping behind him. He walked up to the door and opened it. Nervously, I crossed the street and began my fieldwork in the Caeden SM community.

Methodological Notes

The SM scene in Caeden is deeply immersive. Weekend nights at a club generally began with dinner at a nearby restaurant. Often, this was followed by six hours at the club, and then followed by another several (usually between two and five) hours of socializing over breakfast—which sometimes spilled over into lunch. Other activities occurred on at least three evenings during the week, usually informational meetings and educational demonstrations. These were also normally preceded or followed by dinner. Additionally, I maintained near-constant contact with community members throughout the week via email, telephone, Web blogging, and instant messaging. I attended multi-day events in Caeden and other cities. During the first year I spent most waking hours in the field in one capacity or another. It was not uncommon for me to spend over one hundred hours per week at scene events or in the company of community members elsewhere.

I disclosed my identity as a researcher to everyone I met, normally upon introduction. I was usually warmly welcomed, but a few people maintained a cautious distance.[5] My acceptance changed immediately and significantly after I participated in my first public scene, a few months into fieldwork. Over a short time, my role as a participant seemed increasingly more salient in the community than my identity as a researcher.

I wrote my field notes as soon as possible after the events I was describing, which sometimes meant during activities and sometimes meant a few days later (as in the case of weekend-long events). When I was unable to write copious notes, I often relied on jottings on scraps of paper and phone messages to myself in order to remember observations in detail. (Most nights, I took multiple trips to the rest room in order to accomplish this discreetly.) I usually wrote full notes from these jottings when I arrived home. When I suspected I would be too tired when I made it home in the morning, I dictated notes into a recorder during the drive home.

Although I initially intended to avoid affiliation with one particular SM organization over another, I became much more closely affiliated with Horizons. Within a few months, it became clear to me that Horizons very nearly constituted the Caeden SM scene, while EPP overlapped to no small extent with the Caeden swinger scene.[6] Although this was not how EPP marketed itself, the demographic of the membership (straight male dominants and straight female submissives)[7] as well as the attendance, conduct, language, and activities at their events, parties, and demonstrations, rendered them less representative of the SM scene than of the swinger scene. This, combined with the realization that I was less comfortable in that circle,[8] led me to become more involved in Horizons than in EPP.

After approximately six months, I began conducting interviews. I began with people in my closest circles, waiting until I had established strong rapport with potential interviewees. In most cases, by the time of each interview, my respondents and I knew each other well. The interview conversations flowed reciprocally, and as has been noted elsewhere (Berger 2001), I found that my own disclosure and self-reflection often enhanced the interview relationship. In a few cases, respondents were direct and specific about their interest in this mutual disclosure. In the context of these highly intimate and sexualized relationships, they shared their life histories, and we used our SM experience—common and uncommon—to inspire reflection and discussion.

As is typical in ethnographic interviews, these were not limited to SM-related content; respondents were asked to share their life histories. Interest and participation in SM was an additional, but not sole, or even primary, thematic focus. Interviews were loosely structured; I used a content guideline to ensure thematic uniformity, but interviews were flexible and dynamic in terms of structure, off-topic conversation, and sequence. Most interviews occurred in respondents' homes or offices, and where this was not possible, interviews were conducted at a restaurant or in my office. On average, interviews lasted six and-a-half hours, with a range of between four and eleven hours. (It should be noted that this is "tape time"; interviews often included breaks for lunch or dinner. When this occurred, meal times were not counted as interview time, unless we decided to continue the interview through the meal.) In total, I conducted twenty ethnographic-thematic interviews. Most, including the longest, were conducted in one session; three were continued into a second session because of fatigue or lateness of the hour.

Interviews were tape-recorded, and I transcribed them verbatim, with the occasional exception of a bracketed description of an extremely lengthy and off-topic digression. In all excerpts throughout this book, ellipses indicate pauses in the respondents' speech, and bracketed ellipses indicate editorial omission. I have omitted idiosyncratic utterances such as "uh" and "um." I coded field notes, interview transcripts, and my field journals, multiple times, and recoded as themes emerged and my analysis developed.

I continued my participation in the scene (although not at the level of immersion that I had during the first year) until 2006, when I completed my interviews. Shortly thereafter, I left the field to begin writing.

Scope and Limitations

I was not able to be as inclusive as I would have liked, across sexual orientation or race. Though there is considerable social overlap, the SM community in Caeden comprises a gay male SM scene, a lesbian SM scene, and a pansexual scene, and it was in the latter that I spent nearly all of my time. Additionally, the community is disproportionately white. I was, however, able to be inclusive across gender and SM identification labels.

Because there is so little contemporary work on SM and its participants, it is crucial to note that my discussion of "the scene" is not intended to be synonymous with "people who like SM." The scene in Caeden is a public, social network of people who observe and engage in SM in designated public spaces. The lifestyle in some SM communities in the United States is built around private parties. Throughout my time in the field, I also attended private parties. Although certainly people who play in public also play in private, in Caeden, the private party "circuit" is different in important ways from the larger scene. Private play attracts different people, for arguably different reasons, and it is differently constrained, shaped, and engaged.

In Caeden, at least a portion of the private party circuit overlaps with the swinger community. The broader public scene was, at the time,[9] distinct from the swinger community in notable regards. Public swing parties, for example, may involve "light SM," but are not likely to involve heavier play, and public SM parties do not involve anal, vaginal, or oral intercourse. (Practices at private parties in both groups are dictated by the hosts.)

This book is not, on the whole, about SM as it happens in bedrooms or during private parties. It is about SM as it is engaged in the public SM scene in this particular city. It is about lifestyle in Caeden, the people who live it, and what it is that they do. These differences are relevant to the relationships between eroticism, violence, and intimacy that I explore here. It may be, for example, that gay leather scenes are less likely to frame their SM around the erotic/violent problematic, or that scenes that are more racially diverse are more likely to do so. This analysis should not, therefore, be understood as applicable to other SM communities in a quotidian sense.

Issues of Representation

REFLEXIVITY AND SUBJECTIVITY

The ethnographic endeavor to understand a culture requires what Clifford Geertz described as the experience of anthropology: "[Y]ou put yourself in its way and it enmeshes you" (1973, 44). In some cases (such as when the culture in question is that of an SM community) the truth of this enmeshing can approach the literal. As has been true for other studies of communities and cultures built around carnal experience (Frank 2002; Wacquant 2004), this work necessitated intellectual and theoretical attention to the body as epistemology. In particular, it demanded attention to my body as a source of data and a tool for meaning-making. As both the site of what I needed to understand and how I was to understand it, my body functioned as subject, object, and method, for there is no way to understand SM, or its participants, without a sense of what it feels like to engage in it.

As I explore further in the conclusion to this book, my own participation in SM illuminated dynamics of SM and undercurrents in this community that I could not have otherwise identified. These aspects of SM experience, though common among participants, are not readily apparent in the discourse of the community. Some of these experiences are taken for granted to such an extent that they are uninteresting to community members, and some are simply unexplored. My willingness to examine the very personal sense that I made of SM during my fieldwork—how I responded to it and how it "made me feel"—generated formative insights.

Therefore, in my endeavor to represent (and construct) carnal understanding through words on pages, I have included a prologue at the beginning of each chapter of this book. These sections are depictions of actual events, as I experienced them. These narratives were constructed from my field notes, but they are not necessarily verbatim. In a few instances, they have been edited or blended, resulting in representations not entirely true to time and space simultaneously. They are creative representations of authentic experiences, products far more of my recollection than of my imagination, but products of both nonetheless. In this way I follow Katherine Frank's decision to incorporate creative representation to convey the ethnographer's felt sense (2002).

My use of these narratives does not, in my view, situate this book as autoethnography, in any of its quickly changing senses. As it has conventionally been used by anthropologists, the term "auto-ethnography" refers to ethnographic work in one's own culture (Hayano 1979; Strathern 1987; Dorst 1989). This is the way that I understand this term. This is in part because it is the way I became accustomed to understanding it. It is also because it makes sense to me to distinguish between insider and outsider perspectives when studying communities, and to delineate the movement between one and the other.

In sociology, "autoethnography" has been more recently adapted, with notable success, to mean a kind of writing of the self (Denzin 1989; Ellis 1998, 2004). In this practice, the writer draws heavily on autobiographical narrative; indeed, the deliberate deployment of literary devices is often one of the characteristics of autoethnography (Ellis 2004). Yet there appears to me to be a widespread misperception that all instances of creative representation in sociological writing are also ethnographic.

I do not view this work as autoethnographic because I do not take the "self" as my project or as my analytical focus, and I do not treat myself as a biographical subject outside the context of the field. If autoethnography has become, as Gans understands it, "basically autobiography written by sociologists" (1999), this book is not autoethnographic. I use descriptions of my field experiences *toward* a richer and more sociological understanding of the members of this community and of the social world they inhabit, as I believe ethnographers have long done, whether consciously or not.

Norman Denzin claims that "the work of the good realist ethnographer has always been to study and understand a social setting, a social group, or a social problem . . . these researchers were self-reflexive but not self-obsessed" (2006, 421). It was this kind of ethnographer I aspired to be when I began. Yet all ethnographic work is, on some level, "about" the ethnographer, for reflexivity "makes a problem out of . . . the figure of the fieldworker" (Strathern 2004, 8). During my fieldwork and my writing, I was consistently and rigorously reflexive. Nonetheless, I believe that there is an important distinction, and a challenging balance, to be maintained between subjectivity in the analytical process and subjective focus in the representation of a community or subculture. I am therefore more absent from this representation than I was from my process and from my writing. Barbara Tedlock notes the convention of publishing ethnographic diaries following the publication of a realist ethnography (Tedlock 1991), rather than integrating reflexive insights into the text. In a contemporary twist, ethnographic texts include reflexive insights, but often in the introductory chapter or in an appendix.[10] Subjectivity and reflexivity inform and shape my analysis throughout this work, but they are, for the most part, contained (and constrained) within a chapter situated at the end of the book.

CONFIDENTIALITY

Caeden is a tightly knit community of SM and sex activists, and generally educated and intellectually curious people. They are likely to read what is written about them, and because the prologues are "true," they will likely recognize one another. Though pseudonymous "scene names" (such as Dakota)[11] are not unusual in the community, these obviously do not protect the confidentiality of my informants within the community. Because my interviews were comprehensive life histories, I was privileged with information that is normally not available to other people in the community. I have therefore taken additional precautions to protect the privacy of my respondents. I did not disclose to anyone in the community whom I did and did not interview. This required some juggling on my part, but because the community is so small and because I anticipated that at least some of the members might read this book, I went to considerable lengths to maintain anonymity about who was, and who was not, an interview respondent. Some people were unconcerned with this. Others were highly concerned.

In the text, in addition to the standard protection of changing proper nouns, the pseudonyms I use in the narrative sections (prologues) are not consistent between those and the rest of the text. Pseudonyms are consistent across prologues but not between prologues and text; for example, "Russ" in the prologue is "Russ" in all other prologues (and in field notes in which his actions would be recognizable to community members). If, however, Russ appeared in the text as a respondent, he would have a different pseudonym. For the same reason, dates that appear in interview excerpts may have been changed. Additionally, I make no mention at all of respondents' race or ethnicity anywhere in this book, because people of color are so underrepresented in the community that to do otherwise would itself constitute a breach of confidentiality. However, SM identifications (i.e., submissive, dominant, top, bottom) remain true to the identities provided by my respondents at the time.

Because of these constraints, the people in this book cannot be as richly understood as I would have liked. Ideally, the same people who appear in prologues and in field notes—whom the reader "sees" engaged in play—would be recognizable as people whose life stories provide the backdrop for that play and for this book. The relationships between the life stories of the members of this community and SM play in Caeden are central to my analysis. I regret that I needed to sacrifice this clarity in order to protect the confidentiality of my interview respondents, whose generosity is the heart of this book.

LANGUAGE

I have attempted to convey meanings of perhaps unfamiliar SM jargon within the text, and a glossary is included for reference. However, a few other notes about the linguistic and semantic choices I have made are important at this point.

I use the term "SM," rather than the newer and trendier "BDSM" which seeks to blur the distinctions and subsume all SM activity under one overlapping acronym (Bondage/Discipline/Dominance/Submission/Sadism/Masochism). "SM" is a frequently used catch-all term, particularly among more veteran members of the scene, but BDSM is also widely used in Caeden.

"SM" is used in at least two different ways in the community. It is one of the terms used by members of the community to refer to itself and, inclusively, to its activities, along with "BDSM" and, less commonly, "kink."[12] However, there is a segment of the scene that reserves "SM" for a more specific set of activities, and therefore uses the more obviously inclusive term "BDSM" when referring to the community or to its activities in a general sense.

Perhaps because it is more popular with newer members of the scene, and pervasive on the Web, I have found the use of the term "BDSM" to engender some suspicion on the part of more veteran scene members. Additionally, in my experience, most people who use the term "SM" broadly are not excluding bondage, discipline, dominance, or submission from their frame of reference, as evidenced by the context in which they use it, as well as by the activities in which they themselves engage on a regular basis. I am, therefore, comfortable using the traditional "SM" to refer to *the collection of activities that involve the mutually consensual and conscious use, among two or more people, of pain, power, perceptions about power, or any combination thereof, for psychological, emotional, or sensory pleasure.* This definition of SM refers to SM interaction, rather than to either sadism or masochism in the clinical tradition. It also excludes autoerotic practices that may involve pain or self-induced powerlessness. Further, it differentiates between SM and body modification practices; though piercing, cutting, and branding may be part of SM play, the objective in SM is taken to be, primarily, the experience rather than alteration of the body.

Although SM is sometimes pronounced "S and M" in the community (and sometimes written S/M or S&M), it is more commonly pronounced as two consecutive letters: "SM." I deliberately avoid the perhaps more familiar term

S&M, or "S and M," for two reasons. The separator "and" implies that SM activity hinges on two separate and distinct interests or practices, sadism and masochism. First, it is not my experience that these are in fact two distinct interests or practices among people who engage in these activities. Secondly, SM play may involve activities that are neither sadistic nor masochistic, in the clinical sense. The focus on the clinical dichotomy renders the term "S and M" less relevant to SM experiences that do not involve pain, bondage, or humiliation. In this sense, I view "SM" as a compromise between the awkward, Internet-based "BDSM" and the specific, arguably less appropriate "S and M."

Finally, a note about SM identities is important. The distinctions between identification labels are complex and contested. Not everyone in Caeden, let alone nationally and cross-nationally, agrees on the hermeneutic differences between "top" and "dominant," or between "bottom" and "submissive." I explore some of the underlying issues in these debates throughout the book, but I would like to clarify my own usage at the outset. I use "top" and "bottom" very broadly, as categories of play and players that can subsume other scene identities, including dominant, submissive, sadist, and masochist. Although this may be a contested decision, I do this because, for most people in this community, "dominant" and "submissive" necessarily draw on and connote narratives and discourses of power imbalances. Sadist and masochist, both nouns, involve discourses of pain that not all SM participants share, and thus I view them as more specific terms than top and bottom. "Top" and "bottom," in my view, may incorporate these narratives, but they are not intrinsic to the identities. I view top and bottom as the most flexible terms in the community; they are, for instance, both verbs *and* nouns without changing the form of the words. The way I am deploying them, then, a person submitting is also bottoming, but not everyone bottoming is submitting. I would not subsume "master" and "slave" (also nouns) under the terms "top" and "bottom," for these terms in the community often refer to long-term and/or contractual relationships, or to identities understood as fixed, rather than as kinds of play.

The Objectives of This Book

Because so little is known and understood about SM, one important aim of this book is to represent it to outsiders, illustrating the way that it works and what it accomplishes. In many ways, though, SM demonstrates the complexity of interpersonal and interactional processes in which we all engage, including negotiating gender, managing risk, and constructing intimate experience. It is not my goal to explain why some people like SM and why some do not; as Howard Becker first pointed out in 1953, "the deviant behavior produces the deviant motivation" (in Becker 1963, 42). I have tried instead to render SM understandable in the social contexts in which it occurs. I have also taken it as a case study to illuminate much broader interactional processes.

The life stories of community members figure prominently in the first part of this book, which examines the intersection of social marginality and community in Caeden. Chapter 1 illustrates the marginal experiences common in Caeden among members long before their entry into this community and traces the role of defiance and broader identities of marginality in their lives. In chapter 2 I explore the ways in which these marginal identities inform and shape the meaning of community, and therefore of SM, in the lives of members.

The second part of this book focuses on the varieties, structure, meanings, and social implications of SM play. In chapter 3, I explore the common understandings of SM as sex and as role play, in the context of the complex issue of power performances. I analyze the structure of SM scenes and examine the various strategies employed toward the achievement and maintenance of power-imbalanced experiences. Chapter 4 frames SM as "serious leisure" (Stebbins 1982) and illustrates the benefits and rewards of engaging in play in this community. Chapter 5 provides an analysis of gender performance and symbolism in play, in the context of the many ways in which gender is performed and lived in the community.

The last part of this book grapples with some of the larger theoretical challenges that SM poses and inspires. In chapter 6 I examine and demonstrate the usefulness of SM in understanding and exploring relationships between eroticism and violence, and the role of pain and discourses of pain in making sense of these relationships. In chapter 7, I argue that SM is edgework (Lyng 1990), first through an exploration of particular activities that are intended to transgress or transcend more extreme physical, emotional, or psychological boundaries. Second, I offer a feminist expansion of the edgework perspective. Chapter 8 draws on this analysis to explore broader issues surrounding the construction of intimacy, the erotic and the violent, and gendered negotiations of risk. In chapter 8, I frame SM as the engagement in *intimate edgework,* through which intimate experience is constructed through the transgression of personal boundaries. Finally, the conclusion provides insight into the ways in which this ethnographic text was shaped by particular decisions I made in the field.

Part 1. People

Chapter 1

Defiance

Bodies, Minds, and Marginality

It was the last committee meeting. Tomorrow was the big event. We had rented three floors of a large hotel. One floor was going to be devoted to educational classes throughout the weekend. One floor was going to be devoted to vendors of SM and fetish products, and one floor was to be the dungeon. It was being designed and set up by a man who owned an SM club in another city. I had heard very good things about his work.

It had taken seven months of almost weekly meetings, several hours each. And the IMs and the emails. God, the emails. Seven months of general snippiness and petty arguments. Seven months of asking Noah to relax and imploring Amy to be nice, and trying very hard not to tell everyone to stop acting like the rise and fall of civilization was entirely wrapped up in this event.

The communication was abominable. At each and every meeting lately, I found myself wondering why everyone was so snotty. Was I the only one who noticed? How did they get away with talking to people like this? All of it was driving me nuts: the tension, the drama . . . the body odor.

Wearily, I looked around the room.

Maggie is cross-eyed, and her hair looks as if she never washes it. Jacob weighs over 350 pounds. Dottie is a six-foot-four woman who weighs nearly as much, and Robert has both of them beat by about a hundred pounds. Liam has a severe overbite, and twenty-seven-year-old Malcolm is five-foot-one. Adam cuts off the sleeves of his T-shirts—so that they're what we once called "muscle shirts"—and wears the collar of his jacket turned up. Ellis rocks back and forth when he talks. Trey talks with his eyes closed much of the time. Ronny practices tae kwon do moves whenever he's standing. He smiles a lot at no one in particular.

I started to sigh, but instead I laughed midway through. I couldn't help myself. Sometimes it all seemed surreal.

And really, this event was a big deal. It was a four-day, nationally publicized SM gala, the first for the organization in several years. Though the process had been infuriating and thoroughly draining, I had enjoyed it. I was proud of the planning and the troubleshooting and, ultimately, the pulling it off, with this group of volunteers who found this important enough to devote such tremendous time and effort to it.

I was sharing a room with Adam, Liam, and Phyllis. Faye was going to spend a night on our floor. On Thursday and Friday, I ran around like a maniac, sleeping for a couple of hours here and there. By dawn on Saturday, every inch of my body was desperate for bed. I dragged myself back to my room.

I changed my clothes and slipped into bed beside Adam, whose last shift had ended not long before mine. I sunk into the mattress and closed my eyes. A few minutes later, Liam's alarm went off. I groaned.

From the bed next to ours, Liam rose.

Clink-clank, clink-clank. Clink-clank!

"Liam, what the hell?" I said. The room was dark.

"Sorry," he replied. "I have to be at the programming desk by six."

Adam sat up in bed beside me. "And the programming desk needs the Tin Man?" he asked.

Adam switched on the lamp on his side of the bed. I groaned again, but I glanced in Liam's direction. He was wearing only black briefs and heavy chains around his wrists and neck.

"You wore those to bed??" Adam asked, incredulous.

"Yes. She told me not to take them off," he said.

He headed for the bathroom. Clink-clank, clink-clank.

"Come on, Liam. Just take them off while you're getting ready. They're so loud. We just got back!" I pleaded.

"No, I'm not taking them off! I'm honored to be wearing them. I'll be quiet," he assured us.

I sighed and closed my eyes. A few minutes later, he walked back into the room. Clink-clank. Clink-clank.

"Are you kidding me with this?" Adam said.

I hurled a pillow at Liam. He stepped aside. Clink-clank. *I continued to try to reason with him, though Adam assured me it was futile.*

Somehow Adam managed to fall asleep and was breathing deeply beside me. I was still grumbling into my pillow when Liam finally clink-clanked his way out of the room an hour later.

The people in Caeden view themselves as outsiders. They live their lives on the fringes of social acceptance. For much of this marginal experience, they are indebted to particular and shared characteristics. These characteristics would seem, at first glance, to exist entirely independently of sadomasochism. Many of the members of this community lived on the margins prior to developing an SM identity.

In sociological research, studies of "sexual identity" emerged in response to a broader tendency to ignore the experience of the individual, particularly the sexually marginalized individual. Thus identity research has generally focused on recognizing distinctions between members of groups socially marked as different from the norm (Brekhus 1996) in a climate in which sexual deviance functioned as an overarching marker of pathological difference. While this approach is crucial in addressing inaccurate and destructive assumptions of sameness among members of stigmatized groups, it is primarily concerned with issues of identity that are externally derived, or "other-defined" (Brekhus 1996). For an examination of identity as interactively constructed, the emphasis on individual differences is less helpful.

My objective therefore departs somewhat from the established approach to identity in sexual communities. Rather than seeking to shatter the stereotype of SM participants as similar on any given dimension, I aim to explore the multiple levels of their similarities, which, in this case, converge on the ways in which they perceive themselves as different from others.

Defiant Bodies

In stark contrast to the popular culture fantasies of leather-clad vixens and bare-chested musclemen with black hoods, most of the people in Caeden are overweight. Weight is not a salient part of the discourse of the community; its members are not fat activists, nor do they publicly lament their weights. Though at times weight is invoked as an explanation for lack of attraction to other community members, self-deprecating remarks are rare. During their life history narratives, most of my respondents did not indicate struggles to lose weight nor struggles to maintain body image in their life stories, and this is not a general discursive issue in the community. The issue is sometimes mentioned in the context of SM play; a larger back provides a larger "canvas," for example, and discussions of safety always take into account—respectfully but not particularly gingerly—the size of the players. Apart from these exceptions, however, conversations about weight were relatively absent from community discourse while I was there; it was not treated as a socially interesting or relevant fact.

Though initially I hypothesized that perhaps conventional standards of beauty (and health) were of no concern here, I quickly learned otherwise. While there is truth in the claim that particular SM-related traits often trump conventional attractiveness as social currency, it is equally true that in the absence of a trump card, those who conform more closely to conventional notions of sexual desirability are far more desirable as play partners. Further evidence that I was incorrect arrived in 2003 with the Atkins diet, which several members followed successfully. (Most have since regained their weight.)

Fatness, then, is not particularly desirable in Caeden, but it does not necessarily detract from desirability within the community. It does not appear to inhibit nudity or sexualized presentation in a scene context, and it does not underlie complaints about desirability, fitting into clothing, or athletic ability. Nonetheless, in a community in which fatness is recognized as common but neither reclaimed nor stigmatized, it ceases to be a social marker, at least in the space constructed within and by the group. Instead, thinness is a social marker in Caeden, indicated by the prevalence of comments regarding the smaller size of some participants.[1]

In this context, fatness can be viewed as a means of resistance. If, as Samantha Murray notes, "the act of living fat is an act of defiance, an eschewal of discursive modes of bodily being" (Murray 2005, 155), then the people in Caeden were accustomed to defiance long before their entrance into the SM scene. In this way, many community members identified as nonconformist even prior to their SM participation.

Laura, who weighed 350 pounds during my time in the field, is also over six feet tall. A gender-identified and biological woman, Laura found her height to be a main source of marginal experience. Before joining the SM scene, she was a member of an organization for tall people (Highstanders). Laura told me:

> In Highstanders, one of the things that I got out of that was, not only was I eye to eye and not different . . . a lot of the people had grown up with the same feelings I did, feelings of awkwardness and being different. Feeling accepted there was a very common thread, and it kind of kept people there. And people were warm and welcoming and friendly. So that was what kept me going to Highstanders.

Six-foot-one-and-a-half is, of course, a perfectly acceptable height for a man. The margins on which Laura lives are gendered. Her height positioned her, quite literally, outside the norms of femininity, and therefore outside the norms of the heterosexed female body, in addition to the desexualized space she inhabited as an overweight person.

For women, obesity represents a challenge to identification both as feminine and as sexual (Murray 2004). The overweight female body is not quite "Woman" (Hole 2003). It occupies a space between the femininity of flesh and curves, and the simultaneous symbolic representations of consumption and domination, overtly defying expectations of the sexual female body. The bodies of fat women are "potentially disruptive" in their resistance of both "maleness" and standards for the feminine body (Shaw 2006). Carla Rice argues that fat women are "other-gendered," relegated to gender margins for the failure to meet the standards for attractiveness in girls as well as those for athleticism in boys (Rice 2007). The everyday performances of femininity by heavy women therefore lie somewhere between inauthentic and farcical.

Fatness also threatens masculine performances by undermining hegemonic masculinity.[2] Culturally, fatness is interpreted as a lack of self-discipline, physical strength and agility, and morality.[3]

Greg, who had been heavy since the age of six, said that as a child "some work went into fitting in" and that it took two years for him to "get accepted."

In Caeden, even men who were not overweight structured their narratives of marginality in part around unmasculine bodies. These men regarded themselves as "scrawny" or "puny." Bobby, for example, described himself as

> a little tyke, as a kid. I was advanced in my grade, so I was one of the youngest in there, and also extraordinarily light and small. There were kids two years younger than I was who were bigger than I was. [. . .] The joke I tell—and it's only half a joke—is that I was beaten up every day on the way home from school. And it was quite often; sometimes even by the boys (laughs). And that's the joke, but there was some truth to that. It was just physical fear for my first year in high school. I was in the land of the giants. And asking a girl out or something like that became laughter and joke around the school the next day.

In recounting their failure to meet normative standards of masculinity, both Greg and Bobby referred to being bullied by girls in particular, which they each experienced as especially emasculating.

Similarly, some women structured their narratives around other sources of gendered bodily marginality. At thirteen years old, Lily was heavier than average, but she recalled the transition from a prepubescent body to needing a bra in size DD within a year as far more of an issue. "They got way too much attention. They made me look fatter. They hurt. They were just—grotesque." Nonetheless Lily characterized her social-sexual development as delayed:

> I'm a late bloomer in most everything. I was a virgin until I was, like, twenty-seven. I'm like, so late, it's amazing. So I was like, twelve or thirteen, and I didn't know how sex worked. I had a general idea, I knew the anatomy, but I still hadn't quite figured it all out. And my mom was trying to teach me how to put on a tampon. She was on the other side of the door, and I was trying to feel it, and I'm like, "It won't go in, it won't fit." And my mom said to me, "Lily, a man's penis can fit in there. A tampon will fit." And it was like a light bulb.

If the overweight female body is not quite Woman, the overweight adolescent with extremely large breasts who knows nothing of sex inhabits an especially ambivalently gendered space. Hyper-feminine (and therefore hyper-sexualized) in presentation, Lily lacked sexual curiosity, communication, and experience, contributing to marginal experiences in multiple directions.

Among my respondents in Caeden, narratives of the body are built around deviation from hegemonic gender standards. These modes of defiance are as sexed as they are gendered, defying heteronormative sexual attraction as they defy notions of masculinity and femininity. The members physically defy hegemonic gender standards in two distinct ways: their bodies are fat and therefore inhabit de-gendered spaces, or they are underdeveloped, and thus fall short of the sexualized standards for bodily masculinity and femininity.

Respondents also told shared examples of active performances of defiance, particularly located in and performed through the body. Jack's retelling of an elementary school experience is one example:

> I was a small kid, first of all, I was one of the shortest guys, shortest people in the entire grade, which did not bode well for me as a boy—and there was this little space between a bookshelf and a cubby that was in the third grade classroom. And I wedged myself in between them, and I fit perfectly because I was little, and I wouldn't move. And not just wouldn't move, but wouldn't move. At all. Barely any blinking, staring very straight ahead. There was a point where a girl named Jessica actually came up to me, waved her hand in front of my face and sang a song to try and get me to respond, and I just acted like she wasn't there. So that just convinced everybody that I was literally insane. And then they were like, yeah—don't mess with him. He'll actually hurt you. [laughs] Because you know he's insane.

Here Jack's small size became a source of defiance, as he wedged himself into a space into which he was not permitted, and in which only he could fit. His defiance increased when confronted; his refusal to acknowledge the interventions of others represented a refusal to conform to social expectations.

In the life histories of many of the people in Caeden, defiance is symbolic, in and of the body, and actively performed through the body in ways that are gendered and sexed, and in ways that existed prior to their participation in SM.

Incidental Androgyny

Gender, of course, is "done" not only through the body, but through quotidian actions that construct and maintain gender identities (West and Zimmerman 1987; Butler 1990; Halberstam 1998). In Caeden, these everyday performances of masculinity and femininity are rare. The resulting presentation of selves is gender nonconformist. Yet this implies a deliberateness that is not entirely accurate. Rather than a gender-bending effort or sex-role ambivalence, this nonconformity appears as the absence of either aspirations or traits necessary to conform to conventional gender standards.

This "incidental androgyny" is immediately and physically evident as the absence of markers of femininity and masculinity. Many women in the scene, for example, live their daily lives without makeup and jewelry, have long (often unstyled) hair, and wear clothes that do not fit them well. Most men in the community have little interest in sports, as either participants or fans. They do not have expensive cars (or the ability to fix them) nor traditional good looks, nor the social finesse to banter and flirt. Many dress in ill-fitting, outdated clothing that is often clean but unkempt. Neither butch nor femme, these (usually heterosexual) women and men do not follow or overturn the rules of gender presentation. They simply live outside of them. Understood in the context of West and Zimmerman's work, in which "doing" masculinity and femininity are active, quotidian processes (1987), this "incidental" androgyny is less an actively constituted gender than what we are left with when we do not "do" gender quite so fully or quite so well.

Following their work, several gender theorists have identified examples of, and challenges to, doing masculinity. R. W. Connell's concept of "hegemonic masculinity projects" (1995) inspires Messerschmidt (2000) to what he calls "masculinity challenges," which he defines as "contextual interactions that result in masculine degradation" in the lives of men. While it is likely that most men at one time or another have had experiences of "masculine degradation," many of the men in Caeden have faced several different and repeated masculinity challenges, stemming in part from either being so small that they were bullied and beaten up, particularly by girls, or by being too overweight to do masculinity appropriately. Conventional masculine "successes" such as athleticism, financial success, social panache, aggressiveness, and hegemonic indicators of interpersonal power and physical strength are rare among the men in Caeden.

Though the idea that femininity is affected, performative, and achieved has been widely and well argued,[4] work on "doing" femininity is in its infancy. An application of Messerschmidt's model to women in the Caeden community, then, would suggest that "femininity challenges" include being too tall, too heavy, too awkward, and too inept at feminine adornment for the achievement of socially appropriate femininity, or "emphasized femininity" (Connell 1987). While women in Caeden often do wear makeup and fancy clothing or fetish wear for parties, the lack of primping proficiency is frequently apparent, resulting in a less expert feminine presentation than that of either more conventionally "feminine" women or drag queens. On the occasions during which women in the scene "do femininity," these performances are therefore less than successful.

Gender is not only "done" but also achieved and accomplished; a successful doing is tantamount to the avoidance of lived incompetence. Viewed this way, many of the men and women of Caeden live in gender-incompetent bodies—bodies that defy or ignore hegemonic gender presentations, and bodies that they do not use to engage in conventional hegemonic gender performances at the quotidian level.

Geekiness

Bodies in Caeden are non-normative on several intersecting, gendered, and sexed levels. In addition, community members construct their narratives around life on intellectual margins. More than half of my respondents either had skipped at least one grade in school or had been enrolled in an intellectually gifted program. When asked, generally, to talk about their childhoods, each of my interview respondents reported feeling that they were smarter than average, and all but one used the word "geek" to describe themselves. Geekiness is very much a part of the discourse of the SM community; conversations at a table at an SM event are as likely to be about computer software or science-fiction novels as they are about SM. Generally claimed with pride in Caeden, geekiness serves as the explanation for several aspects of SM interest: the affinity for complicated techniques and well-made toys, the stamina to practice skills to the level of mastery, and the desire and ability to deconstruct meanings and experiences of SM.

Yet in the narratives of my respondents, geekiness also served as an explanation for victimization. For example, when Laura told me that in high school, someone had thrown a match into her hair, her explanation followed immediately: she was a member of her school's Academic Olympic team. Juxtaposed with a discourse of geekiness as cool in the community, the narratives of its members reflect both intellectual loneliness and social isolation emerging from their geekiness. Perhaps one of the most poignant instances of the latter was an excerpt from my interview with Greg:

> [I had] lots of imaginary friends as a child . . . mostly made up of characters from novels . . . I had that up until college, and to some degree, I still do it. I can't do it for you consciously, but if I'm alone, watch sometimes. Ever see me talking to myself? I try not to do it in public . . . talking with them. Not creating dialogue—using them as a sounding board. There's another person there to talk to. [. . .] It's not John Nash, it's not schizophrenia, I don't see somebody else—I create the space for that person to be there. Most frequent character—they're all characters [. . .] is Val Kilmer's character from Real Genius. Chris Knight. Because he was—he is—smart, cool, a little older, and nice to the kid who was new and younger and uncomfortable. And I was always the kid who was new and younger and uncomfortable. I skipped two grades.

Self-understandings of intellectual marginality often intersected with bodily marginality. Experiences of nonconformity to standards of the body were shaped by these impressions. Additionally, the identifications themselves contributed to the constructions and maintenance of each other, as Seth illustrates:

> I was always pretty bright, as a kid, and so my reputation became as the kid who was the smart guy. You know, geeks are generally not sought after for the looks. And I wasn't—you know, I really wasn't a bad-looking kid, but I wasn't particularly attractive either, as a child. Buck teeth were really an issue. [. . .] If someone had simply taught me how to tie my shoelaces correctly, okay, with, you know, with the string in the right way, and the double-loop . . . I would have gotten laid in high school! . . . It lent very much to my slovenly appearance. And since I wasn't convinced that I was attractive, I put no effort into making myself so. It was a very self-fulfilling prophecy.

The perception of an inverse relationship between geekiness and sexual attractiveness magnifies feelings of marginality for people who viewed themselves as intellectual outsiders. From this perspective, "too smart" easily translates into "too smart to be bothered" with the trappings of physical appearance, thereby reinforcing the smart/sexy binary by which adolescent social life is often structured in the United States. Seth's "self-fulfilling prophecy" is an acquisition of two distinct but intertwined marginal identities; geekdom conflates the bright kid with the unattractive kid.

Closely related, and even more frequently, intellectual marginality intersected with incidental androgyny. For those who were accelerated in school, the sense of being smarter than others was accompanied by a gendered marginal position throughout most of their academic lives. Men who were smaller than average and women who regarded themselves as "late bloomers" were comparing themselves with their peers, who, in these cases, were older. Their advanced placement in school thereby conflated bodily marginality with intellectual marginality. Because they were significantly smaller and less sexually developed than their peers throughout childhood and adolescence, their intellectual abilities contributed to lives lived on the margins of hegemonic gender categories. Sophie, who, like Greg, had been advanced two grades, explained her challenges:

> I never had a problem as far as course material went, not only keeping up with my classmates but being at the top of my class, but it was a real pain in the ass emotionally. Being two years younger than everybody and just as I developed mentally, it caused a lot of problems . . . I was always behind, socially and physically. So I was always runty, even if I wasn't really for my age. And then of course the fact that I was a straight-A student didn't win me any points either. [. . .] So I got picked on a lot. And I lacked the—because I didn't go through kindergarten, which really, it's not about learning much except how to socialize with other children, and I had never had that. So I was always massively lagging in basic social skills throughout grade school. It took me a long time to get caught up with that. I always really, really resented the fact, especially by the time I got to high school, that I had been accelerated.

Having made a conscious effort to "catch up" on her social skills, Sophie has social panache that is notably uncommon among the people with whom she now spends most of her time. Pervasive social awkwardness in Caeden includes excessive fidgeting, disclosure of highly personal information to strangers, and behaviors that would suggest an inability or disinclination to listen to others (such as avoiding eye contact and nodding randomly while engaged in a one-on-one conversation). This social awkwardness is normative in the community, but more extreme examples—what would likely be considered social ineptitude outside of the community—is also common. For example, the tendency to speak one's mind bluntly and without qualification is typical, and, importantly, usually appears to escape notice. Further, what would elsewhere be called "boasting" is a primary means of communication in Caeden; popular topics of conversation include what the speaker does well and what impressive things the speaker has done. This communication pattern is an accepted part of the discourse of the community; it is not identified as bragging and does not prompt negative responses.

Even more extreme social challenges involve issues of personal space and nonverbal communication. During my time in the field, I frequently found myself unable to communicate effectively through normative bodily cues. Backing away from a speaker who was standing too close often resulted in the speaker closing in on me, and even walking away sometimes led to being followed by the busily chatting "offender."

Poor social skills are sometimes interpreted as a general lack of intelligence. Outside the realm of the social, though, the people in Caeden are articulate, well-read, logical, and creative. The problems with "intelligence" measures (and kinds) notwithstanding, many of the members of this community are what we normally and culturally understand as intelligent.

In the narratives of my respondents, this had two distinct impacts on their lives. The first, depicted in the excerpts above, emerged from the external identification of their intelligence, which began early for many. The second impact is the experience of this identification as marginalizing. Specifically, life stories continually reflected the sense that the respondent had always been surrounded by less intelligent people.

Bobby's narrative consistently returned to this theme:

> My senior year in high school I was reading what an American history master's program [would involve]. I was reading all the books, as my mom would bring those books home, I was chewing through them, at age sixteen to seventeen. And my history teacher in high school had a degree in fashion design. I, hands down, knew more about American History than she had ever encountered. After I took her first exam in my senior year—and again, I don't want, I don't talk about this with guys, my senior year at school, I took her first exam, and I ran across the third question, which had a triple negative in it, I said "we have to talk." And I handed

in my paper best I could, but I went over the grammar of the paper and the intent and the writing that was on there and I said look, and she said, "Look. Let's not tell anyone else. You're going to write the exams for me for the remainder of the session. And we'll just give you [an] A.

Replete with examples of his educators' intellectual inferiority, Bobby's narrative reveals a frustration that no one else seemed able to keep up with him. Moreover, his teacher's inclination to deceive the other students did little to restore his faith in education, and his collusion in her scheme served only to reinforce his belief in his intellectual superiority. This provides the backdrop for his rejection of mainstream education:

> So I was a terrible college student. I just didn't follow the protocol. [. . .] And I would also challenge; I wasn't popular with the professors. 'Cause I challenged them. I was much better read than anyone else who was sitting in that room . . . and I'd want an intellectual exchange, and they didn't appreciate that. [. . .] You don't need college to learn. Once you've got the habit, you know how to do it. I read nonfiction, and fiction, and just switch 'em off. And I will go into a store and buy a book on chaos theory or quantum physics, and just, for fun. And I read this stuff. And I don't know anyone else who does, and I get some looks when I sit at a restaurant and I'm reading a book on quantum theory, but this is just what keeps my mind active. I'm just intellectually curious. And I just wander into stuff.

Bobby was not atypical in his view of himself as exceptionally intellectually capable, nor was his subsequent defiance of what he saw as the intellectual and educational "system." Laura described herself as being able to "run circles around" everyone she knew, and Jack's resentment of the inadequacy of his teachers began in second grade. In Jack's case, this fueled a more generalized and conscious defiance:

> I hated the teachers. They sucked. School in general, I couldn't—there were specific things I hated about every school. In each one there were things I didn't like. But the general concept of school was something I also hated. I didn't like the idea of being forced to study, out of a threat to a family unit . . . if I don't go to school, my parents will be fined, sent to jail, whatever. [. . .] Also, the way in which I was being made to study, and what I was being made to study, in every school that I ever went to, was horrible. Horribly chosen and horribly executed, and I knew more than some of the teachers did and I certainly was able to organize [ideas] better than they were.

Thus Jack spent the remainder of his formal education (which lasted until he was sixteen and able to arrange alternative schooling) refusing to do as instructed. He changed many of his assignments to things he thought were more logical or productive, and completed them so well that none of the four schools he attended was willing to give up on him entirely.

In her study of identity projects in three different youth communities, Amy Wilkins finds that the Goth scene she studied consisted largely of former geeks (2008). For her, geeks "are marked by over investment in adult middle-class values—studious, industrious and often technologically adept" (2008, 27). In this view, geeks are a contemporary incarnation of the "nerd" of the eighties. The self-defined geeks in Caeden are neither studious nor, in many cases, particularly industrious. Perhaps the mainstream stereotype that captures geekiness as I intend it here, distinct from Wilkins' geeks, is that of the gamer, then—well-read in particular realms, technologically proficient, but academically and socially less so. Geekiness in Caeden is characterized by a resistance to conformity and rule-following, at least in regard to education.

Despite their rejection of conventional approaches to intellectual development, most of my respondents identified as "good" kids. When Frank identified himself as a misfit, I asked whether he was one in high school. He responded: "I was too good to be a true misfit. But don't forget, I was a misfit because I was fucking since I was thirteen." Similarly, my respondents generally viewed themselves as cooperative and rule-abiding:

> I think I was a pretty social kid. I mean, generally I was the brain kid, amongst the crowd. I was totally—at least I felt this way—I felt totally awkward as a child. But. . . I was somewhat of a klutz and a brain and I was awkward and wickedly sarcastic and alienated, and I probably would've become Goth if Goth had existed. But I was too straight-laced. You know, any opportunities that I had for drinking or drugs, I was like, no, I don't do that. (Interview transcript, Seth)

> [When I tell people I'm a good girl] it just sounds geeky. I was a good girl. I was a very good girl. I was a good student. I was a good daughter. My brother has some developmental issues, so I was the perfect child also. [. . .] Even if I was an only child, had to get the grades, never got below a B, you know, did as I was told, I'd say 98% of the time. (Interview transcript, Leah)

There were exceptions, however. Jeri, Jessica, and Shane all had histories of poor performance in school and drug use.[5] Jeri, who was overweight and identified as a lesbian, is also of mixed identity. She recalled:

> I've always been an outside the box. I mean, literally, no matter what it was. In high school, you know, I was a smoker, I did drugs, you know, whatever was outside the parameters of normal society, I always did that. I got a tattoo, I got a nose piercing, I—whatever.

Feelings of social marginality among American children are not unusual, but the collective marginal experience of the people in Caeden is profound. Distinct in scope from typical adolescent angst by bodily nonconformity and social awkwardness, many people in Caeden did not feel like outsiders merely at an awkward point in their lives; they were outsiders throughout their lives. Emerging from their preadolescent years without "corrections" to their geekiness and incidental androgyny, they were outsiders, and they remain outsiders as adults—quite apart, at least it would seem, from their interest in SM.

Throughout their lives, the members of Caeden have inhabited non-normative bodies, have maintained incidentally androgynous presentations, and have—always—felt much too smart for social acceptance. Even beyond these characteristics, however, interview respondents' narratives of marginality included feelings and perspectives about their families. More than half of them felt that, during childhood, it had been necessary for them to take care of themselves, their parent/s, or a sibling. In most cases, this reflected the circumstances, most commonly, a parent with addiction, bipolar disorder, or depression, or a sibling with a developmental disorder. In other cases, the adults in the home could not be trusted to care for the children; five of my respondents disclosed either physical or sexual abuse in the family. In addition, six had experienced the death of a parent at a young age, and three others had parents who divorced. Of the twenty people who participated in formal interviews with me, only one did not fit at least one of these profiles. My conversations with members of the Caeden scene even outside of formal interviews revealed similar family histories throughout the community. These stories are filled with tumult and trauma, leaving many of the people in Caeden deeply convinced that their lives were vastly different from the lives of everyone else, and feeling profoundly socially isolated.

Marginality: Narratives and Identities

At a Horizons meeting I attended, a man named Jonas was to demonstrate how to throw a single-tailed whip. He was a large, awkward man with long hair and a lumbering gait. He wore old black jeans that hung sloppily from his waist, and his shoulders were slightly hunched. Without the usual greeting or verbal introduction, Jonas immediately turned his back to the audience and pushed a button on a portable compact disc player. A tall thin woman stood with her back to the audience, and Jonas began to hit her back lightly with the whip. As he whipped her, he began to move, increasingly, rhythmically. He was not quite dancing in the performative sense; it was as if he were unaware that he was even moving to the music. He circled the woman, repeatedly throwing the whip in such a way that it curled around the woman's body, appearing deeply engrossed. His movements were unconventional but unselfconscious and entirely in rhythm with the music. After the demonstration had ended, in a small, soft-spoken voice, he explained, "Words fail me for the most part, but this doesn't." He said little else.

The experiences of geekiness, obesity, incidental androgyny, and social awkwardness are potentially so closely linked that it can be difficult to extricate them from one another. Yet each is distinctly marginalizing, and their conflation results in a multi-layered sense of marginality, as Laura illustrated:

> I didn't have a lot of friends. People didn't like me; I was the kid people made fun of. I was tall, I was fat, I was a geek. I was smart, which was probably a really bad combination. And kids are cruel. I was always the kid that had the answer. I fit in better with the geeks, but I wasn't completely accepted. I wasn't invited to things. Even when the geeks got together, I wasn't invited. I was not a social person. I didn't know how to be. That's what it kinda came down to. I didn't know how to be. I just didn't fit in anywhere.

Experiences of life on the social margins are pervasive in the life stories of interview respondents, salient in the conversations among community members, and a generally assumed aspect of community life in Caeden. Whether these marginal experiences were meaningful for the members of this community before they arrived, or have been jointly constructed through community narratives since, the stories of marginality resonate very strongly for people in Caeden. The loneliness captured in many of these stories is striking, as is the framing of marginality as an affinity for nonconformity:

> I would have these things that I was weird about, but I liked being weird about [them]. I would bring a book sometimes during recess and I'd get like friends to do it too; I'd be like "bring a book at recess and we'll sit by the dumpsters and read!" I wasn't a loner, I was just—I liked being different. There were usually like sixty kids in a class, in a grade. I was always, though my whole life, somewhere in the middle. (Interview transcript, Lily)

Membership in the Caeden SM community cultivates, reinforces, and sustains identities of marginality that draw from sources far beyond members' interest in sadomasochistic play. Entrance into the community provides immediate reassurance that kindred spirits—and bodies and minds—exist. This observable validation suggests to participants that their interest in SM must somehow be connected to their other marginal experiences. By providing them the chance to cast SM as the (essentialist) explanation for why they have been different all along, the community reaffirms a broader and farther-reaching identity of marginality. This identity trumps the pre-community sources of nonconformity and highly values living life "outside the box."

The members of this community make unconventional life choices at almost every turn. They generally view themselves as especially sexually libidinous. Many were sexually active earlier than average and engaged in less normative sexual activities at a young age. Careers (and career paths) tend also to be unconventional; many people work at home, freelance, or live off passive income of one sort or another. They participate in a broad range of other nonconforming, extreme, or marginal activities, including Wicca, Satanism, the Society for Creative Anachronism, civil war reenactments, shamanism, fencing, barbershop quartets, marathon running, skydiving, and vampirism. In their livelihood and in their hobbies, the members of this community are nonconformists. They are accustomed to defining themselves as outsiders.

Importantly, the alternative movements that attract the members of this community are pastime or hobby-based, rather than aesthetic or stylistic. Many members of the community reported having "Goth" friends in high school; Seth was not the only one to remark that he could have been Goth. In some ways, they bear strong similarities to members of the Goth communities (Wilkins 2008). Yet they are not Goth; they do not conform to a countercultural fashion style that would contextualize and present their outsiderness to the world. Their freakiness does not "resolve the dilemmas" of coolness that Wilkins observes for Goths, who consciously and deliberately construct their freakiness on their bodies as they move through heteronormative spaces from which they may have previously been excluded. The members of the Caeden SM community do not make these stylistic and declarative choices regarding self-presentation. Even when they are "out" about their SM identities, this declaration does not resolve their dilemma; they continue to live on the social margins everywhere other than within the SM scene itself.

In this context, community identity becomes important not merely because it represents shared interest in SM, but because it represents shared histories of living on the margins—of having been, for much of their lives and for multiple reasons, what Erving Goffman called "disqualified from full social acceptance" (1963).

Chapter 2

Geeks and Freaks
Marginal Identity and Community

In celebration of Raven's birthday, several of us were meeting at a restaurant in the vicinity of the club before the Horizons party. When I arrived at seven o'clock, twelve people were already seated. I waved to everyone and went to sit beside Elise, who jumped up to hug me as I approached. Four more people entered before we ordered.

The place was busy, and the din made it difficult to hear each other. It was not our usual spot. The wait staff seemed slightly contemptuous, perhaps noting the preponderance of black leather—or the popularity of the fettuccine alfredo dish with extra garlic bread—in this particular crowd.

At 8:30, the four of us who were scheduled to set up for the party prepared to head out. As we each rounded the table to give individual hugs to people we would see again in approximately ninety minutes, Sheryl stood up and yelled, "Wait! Wait! I won't be there!" and rushed all of us to give a proper good-bye.

Adia, Kim, Larry, and I walked up to the club and set about hanging decorations, putting out prizes, setting up the food—cold cuts and shrimp, candy and cookies. The CDs needed to be queued in the disk player, along with whatever special instructions James needed to cut and cue the music for special events throughout the evening.

At 9:30, we were nearly ready for the 10:00 start. By 11:00 the place was packed—wall to wall people—and several scenes were underway. I sat at a booth next to Jesse and across from Adam, and we caught up on the day's events.

After a few minutes, Jesse asked me, "Do you like knives?"

"Sure," I replied.

"Close your eyes," Jesse said. She took my wrist. I felt a dull blade trail along the inside of my forearm. I opened my eyes and saw that it was not a blade at all, but a paper-thin, plastic card. We marveled at how like a blade it felt.

Adam began to dig all of his sharps out of his bag. He held out his hand for mine. I gave it to him and watched as he placed a two-bladed finger cuff over his index finger. I had not seen a cuff like that before. It was a new toy for Adam also. He dragged it along the back of my hand. We discussed how to make them, how expensive they were, and where to find them.

Handing the cuff to Jesse, he said, "Here, try it on her neck."

"Do you mind?" Jesse asked me.

"No, it's okay," I replied, piling my hair atop my head with a hair band so that my hair wouldn't cause the blades to skip.

Jesse dragged the blades up and down my neck, softly at first. It gave me goose bumps. When I shivered, Adam wrapped my arms in his. Within a few seconds Jesse was no longer using the blade lightly enough to tickle, and I was no longer shivering. Adam reached into his pocket, removed his pocketknife and flipped it open. Taking my wrists in one hand, he stretched my arms across the table, palms up.

In soft voices, just above whispering, Jesse and Adam talked as they used the blades on my skin. I kept my eyes closed and focused on the feeling.

"She marks so nicely," Adam said.

"I know. And look at her face. It's like it's putting her to sleep," replied Jesse.

"Except when it hurts," Adam said as he pressed the knife into my skin.

The three of us played at the booth for a while. When the impromptu scene ended, Adam stood up with his toy bag, gave me a dramatic look and said, "You ready for me?" I smirked and said good-bye to Jesse. As we wandered around, looking for an empty play area, several people called out, "Have fun!"

"Don't let him be mean to you," called James, the owner of the club.

Lars smiled as we passed him. "Always with a full dance card," he complained jovially. "Let me know when it opens up!"

When we found a play space, Elise was sitting in the room. She squealed and clapped loudly.

"Oh goody, Dakota and Adam are going to play! I love to watch you guys play! Oooh, wait wait wait! I gotta pee! I'll be right back!" She dashed off. Adam and I exchanged surprised and flattered smiles.

About an hour later, our scene was interrupted by an announcement over the loudspeaker that the club was closing. We ignored it. James, the owner of the club, played "Cotton-Eyed Joe," a loud, fast-paced, grating bluegrass song intended to put a quick end to the scene. James lived far away from the city and had a long commute home. Disregarding the not-so-subtle hint, Adam danced a mock two-step as he swung his flogger.

The club went black. Startled, I gasped. James, a longtime community member and well-known spanking aficionado, sighed tiredly into the microphone.

"Okay, everybody. No more, you freaks!"

We laughed. I sat down and Adam hollered, "All right, old man, all right." He began gathering our things in the dark. James turned the lights back on. We made our way to the front of the club.

It was nearly four o'clock in the morning. Only about twenty-five regulars were left. It appeared that everyone else had finished their scenes and was sitting around, glassy-eyed from either play or exhaustion.

As we made our way to the booths where we had left our things, Jacob commented to me, "Hey, I didn't know you liked knives. I'm really, really good with knives. We should play sometime. Seriously. I make people faint!"

I smiled and thanked him for the offer, but did not accept his invitation to unconsciousness.

We arrived at the booths, and the ritual chatter began. Planning the post-club diner visit involved multiple simultaneous conversations that generated the same result almost every weekend night.

"Who's going for breakfast?"

"Hey, are you guys going to Sully's?"

"You two going for food?"

"I think Joanna wanted to head over to Paradise."

"I'm going home. I'm exhausted."

"Who just said home?? It's only 3:30!"

"Hey, you guys going for breakfast?"

"What's wrong with Paradise?"

"Schuyler's my ride. Where is she? Oh, she's over there—hey, can one of you guys ask Schuyler if she's going for breakfast?"

"We're going to go to Sully's. We'll save a booth in case you end up over there."

In the end, we all ended up at Sully's, as we had the night before, taking up several tables and annoying the wait staff with individual checks. I left the diner at seven and crawled into bed, thoroughly exhausted, at eight o'clock in the morning. Again.

Like "identity," the term "community" is contested in the social sciences. Its meanings vary widely, and criteria for its use are elusive.[1] It is always, however, about boundaries. The notion of community is used, in academic writing and in American discourse, to draw lines between insiders and outsiders. This division is what brings the members of Caeden—and what compels me—to consider it a community. Used interchangeably with "the scene" in the discourse, "the community" serves as a source of a good deal of personal meaning. Participants in the scene find in the community a bond created by shared life experiences and shared objectives.

Though the concept of community remains particularly nebulous in both sociology and anthropology, in psychology in recent decades it has been subjected to valuable hermeneutic shifts, from community as geographical and cultural territory to community as social-psychological responses to social spaces. This has allowed for the study of the "sense of community" (and, later, the "psychological sense of community"), considering the roles of identification and identity, community seeking and community building, and, ultimately, the intersection of community, identity, and interaction.[2]

McMillan and Chavis (1986) propose a definition of sense of community with four elements—membership, influence, integration and fulfillment of needs, and shared emotional connection. These aspects of life in Caeden are important to its members; the community is built around these experiences and understandings, through discourse and through SM play. It is not simply that the community offers these emotional benefits, but that it exists in order to provide them.

Membership: Coming Home to Caeden

When asked about the role SM played in his life, Seth's response focused not on SM itself, but on the community:

> BDSM is home. BDSM is being amongst people who stroke each other's hair. Give each other backrubs. I think it's inherent in the BDSM community, a willingness to be more open about contact. I need contact. My deepest desire is driven by contact. It's where I found it—and it's home. . . . It's the place where I've really felt the opportunity to be myself, the person I've been my whole life, amongst people who understand the nature of freaks and geeks . . . people are much more open about touching each other, more than anywhere else I've ever been in. I'm a touch slut . . . that's the way I would describe myself. I'm a touch slut. I mean . . . my life has been very touch denied.

Despite Seth's conceptualization elsewhere of BDSM as a primal need, he entered the SM scene in order to find companionship—to be touched. With his acute awareness of a loneliness that came from feeling like an outsider in all other social situations, Seth's decision to join the SM community was fueled, consciously, by a desire to join a community.

> In high school I was a total loser. I struggled a lot with my sense of not being particularly attractive, not really knowing how to deal with people on a human basis. I was like . . . I spent my teenage years being the guy at [The Playground] who can't talk to anybody. . . . Except on an intellectual basis, I really found no way to breach [sic] the subject of relationships or even friendships with women. I had a very hard time accepting that anybody would want to, you know, interact with me. It was very lonely. It really was.

Then, at twenty-three, according to Seth, someone took an interest. He and Sara, twenty-five, had been a couple for several months and planned to get married. On the day Seth planned to propose, he and Sara were on his motorcycle when a car plowed through a stop sign and hit them. Seth awoke in the hospital a few days later, engagement ring still in his pocket, and learned that Sara had been killed.

Having lost his brother and his almost-fiancée within a year of each other, Seth again tried to find a community where he felt comfortable. A longtime science-fiction fan, he attended a sci-fi convention, and the program included a stage show with whips, chains, and leather. Seth viewed the show as something separate from the topic of the convention, and it marked his introduction to the SM community; he said he now had "a place to go."

The SM scene interested him because it was unfamiliar and required an intellectual investment. Although he and Sara had experimented with SM, Seth considered his interest fairly newfound, describing his discovery of the complexity of SM as "Oh, look, something to learn about! Something to read!" He bought several SM books, began to identify as "kinky," and began to search for other kinky people.

Newly anchored in the SM scene, Seth found a space for socializing, people to touch, and new material for intellectual exploration. The community brought an end to his loneliness and rendered his social marginality less relevant. He was "home"; for him, the community was a sanctuary of unconditional acceptance and emotional opportunity.

Reflections like this are typical in Caeden; the "how-I-found-the-scene" narrative seems obligatory in introductions and discussions of identity, and the metaphor of the SM community as home is a widely accepted component of community discourse. Greg felt that his life changed when he went to his first Horizons meeting:

"October 9, 2001,[3] and the rest is all good . . . I had heard wonderful things about it. Discovered I liked the people. And it was just home . . . immediately."

Frank went to his first Horizons meeting at eighteen years old. He had brought a friend with him who wanted to leave early, but Frank refused: "I looked around and I said 'I'm home.'"

In light of identities of marginality, it is not surprising that the entrance into the community is a metaphor for finding a home. Members of the scene readily share the perspective that they did not belong anywhere prior to finding the SM scene. They frequently assert that "people here *get* it," and the "it" refers not narrowly to SM interest, but to marginality more broadly, for the reasons and in the ways that are so common in Caeden. The sense of being understood, of being known, underlies the importance of community for many people in Caeden. By subsuming the marginalities under one overarching identity, the community offers understanding of the experiences of outsiderness that many have lived. The metaphor of home conveys not only like-minded people, but a belief in kindred spirits, acceptance, and connectedness.

Membership involves a "sense of belonging and identification," a category in which they include the feeling, belief, and expectation of fitting in, as well as a sense of acceptance within the group (McMillan and Chavis 1986). The search for an in-group, a place where we belong more than others do, is central to the experience of community membership. McMillan and Chavis use "It is my group" and "I am part of the group" as indicators of this identification. The arguably more romantic "I am home" is especially powerful in light of the rarity of the home as sanctuary in the lives of the people in Caeden.

As much as community membership is derived from identification, it is defined by drawing boundaries between people who belong in a group and those who do not. These lines are linked not only to familiarity, but to trust; the shift from outsider to insider begins with visibility and moves quickly to immersion in the public scene.

For the people in Caeden, the most common criterion for inclusion in "the scene" is involvement; unknown SM participants may be "kinky," but they are not considered part of the community. Opinions vary about whether participants need to play in public to be considered part of the scene; although several people did argue this, most felt that regular community involvement constituted membership.

Players are able to, and many do, successfully arrange their lives around scene activities—politically troubling as the term is, avoiding "normals" (Goffman 1963) is often achieved through participation in the Caeden SM community. It is a well-established and multi-faceted group. During any given week, there are at least five SM-related events one can attend, of varying types—educational, activist, social and/or play-oriented. Most of the time, there are more than five; the more active one is in the community, the more opportunities exist for participation.

Immersion in the scene is common and easily achieved. Through Web blogs, organization discussion lists, instant messaging, and organization volunteerism, the most involved members of the community spend most of their waking hours interacting with other members. In addition, several times a year, multiday, multi-level SM events provide the opportunity for complete immersion in the social, political, educational, and sexual milieu of the scene. Though many of these events do not take place in Caeden, many members of the community frequently travel across the country, and more commonly along the East Coast, to participate in these events.

Several people in the scene also travel frequently to teach and speak at regular, smaller-scale meetings and events of other organizations throughout the year. They invest a considerable amount of time in networking, planning, and participating in these events.

In 1963, Howard Becker's pivotal work shifted academic focus from why people engage in "deviant" behaviors to why everyone else follows "the rules." He argued that we must ask how a person "manages to avoid the impact of conventional commitments," and posited that "a person who does not have a reputation to maintain or a conventional job he must keep may follow his impulses. He has nothing staked on continuing to appear conventional" (Becker 1963, 28). The fact that careers (and career paths) tend also to be unconventional among people in the Caeden community is highly conducive to immersion in the scene. It is also the case that people sometimes structure their work lives around their involvement in the scene, even declining opportunities for income that would interfere with their volunteer responsibilities and participation in the community. It is not that the members of the Caeden scene simply have nothing staked in appearing conventional; it is that they are quite deliberately rejecting the conventional as a legitimate place for a stake.

It is not unusual for community members to have relatively little everyday contact with people outside the scene. Even among people with conventional work lives and contact with their families, many report that their "vanilla" (people outside the community) friendships have dwindled or disappeared since joining the community.

Social status in Caeden is linked to the extent of immersion in the scene. The relationship of this link to play and status will be further explored later, but in general, one's social status increases as one's involvement in the community increases.

In drawing these boundaries, the community reinforces and legitimizes group identity, and creates a safe social space for participants. Lily explained the value, for her, of the interplay between SM itself and the social-psychological appeal of a community of people who accept SM:

> I enjoy the combination of meetings where I get to learn and socialize and club time where I get to play and see friends who I might also play with and I like that it's not just play. [. . .] I always kind of said I wanted a group of friends who could make an offhand joke, like somebody cuff that girl, you know? And I remember saying early on, I was like, wouldn't that be great? To be part of a group that could just like joke about it, it was so commonplace. And I'm part of that now. I'm part of a group where like Richie can give me a spank when I walk in the door, and that's common. That's us. It's not scary or weird or odd. I love that . . . [. . .] I like community, I like having friends who are into it the way I am, in a lifestyle way. [. . .] It's a big part of who I am, and I don't think I can change that. I don't think it's a phase. I think it may be something I go in and out of throughout my life, like, there may be years where I'm not submissive someday. But I think it'll always be there, as a part of me.

Identities of marginality in the lives of the members of this community are recast, blended, and romanticized; in and through Caeden, to be a "pervert"[4] is to be open-minded, geeky, and creative. Though a good deal of this is accomplished through play itself, the potential for this identity shift has much to do with members' immersion in the community itself. The mitigation of the stigma of SM participation, then, is part of the value of the community to its members.

The paths people take to the SM community in Caeden reveal the interdependence of identity formation, community seeking, and community building. Some, like Laura and Jack, sought the SM community specifically in order to validate and share an SM interest they had already recognized. Although Laura viewed her SM as simply an "alternative interest," she wanted to spend time with people among whom she felt less conspicuous:

> I wanted people like me, who were essentially normal, living normal lives, who just had alternative interests. And that behind closed doors they liked certain things . . . I felt like I didn't stand out for the first time. It was a very comfortable place to be. I just remember the not-standing-out part. I'm the same here.

Jack joined for similar validation:

> Well, when I first figured out that there was actually a scene, I was like okay, that's what I gotta find. Because . . . as you already know, I've been interested in this lifestyle and the whole S&M thing ever since I can remember . . . so the scene was just kind of the natural development of that. It was like, if there's an organized group for it, then I might want to join it . . . kind of thing. Same reason why soccer players join teams. I wanted to join the team. That, and also just to find the sense of, I'm not actually a creep.

Aware of the marginality of SM, Jack found reassurance in the community. Diagnosed with bipolar disorder by then, Jack understood himself as different in several ways. Although he was not looking to feel "normal" by joining the SM community, he frames his motivation in terms of social acceptance of a stigmatized—and pathologized—interest in SM.

Others, like Frank, cast their finding of the scene as a happy accident, but nonetheless understand the value of the community to them as one of validation and reassurance at the stage of entry:

> I stumbled onto [the scene]. Probably searching for perverted things because I was perverted. But I stumbled onto SM and then it was the finding other people, going "wait a minute—maybe I'm not that fucked up. Or, if I am, there's a lot of other people who are fucked up. Like me." And that was a big, big, big deal.

Community and Identity

Although many of the members of this SM community subscribe to a belief in a preexisting (often essentialized) interest in SM, many also understand their interest as part of a larger creative epistemological approach to the social world. This paradoxical juxtaposition transpires not only in the discourse of the origins and importance of SM identity, but also in discourses of nonconformity and marginality in Caeden. For most members of this community, SM identification is a salient part of their larger social identity. Greg's description is typical:

> I identify as someone who is leather, who is a scene person, who is a pervert. And who is happy being one. And that part about it's self-acceptance, and not rejecting myself. . . . It's where I'm happiest. If I was

> in a vanilla—I would probably not choose to be in a vanilla relationship at any point in the foreseeable future in my life. And I can understand people do. I personally find that this works better for me and I'm staying with it as long as I can.

In recent years, work on identity has proliferated, but scholars have objected to its overuse, vagueness, and general weakness as an analytical category.[5] These are astute and important criticisms, and throughout this work I have endeavored to be diligent about the use of the term, opting for clearer and more precise concepts such as "identification" and "self-perception" where appropriate.

However, "identity" is useful even as it is nebulous. There is no alternative to capture the sense of self that is, at once, constructed through interaction, influenced by the responses of others, presented to the social world, and invented, evaluated, maintained, and reinvented "from within." Whatever it includes or does not, identity scholars use it to suggest that the social-psychological implication of "identity" is greater than the sum of its parts. I find "identity" valuable in conveying the importance of *relationships between* particular self-understandings, identifications, experiences, and community memberships for individuals, and the centrality of these relationships in their lives.

Narratives about discovering Caeden are constructed not around a particular identification, but around looking for a sense of belonging. Some people in the community maintain that their SM interest developed *after* finding the community, though this is almost always accompanied by the assumption that they are unusual in this regard. Further, even when community members discuss having known about their SM interest or having sought out the scene because of it, SM interest is often conceptualized broadly, as if it mattered little whether the interest was in topping or bottoming specifically.

Many people in Caeden believe that SM proclivities are innate. Borrowing from the rhetoric of gay and lesbian activism, SM is an orientation, and for most members of the community, concerns over "sexual freedom" are central to participation in SM. Jack, for example, views his SM identity as an essential component of himself. It matters less whether people believe that their SM interest is inborn (which may be the most pervasive perspective) or comes out of life experience than that they commonly view it as inextricable from the self:

> The interest for me was literally the first thing that I can remember about most of the world. It's why I say it's so deeply ingrained in who I am, it's more today than a sexual orientation, than a gender identity—it's SM. It's really where I identify with; it's that strong. And no one really quite gets

> just the power of that until they actually have this conversation with me; 'cause it's like okay, he's just really into SM. NO. That was like my first few experiences with the world. That's how strong it is.

Frank's perspective on his SM identity is also essentialist, and, having always been aware of his alternative sexual interests, he views the Caeden scene as emancipating:

> Look at all those years I was depressed and low self-esteem, because I thought I was bad because of it. Once I found it was a positive thing, I lost thirty-five pounds. I all of the sudden had a self-awareness, I all of a sudden had a self-identity, I had pride for who I was. I'm proud of this. It is my social universe. Sexually it excites me. Psychologically it balances me. Spiritually it completes me. It's in my genetics.

The idea of SM identity as both essential and meaningful is pervasive in the community. In one major SM organization, meeting attendees take turns introducing themselves, and almost without exception, use a social script: "My name is Jane, I've been a member for two years, and I'm a submissive."

Further, although it is common for people to top when they had previously only bottomed or vice versa, the typical response highlights essentialist views of identity: "I knew you were really a switch!" References to fixed SM identities waiting to be discovered are also typical, such as "a submissive and doesn't know it yet," or a "top who can't admit it."

Despite these essentialist beliefs, SM identities are also understood as changing over time. The ubiquitous metaphor for SM as "the journey" not only involves the transgression of boundaries and introspection, but also implies that the destination is less important. Stories about identity in the scene very often include change, and identification shifts are both recognized and encouraged, even as members adhere to essentialist ideas about identities. The essentialism shifts from particular SM identifications to more profound identities as SM and not-SM (kinky versus vanilla) and allows for flexibility in the particular SM roles. This fluidity of identity is not an implicit contradiction in the analytical construct of identity (Brubaker and Cooper 2000), but an indicator of the importance of possibilities for meaningful change in selfhood throughout the life course.

The persistence of an essentialist understanding of SM in the face of this variability evidences SM identity as immutably central to self, and underscores the importance of the community in the lives of its members. Further, the essentialist perspective thrives alongside the contradictory belief in SM as yet another exploration undertaken by people whose tendency it is to explore. In a radical departure from the clinical model, it is not the belief in a particular kink itself that is essentialized, but the propensity *for* kink—the interest in SM as a nonconformist activity. The narrative is not built around wanting to take a particular action, as in "I just need to be tied up," but around being a part of this community, and being different from those outside, thereby reinforcing their sense of membership in Caeden and, simultaneously, the importance of that sense.

The Romanticism of Marginal Identity

The overlap between the SM community and science-fiction fandom is notable in its own right, but it is especially striking against the backdrop of these essentialized perspectives of SM interest. Not being especially familiar with science-fiction film or literature, I was continually surprised at the unquestioning acceptance of this relationship. Despite its absence from the discourse, when asked about the overlap between the two communities, people in Caeden offer surprisingly similar explanations, as easily as if they were intuitive. While models of alternative sexuality are common in science-fiction literature, so, of course, are alternative worlds. Science-fiction fans in Caeden do not usually trace the relationship between SM and science fiction to the alternative sex in sci-fi, but to its imagination. The most widely held of these views was articulated especially well by Seth:

> I think unusual ways of thinking attract the science-fiction and fantasy crowd. So that's what they read, that's what they enact. . . . I don't think that that's a very far jump at all to being more open about sexual desire. I think people who are attracted to freedom, to the freedom to be themselves, are attracted to the freedom to be themselves in a variety of different aspects of their life. And science-fiction and fantasy people really consider themselves outsiders to begin with. Doesn't matter whether it's an outsider in terms of politics or outsider in terms of sexuality or wanting to go to the stars. All being outside the norm, you don't . . . I mean, really . . . the term "geek" has been really reclaimed. But it still implies outsider. There are an awful lot of geeks in the BDSM scene. But I think the turning point . . . when geeks become masters is when they realize that it's okay to be outside. Being outside is cool. One can be geeky and cool. And outside. And powerful. All in the same package. And that's extraordinary.

From this perspective, interests in alternative literature and film, particularly sci-fi and fantasy, not only precede but also set the stage for other alternative interests, including SM. Outsiderness cultivates open-mindedness, which in turn reinforces outsiderness. Nearly everyone I asked in the community shared a similar perspective (and I asked almost everyone I knew). Some accounts included the potential for science fiction to create open-mindedness. Greg found in science fiction a means to an end, a mechanism for achieving the level of imagination and tolerance he feels is found in the SM scene:

> I think [science-fiction literature] helps open your mind. I think it helps prepare you for anything. Like, there's a novel on that shelf about a woman who crash-lands on a planet which is populated by small . . . creatures, and to be able to survive on the planet, she's turned into one. You have to be open-minded to read sci-fi. The same way you have to be open-minded in the dungeon. You see somebody doing something extreme, that you would neevvvver do. And your first reaction might be repulsion, your second reaction should be observation, and your third reaction will probably be acceptance. But if you can get to observation and then acceptance quicker, then you're saving yourself a lot of self-battling, you're saving yourself beating yourself up. And it's easier to accept than reject; rejection takes more work, and is ultimately less helpful.

Greg's perspective posits science fiction as a virtual training ground for the tolerance necessitated by SM participation. Yet the pragmatism of this perspective is not inconsistent with the romanticism of Seth's. In both views the appreciation of and attraction to science fiction and SM are fundamentally the same. They cultivate and *require* imaginativeness, creativity, and social acceptance.

Kyle made the argument even more broadly:

> The people that are willing and courageous and able enough, and have the willpower and the strength to question themselves, and to question the way they were raised, and the way that they're living—the people that have the courage to admit maybe we're wrong about this and maybe we need to look elsewhere and get new information, new ideas, and maybe try something new—those people have an affinity for one another. Whether they did that kind of questioning through sci-fi, through religion or spirituality, whether they did it through SM and alternative sexuality, whether they did it through really anything—it—once a person questions their basic tenets of existence, and questions them successfully, and says you know what,

maybe—by successfully I mean they actually do admit to themselves maybe they're wrong. They have one chance in hell to rebel against themselves. And if they can do that, and by doing so they can find a way of life that makes them happier, um . . . then they're forever open-minded. And open-minded people have a great affinity for one another, because they don't shut down when they're talking to one another about their way of life.

For Kyle, it might as well have just *happened* to be SM. Interestingly, he does not ask why people come to SM, but instead frames human behavior in terms of surrendering (or not) to social inhibitions. SM interest, in this view, is not at all rare, but pursuing it is; therefore, the scene consists of people who have the courage and, presumably, the impetus, to seek it out. From this perspective, people engage in SM, or science-fiction reading, or pagan religions, or vampirism, or a host of alternative activities, because they were open-minded enough to try new things. That some of them "stick" and some of them do not, for Kyle, amounts to little more than chance.

Many members of this community believe that their own interest in SM is inborn. Kyle's implication that an affinity for experimentation perhaps supersedes the affinity for SM threatens the essentialist beliefs that permeate the community, and most certainly threatens the romanticism of the good/evil binary that provides the backdrop for much SM play.

Regardless of whether SM exists as one of a multitude of new "flavors" of life one might (or might not) be inclined to try, or as a preexisting proclivity for the activities themselves, Kyle's observation is consistent with the life stories of my respondents. Because outsiders find each other in the SM scene, immediately and easily, they cease to be outsiders just as quickly. If overlap between interests in alternative lifestyles exists because of dialectically expanding horizons among people prone to experimentation, this cements the bonds between community members; SM, therefore, is not the only interest they have in common. SM becomes, for them, the symbol of home—they are familiar, safe, understood, and accepted unconditionally.

This view of SM—and of social life—makes sense in the context of identities of marginality and lived defiance. Marginal status, on multiple levels and in multiple ways, takes precedence over any particular source of outsiderness. This status either leads to or is framed as the explanation for marginal interest and pursuits, rendering a nonconformist life—the romanticized, open-minded, creative rejection of social imperatives—the overarching explanation for the connection among community members.

The open-mindedness that is taken for granted among community members is clearest when outsiders venture into the community for the first time. While some newcomers integrate fairly seamlessly, others, particularly those who do not appear to necessarily live lives on the margins of social acceptance, find that the scene is not what they envisioned. During a major multi-day event, I was wandering through the dungeon, stopping occasionally to chat with people, when I was approached by a clean-cut, good-looking man in his mid-twenties. Appearing frantic and highly agitated, he asked me to point out "Miss Danielle" to him. "Miss Danielle," who was known as Danielle in the scene, was ten feet away from us. I explained that I was unwilling to identify her because I did not know who he was, but I said that I would be happy to give her a message when I saw her. He grew increasingly agitated, his voice raising in pitch and his eyes darting around the room. He did not seem angry, only profoundly uncomfortable and slightly fearful. I told him that he seemed highly agitated and asked what the trouble was.

He finally looked me in the eyes. Though a bit reticent at first, he agreed to accompany me to a quiet corner with a table, where we sat down together and he told me his story. Danielle, whom he had met through a personal ad, had told him about the event, and he had come to meet her. It was his first time at an SM event. Having paid a good deal of money to attend this event, he (Scott) was shocked by the sight of so many conventionally unattractive attendees, and he was afraid to meet "Miss Danielle" without knowing what she looked like.

Further, he explained, he was extremely uncomfortable with the activities he was witnessing. He was interested in the light bottoming known in Caeden as "slap and tickle"—ice, silk scarves, and light spanking. He thought everyone around him was insane, and the fact that he found so many of them unattractive rendered everything even less understandable to him. As I later wrote in my notes, all of this "clearly freaked him out." He made no mention of leaving the event, but he paced, tapped his hands and feet, and all but trembled with anxiety.

As we talked, I found his agitation unsettling. Hoping to calm him down, I introduced him to several strategically chosen members of the local scene. At one point while we were talking, Kevin approached me and commented on the scene I had done the night before (described in the prologue to chapter 4). Scott, who had finally begun to seem more settled, asked about the scene. I changed the subject, but he pressed for details. When I described the scene, as generally as I could, he asked to see my back.

I lifted my shirt. He gasped and stammered, "But . . . you seem so . . . so . . . so . . ."

"Normal?" I asked.

He grew flustered again, afraid, I think, that he was offending me. "No, no, I didn't mean that—I didn't mean that at all. You just seem so . . . down to earth."

Out of a sense of loyalty to the community, I regretted confirming his sense, on the basis of my appearance, that I was anomalous, but when I told him that I was a researcher, he appeared confused. For him, that explained why I was not the same "type" as most of the other attendees, but not why my back was welted. Scott and I talked for most of the night. When Danielle was free, I told her that he was there, but she had just finished playing and was not up to meeting him. They never did meet, and as far as I know, Scott never attended another scene event in Caeden.

Scott's response to the social setting in which he found himself underscores not only the marginality of the people in Caeden, but the absence of a space for them outside of this community. Scott, mainstream in his appearance (and arguably in his "SM" interests), despite the interest or openness that had brought him to the event, embodied the antithesis of the "open-mindedness" that community members attribute to one another, and so highly value in the community.

Anthony Cohen has argued that, given the symbolic nature of the opposition of any given community to the larger society in which it lives, "people can think themselves into difference" (1985, 117). In Caeden, intersections of marginal experiences on multiple fronts coalesce into identities of marginality that underlie participation in the SM community and in SM itself.

To some, the community serves as a place to conform to the standards and expectations of those around them. To others, it serves as a place where rebels go to find new ways to rebel. Regardless, the "how-I-found-the-scene" stories are constructed and retold precisely because many people view their discovery of this community as a pivotal moment in their lives. Although some narratives are constructed around top/bottom identities, many are not. Moreover, among narratives in which an essentialist SM identity figures prominently, many are tales of finding the scene and meaning in the community, quite apart from topping and bottoming specifically. The members of this community tell stories of coming to the community not because they felt like sadists and masochists, but because they felt they were different.

The feeling of social acceptance many people reported upon entering the scene, then, was an acceptance not of their SM interest, but of their more general outsiderness. Even if these narratives are cultivated or nurtured in and through the community, their resonance is a testament to the marginal experiences of community members long before their entrance into the scene.

This is not to say that the members of Caeden are, simply put, sadists and masochists because they are misfits, nor the reverse. It is instead to illustrate the ways in which marginal identities and experiences have intersected in the lives of its members, to cultivate a creative worldview and an exploratory approach to social relationships. It is also to deny, along with others, that the social pursuit of SM emerges directly from a fundamental interest, whether sourced in genetics or childhood trauma, in that which we know as sadism and/or masochism (Weinberg, Williams, and Moser 1984; Langdridge and Butt 2004; Langdridge 2006; Weiss 2006b).

The Caeden SM community serves its members in ways beyond providing a social network and opportunities and partners for SM play. In the first place, it is a place of support, where in-group identities of marginality are cultivated and maintained in contrast to out-group identities of conformity. Secondly, it is a marketplace for particular social currency elsewhere unrecognized, and as such it offers pathways to prestige and status often unattainable to its members in other social settings. The conflation of these pathways to high status with identities of marginality, in turn, provides a sense of acceptance powerful enough for members of the scene to refer to the community as “home.”

Part 2. Play

Chapter 3

Tipping the Scales

Striving for Imbalance

I stood facing him, trying to keep my abraded back from brushing against the rough concrete wall. I was exhausted. We'd been playing for a long time; it must have been at least two hours. I think he used just about every toy he owned. My legs were stiff. My arms ached from straining against the cuffs. I was depleted from the scene, ready to go home and crawl into bed.

He set his flogger on the table beside him. He moved close to me and stroked my hair.

"How ya doin'?" he asked softly.

"Good . . . ," I responded, ". . . sleepy." I smiled and he laughed at me.

"What?" I asked, half-dazed.

Mimicking me, Adam smiled—a wide, spacey, extremely goofy grin.

"Here, let me get that," he said, miming wiping drool from my chin.

I laughed. He laughed.

Then he hit me, open-handed, across my left cheek, probably about as hard as I had ever been hit. My face swung toward the wall.

I was stunned. I stared at him in disbelief, recognizing nothing in his expression. I was silent. No words came to mind.

I felt something like fear, though fear doesn't quite describe it. I wasn't worried about any particular consequences; I wasn't clear-headed enough for worry. I was on edge—not quite needing to run, but wide-eyed and vigilant. I had no idea what he might do next. It bred a strange state of something akin to fear, without the consciousness that fear normally requires.

As I stared at him wordlessly, he hit me again. Then again, almost as soon as his hand left my face, another, followed by a dizzying series of rapid-fire slaps.

He stopped and looked at me. He hit me again, followed by another pause, more time between slaps—then faster, then slow again.

Completely off-kilter, I winced in anticipation of slaps that never came—relaxing my body just before they landed. I was overwhelmed by the constant barrage of blows, the never having had the chance to get my head together in the scene, no chance to shake my mind clear, assess how I was feeling—too much, too fast, all on top of itself.

I don't remember how it ended, exactly. He must have uncuffed me . . . he hugged me and we walked over to the booths. He kept his arms around me and stroked my hair. After a while, I started to talk.

I couldn't really communicate. I kept losing the words I wanted, and instead I started to giggle. The giggling became uncontrollable. I felt completely intoxicated. Every time I opened my mouth, I found the situation hysterically funny.

He rubbed my back and smoothed my hair silently for awhile, and then conversations began to crop up around me. I remember none of them. I lay there feeling relaxed—drained—trying to get back into my own head. When I was ready to sit up, I did so. He kissed my forehead, near the temple.

SM is often viewed as an alternative sexual practice. It is also frequently understood as role play. Neither of these, by itself, is an especially useful frame for understanding SM play. Perhaps partly in an effort to avoid miring current SM research in longstanding feminist debates over patriarchal gender performances, the view of SM as either (simply) sex or (simply) fantasy is implicit in contemporary work on the topic.

The Role-Play Problem

In the perspective of SM as role play, consenting adults are free to suspend their individual lived realities for the sake of erotic enjoyment; the teacher spanks the misbehaving student in order to enhance the sex life of the couple. Role-playing, as Gary Alan Fine illustrates in his study of fantasy gaming, involves a distancing from their roles even as they are engaged; during play, they say, for example, "I hit him" rather than actually hit him (Fine 1983). These roles are not the everyday performative roles that Erving Goffman regards as comprising all social interaction, but "contrived performances," in which the actors are insincere (Goffman 1959b).

Contrived performances do not typify SM interaction in Caeden. Real-life SM, at least in this community, is rarely role play. Scenes do not typically involve the adoption of alternate personae or plotlines. SM is not fantasy, but the enactment of fantasy. For many, it is the transformation of fantasy into reality—or the closest approximation of it in which they are interested, or that they are willing to achieve. SM scenes are unscripted and unrehearsed, and participants experience them as interpersonal adventures rather than performances. When roles are adopted, pain is often a central aspect of the scene. During one of the few scenes I saw that might be understood as role play, Russ used more than forty clothespins on Heather, clamping them around the outside of her breasts, areolae, and vaginal lips. He left these on her as he flogged her with several different floggers. Throughout the scene, Heather screamed several times, and called Russ "Daddy."

Russ was, of course, not Heather's father. In this sense, this particular scene can be understood as role play. Importantly, though, Russ and Heather were not pretending to be father and daughter, but drawing on language and meanings surrounding power, abuse, and incest to form the narrative of their pain play. Nils-Hennes Stear maintains that SM is "relevantly similar to reading a book or watching a film, for example" (Stear 2009, 23). Even as the contexts are (merely) *simulations* of dominance and submission (Hopkins 1994), the pain in their scene was quite real.[1]

When these kinds of scenes do occur, they occur as sites of spontaneous interaction within a general set of rules. In this regard, they are more akin to improvisational theater than scripted performance. In improv, performers (who refer to themselves as "players") create, and they often do not know what the scene will involve or where it will "take" them. The success of an improv scene depends in part on the "agreement" of the players, generally and before the scene. This "like-mindedness" refers not to the procession of a particular plot or the development of particular characters, but a willingness to follow one another for the sake of the scene (Seham 2001). SM participants enter into play from a similar perspective; negotiation and consent set the parameters for a scene, and participants regard their interactions within those constraints as spontaneous, pure, and authentic.

Yet the "performances" of SM differ even from improvisational theater in important ways. During an improv scene, actual characters, complete with fictional names, histories, and plotlines, often emerge. Unlike SM, improv players play roles that they develop as such, however spontaneous and fleeting these roles might be.

Further, in improv, these roles exist for the sake of the audience. In SM, in contrast, there is no "audience"; the significance of bystanders or even spectators is not that of the improv audience. For SM participants, there is no "show" for which to prepare on a conscious or discursive level. Nearly all SM scenes begin without onlookers. There are no curtains to raise nor lights to dim. Observers drift from scene to scene, moving through an SM club and sampling the goings-on, rather than witnessing a scene from beginning to end. Often, the most private play spaces in a venue are the most desirable, and at times players even enlist friends to help direct potential onlookers elsewhere.

While the presence of onlookers certainly impacts public play in numerous ways, SM participants are not playing *to* the audience. In fact, participants' reputations can be harmed by appearing aware of spectators beyond the extent necessary for safety. A top must be vigilant enough that she checks behind her before she throws a whip, but she will be sanctioned for appearing distracted, preoccupied, self-conscious, or otherwise inappropriately concerned with onlookers during a scene. SM is unlike other spontaneous performances such as professional wrestling and improv, in which players generally attempt to affect the audience together. SM participants seek instead to affect *each other* in the presence of onlookers. The goal in SM experience is a successful performance not for the sake of the audience, but for the sake of the players. For Stear, the performance metaphor of SM breaks down for this reason. The emotional engagement of SM participants, he argues, is akin to that of the audience: "an audience member's game of make-believe is dependent on her or his psychological states, just as a role-playing sadomasochist's game is" (Stear 2009, 29).

Some people do adopt a pseudonym upon entering the Caeden SM scene, to minimize potential damage to their personal and professional reputations. Most of these pseudonyms, however, are simply that: Larry instead of Joseph. Alter egos entrenched in fantasy characters—Dark Lord and Mistress Pandora, for example—are products far more of online chat rooms and email discussion lists than of the SM life in Caeden. Moreover, pseudonyms are adopted as an overarching identity in the community; while Joseph might be Larry "in the scene," he is not Bob in one scene, Jacob when he plays with a different partner, and Thomas on Friday nights. To the extent, then, that pseudonyms reflect and create respite from one's "other" life, the Caeden community does provide a space for that. However, the "identity" is consistent across all interactions in community space. Community space spans dozens of places and times and kinds of events, and for many, community time is all waking hours. These "identities" are therefore the very same "selves" from which SM participants are presumed to be stepping back when they play.

SM and Role Play in the Literature

Early sociological research on SM has helped to shape the perception of SM as role play. In a pioneering study, Weinberg, Williams, and Moser argued that role play is one of five "components" of SM (1984). This work was based on SM as it was practiced in cities on the east and west coasts of the United States between 1976 and 1983. Since then, profound cultural changes, especially regarding gender relations and the advent of the Internet, may have resulted in a different SM, or at least in a different understanding of it. Importantly, the study included members of two particular groups whose SM is not included in the Caeden SM scene: (1) people whose SM activity occurs around economic relationships and (2) leathermen.

Professional dominatrixes (pro-dommes) and their clients, who are by definition engaged in role play, are rarely considered part of the Caeden SM community, though some work suggests this may be different elsewhere (Sisson and Moser 2005). In Caeden, on the whole, pro-dommes do not attend "lay" SM events, clubs, or meetings, and though pro-domme clients occasionally drift through the club or a party, most are not active members in the community. Pro-dommes and their clients are therefore not represented in this book, except in rare cases in which individuals are also members of the larger community.

In Caeden between 2002 and 2006, the pansexual SM scene was separate from the more exclusively gay scene. The two were distinct in several regards, including SM practices and discourses about play. Weinberg, Williams, and Moser's work focused on SM as it occurred in gay SM communities. The leathermen in the Weinberg, Williams, and Moser study engaged in behaviors that are considered SM in Caeden (fisting, whipping, scat,[2] and beating with chains), but they did not view these activities as SM. It may be that because these activities did not occur alongside fantasies about hierarchical relationships, these men rejected the term "SM" precisely because of the role-play frame, in which SM is understood as a game of pretend.[3]

SM play does occupy an ambiguous space between role play and reality. On the night of my first foray into the SM club, I walked through the door and into the main section of the Playground. Having never watched an SM scene before, I was not surprised to see a woman sitting on top of a long table (which I later realized was a rack) wearing a nurse's uniform. I could see only her back, but she wore a nurse's cap, dress, and white shoes. My assumption was that they were "playing" nurse and patient (or perhaps nurse and doctor). I walked around the table to watch the scene, and was taken aback to see her quietly nailing a man's scrotum to a wooden board. The man (her patient, I suppose, if they were indeed role-playing) hissed and screamed. She said nothing, methodically spreading the skin of his scrotum between her fingers, in order to drive each nail through with one or two quick swings of her hammer.

Costumes in scene are rare in Caeden, and when they are worn they are worn as fetish wear rather than as costumes. Nevertheless, outside of a medical setting, her uniform certainly suggested role play. The bottom, however, was not calling her "Nurse," and she was not addressing him as a patient. And she was, in fact, *actually* nailing his scrotum to a wooden board.

In one particular kind of SM (known as "D/s," for Dominance/submission), scene activities approach "role play" more than elsewhere in the SM community. However, for many of these participants, these practices are manifestations and strategies of the *relationship* the players are attempting to create. They are as likely to be engaging in a similar style of interaction at a coffee shop or a family gathering.

Other participants eschew the symbols of performance and focus on the carnal experience of play. Early in my fieldwork, I attended a singletail demonstration by a man well-known in the national SM community for whip-throwing. The presenter, Dean, had much to say on the topic of safewords—the community-wide practice of using code words in order to change the course of a scene without detracting from the various illusions being constructed. My field notes described his perspective:

> Dean was [also] against safewords as a rule, insisting that clear communication between people who know each other makes the most sense. His position was that safewords are silly and unsafe—they can be difficult to remember and therefore dangerous for the bottom. An audience member pointed out that people like to play in situations in which no does not mean no, but he either didn't understand her (she wasn't very clear) or didn't want to deal with it. He harped on the idea of saying what you mean to each other—play for him seemed very straightforward and technical—there was no room in his view for struggle or nonconsensual fantasy—and not much room for anything D/s oriented, either.

Though Dean's "realist" perspective seemed to me to be more extreme than that of some of his audience members, the realist approach is the more common perspective in the scene. For most players, SM is about constructing experiences of imbalanced power relationships at least in part through actions on the body. This is not to say that SM play is identical to the authentic experiences of the narratives with which it engages, but to worry the binary between pretense and reality, to which debates about SM still so often resort.

The Sex Problem: Gawkers and Wankers

One night, several months into my fieldwork, I arrived at the club to find it markedly different than usual. After making my way past hordes of relatively young, good-looking, well-dressed "gawkers," I located several disgruntled regulars and asked what was happening. The club, I was told, had just been featured in some "Erotic Guide to (Caeden)" book. The inside word was that the place would be overrun with the "stand and model" crowd for a while.

"See ya!" said Adam, and headed off in search of female college students, a group with which he frequently had success initiating spanking scenes on nights like this. I wandered around trying to ascertain why it was, precisely, that the place suddenly seemed so unfamiliar.

Some of the gawkers were no longer gawking, and instead were draped over one another's knees. Though spanking scenes are a part of everyday life in Caeden, these were different. They were lighter and punctuated with feigned protests. It seemed, too, that there were generally more woman-woman scenes going on in the club that night than I had seen in total thus far. I stopped to watch a light flogging scene between two young women.

Within moments, James (the owner of the Playground) entered the room, strode purposefully over to a man near me and said loudly, "Hey—knock it off—this is not that kind of place." I whipped around to see the man yank his hand out of his pants and slink away. *The wankers are here,* I realized.

In the city of Caeden, the wankers (men who attend SM clubs to masturbate while watching scenes) most clearly represent the boundary between the SM community and outsiders. Wankers never play, or introduce themselves to people. They do not attend meetings or other social events. They are phantom cultural parasites, drifting in and out of view just long enough to ejaculate in their pants and leave. Wanking had been permitted at a club that had been closed down by the city a few months prior, and since then James had been "battling" them on a regular basis, posting "NO MASTURBATION" signs around the club and policing the scenes systematically. Because the wankers generally caused resentment and uneasiness, they were bad for business.[4]

I wandered to the stage, where a man and three naked women were doing something that looked like a flogging version of the seventies dance I knew as

"The Bump." The women hopped around, breasts bouncing, and took turns wiggling their asses in the direction of the flogger. Several of the regulars at the club looked and shook their heads as they passed. A few rolled their eyes. Suddenly, I realized what the difference was: this was *pornographic* SM, the stuff that sold videos and fueled the fantasies of the hundreds of people who had, apparently, read "The Erotic Guide to (Caeden)."

The perception of SM as alternative sex is woven through the academic literature on SM. Early depictions of what we continue to consider SM frequently involved the eroticization of nonconsensual relations. Our contemporary understanding of SM is indebted to various works by de Sade (1795, 1797), Sacher von Masoch (1870), and early psychologists and sexologists (Ellis 1927, 1938; Freud 1905; Kraft-Ebbing 1886, 1912).

Later, SM entered both mainstream consciousness and academic literature through the gay and lesbian communities (at a time when homosexuality was also assumed to be unequivocally about sex), further ensconcing SM in discourses of sexuality. The view of SM as sexuality persists in contemporary work despite recognition that SM is not always considered sex by participants. This both presents and represents a significant obstacle to understanding play. For Weinberg, Williams, and Moser, another of the five components of SM was "a sexual context." This was again informed by the inclusion of pro-dommes; the fact that paying customers masturbated at the end of their sessions evidences a sexual context. This distinction, however, might well be among the reasons that these interactions are not considered part of the larger Caeden SM community. Relevantly, much as I am excluding professionals from my analysis, Weinberg, Williams, and Moser drop from consideration lay people who rejected a sexual context for their participation in SM: "Some people engaged in SM-type activities but did not give them sexual meaning and thus were not considered to be 'into SM'" (1984).

This reflects a narrower conceptualization of SM than their respondents held, and certainly than the people in Caeden hold today. Having excluded the activities of leathermen from their analytical category "SM" on the basis of self-definition, the authors retained "sex" as a fundamental and necessary characteristic of SM, despite the denial of this by some of their respondents. In light of their understanding that the social construction of SM as pathology "makes sense of what appears to be bizarre behavior" (Weinberg, Williams, and Moser 1984, 380), the adherence to a sexual model is noteworthy. The framing of SM as sex makes a new "sense" out of what would appear to be, at this point, perhaps even more bizarre: SM activities outside the contexts of role play and alternative sex.

Another recent study follows Weinberg, Williams, and Moser (1984) in restricting eligibility for selection to people for whom SM is experienced as sexual. Taylor and Ussher's respondents "were required to define their sexualities or sexual practices as SM . . . it was to be their preferred means of sexual arousal" (Taylor and Ussher 2001, 296). Not surprisingly, given the exclusion of all SM-identified people who define their enjoyment differently, all of the respondents maintained that the enjoyment of their activities is dependent upon a sexual context.

This conceptual framework for SM has recently shifted to an assumption of primacy. Darren Langdridge observes that, despite "some recent moves within SM communities to minimize the sexual and instead focus on identities and practices that are more relational . . . at its core, SM, at least, appears to be *about* sex and this cannot and, I would argue, should not be denied" (Langdridge 2006, 380, emphasis mine).

For researchers committed to sexual rights and sexual citizenship, to understand SM as something other than sex is to sweep under the rug the very real and consequential problem of sex-based discrimination. Yet, and especially in this effort, it is relevant that some SM participants reject a sexual context for their SM participation. Langdridge reads this rejection as a movement in the community, which would seem especially important given his concern with sexual rights and citizenship, but it is dismissed. Having been socially constructed within and for a discourse of sex, mainstream conceptualizations of SM ought to be engaged critically and theoretically before being adopted by scholars. We should endeavor to understand what SM is "at its core" that we believe makes it necessarily "about sex."

The characterization of sexual fulfillment as a motivation for SM is problematic for several reasons. The dismissal of the members of the community as denying their "true" motives evokes the very same essentialist identities against which Langdridge is arguing. The rationale for privileging the paradigm of sexuality as the motive and reward for engaging in SM appears to be that it is the more common paradigm among participants. Yet SM participants who reject a sexual frame are excluded from studies of SM participants. Given the paucity of research on SM, and on play in particular, this assertion seems premature. However, even if it is the most common paradigm among participants, the uncritical procession from this assertion as the starting point is concerning.

It is of course likely that SM differs, to some extent, by community. Much of the recent work on SM has been conducted in the UK. It is possible that British SM is unequivocally about sex, and that, in turn, British participants are disavowing this. It is also possible these participants should not "count" for reasons that have yet to be clearly demonstrated. Since, however, SM researchers consistently note the rejection of a sexual context for SM play among participants, one must wonder what is behind these would-be denials, and how the "deniers" differ from the "accepters" of the sexual context. We might further wonder why it is that researchers are compelled first to mention them, and then to dismiss these particular "voices from the margins" (Langdridge 2006).

In Caeden during the time I was there, SM was neither a precursor to conventional sexual activity nor a replacement for it, but an end unto itself. Although SM is most often understood as having some erotic component for participants, several things trouble the unequivocal understanding of SM as sex. At least one person in any given SM interaction is almost always dressed, and sometimes all are, though nudity is generally permitted in play spaces. Kissing during play is rare, and genital play is much less common than other kinds of play (such as back-flogging). Participants often play with people they do not (initially) find sexually attractive, and with whom they are not interested in being sexual. After play, participants normally go out to eat or home to sleep.

While SM communities certainly include people who engage in sadomasochistic sex, they are also sites of engagement in sadomasochistic activities that are not so clearly or necessarily experienced as "sexual." Some SM participants insist that their play has nothing to do with sex at all, and there are community members who decry the presence of any sexual activity in SM clubs, lest SM be conflated with "kinky sex." Others view SM as potentially sexual, but not a core aspect of SM experience. Sophie explained, "I haven't actually had the experience of it having very much to do with my sexuality—I can get aroused, but it's not a default position."

Either SM itself has changed, or SM participants are now renouncing a sexual explanation for what they do, or the sexual context has never had the stronghold that has been assumed. Yet SM communities are flourishing and SM participation appears to be increasing in frequency. It may be that, as Plummer (1995) predicted, another kind of sexual story is proliferating in late modern discourses of sex, one in which the erotic is desexualized. The divorcing of sensory, carnal, and potentially erotic experience from all that is culturally subsumed by the notion of "sex" may be one indicator of changing criteria for what is sexual, and a widening perspective on carnal pleasures. It may also signify a response to changing gender scripts—strategies for negotiating the anomic state of gender for middle-class straight men and women. It may also be that SM is not—at least not simply—about sex.

In part, then, this is an issue of narrative and meaning-making. The extent to which SM participants understand their experiences as sex or as not sex is important, as are the social contexts in which they come to make these meanings. These questions cannot be adequately addressed outside an understanding of what it is SM participants actually do during SM play.

Understanding Play: "Straight" SM versus D/s

The members of the SM community in Caeden categorize play along multiple axes. On the simplest level, play is defined by the toys used in the scenes—knife play or spanking or a bondage scene, for example. Play is most easily defined as one of these types when it is either the only or the principal activity in the scene. This choice is also subjective; a scene in which a top singletails a bottom after intricately tying her with rope may be referred to as a bondage scene by one and a singletail scene by the other. It is further contextual in place and time; at a bondage meeting, the same person who last week called it a singletail scene elsewhere may now call it a bondage scene.

The most salient distinction between kinds of play hinges on the role of power in the scene. Issues of power are at the core of SM play. For most people in the community, the illusion of an explicit power differential is crucial for the enjoyment of play. In this kind of play (called "D/s," for "dominance and submission"), participants incorporate inegalitarian power dynamics. This can be accomplished explicitly in and for the scene itself, as, for example, when one player is fastened to the end of a leash held by another player. It can also be incorporated into a relationship built around a D/s dynamic, wherein all scenes are understood and experienced within this context.[5]

D/s takes for granted a hierarchical status between players even before a scene begins. In contrast, "straight" SM,[6] neither assumes nor seeks a hierarchical structure at the outset. For this reason, "straight" SM is viewed as being about pain *rather than* power. D/s is therefore usually understood as potentially more inclusive than other kinds of play.

In practice, the distinctions are often evident. The use of honorifics (e.g., Mistress, Sir) during play, for example, can characterize a scene as D/s. Similarly, one player might carry the bags of the other to the play space, abstain from speaking until "permitted," or sit at the feet of another. Arguably, D/s more closely resembles the mainstream idea of SM as role play than does straight SM. Even in D/s, though, this is a more complicated issue. Early in my fieldwork, during my second scene with Liam, this became clearer to me:

> Liam said that wearing his collar was important to him, and I had, after much conversation about it, agreed to wear one. He gave me a choice of four collars—three were rope, one was leather. The leather was the smallest, and I chose that one without hesitation. I didn't like any of them, and I didn't like the implication. [. . .]
>
> He had some kind of protocol for handing it over—he wanted me to take it from him, and then hand it back or something—I don't know. I was supposed to say please, I think. I shot him a look that made it clear that I was humoring him, but I did what he asked and put it on. [. . .]
>
> We had this incident once . . . he'd moved me to the opposite wall, for no apparent reason. He caned me, and I guess he wanted me to ask for another. He'd been big on the asking for another thing, and I felt like I'd been a good sport about it. But then he wanted me to ask for another and—I don't know what happened . . . I just really didn't want another, I guess. In any case, I said no, and he sat himself down on the chair and didn't move. I could see him in the mirror. I turned around to look at him a couple of times and said nothing. It was extremely awkward and very annoying. I was self-conscious and irritated with him. (Field notes)

Liam wanted this to be a D/s scene, a kind of play with which I had had no experience and which I assumed was essentially role play. Had I safeworded (the utterance of "yellow" would have signaled to him that he needed to change course), Liam would have been able to redirect the scene. Instead, I directly and overtly challenged the power performance by simply refusing to do what he asked. Liam was uncertain about whether I was playing a power game, wanting him to force the issue somehow. He did not step out of his role because he did not understand himself to be *in* a role. He was still Liam, trying to construct a particular dynamic in the interaction between Liam and Dakota that would, if it succeeded, be experienced by each of us as authentic.

This anomic situation emerged from my refusal to employ the normative strategies of the community in D/s play, while failing to communicate productively with him. Without the power performance, the D/s aspect of the scene lost its meaning entirely, leaving both of us without a clear sense of how, or even whether, to proceed. Had Liam shifted to a "straight" SM scene, the expectations would have been clearer. In most D/s scenes, these "roles" usually reach beyond the finite space of the SM interaction itself. The dynamics that players create and maintain through these strategies during play are carried through to community interaction. They are intended to structure the interaction between dominants and submissives more generally. For this reason the consideration even of D/s as role play obscures important dynamics in the community.

Because "straight" SM does not incorporate these power performances, many members understand it as being "only" about pain, for its own sake rather than for experiences of inequality. Straight SM is therefore often regarded as *less* than D/s.

The argument that playing with physical pain is not *also* about power is of course problematic, for SM is about the *infliction* of pain on one body by another.. Contrary to popular stereotypes, bottoms in SM scenes do not enjoy hurting themselves; the appeal is at least as much in the infliction as it is in the sensation.[7] The infliction of pain—injury, in the broadest sense, to one body by another—cannot be extricated from power. There is power in the intent to injure, the intent to withstand injury, and the responses to injury. While D/s play renders explicit the ideology of domination through rituals of hierarchy, straight SM necessarily manifests *consequences and symbols* of this ideology on the body.

The ideology of domination is not carefully preserved in this kind of SM play precisely because straight SM is, inherently and carnally, about domination. Where straight SM play is defined in the community by the absence of a D/s "dynamic," D/s play may or may not include SM. This leaves straight SM play as the only kind that *necessarily* mimics assault. As explicit as the ideology of power is in D/s play, it is based on the acceptance of a hierarchy for the purposes of the scene. D/s performs dominance and submission where SM performs conquest and defeat.

Protecting Performances of Power

These power performances are symbolic. Unlike contrived performances, the objective of SM play is the achievement of emotional, psychological, and physical experience of the *actors* as *authentic.* To that end, participants expend a good deal of effort creating and maintaining perceptions of power differences *outside* of SM scenes. The suggestion that these inequalities are illusory meets with impassioned resistance. More a script than a debate, these conversations normally result in identity policing; inevitably the challenger learns that she must not be a "real" dominant or submissive if she believes that the submissive is "in charge."

In more private settings, however, where the illusion on which the community is based is not threatened, most people entertain the complexity of the power paradox, as Laura did:

> You are putting yourself in a situation where you could truly be powerless. Most of the time, people are responsible and know that you're playing a game. Most people know this, and aren't going to do those things. It's possible that they can, absolutely, and you don't want that, but it is possible. But the more likely situation is that they're gonna respect your limits, and you'll get your illusion and enjoy it. It's an escape from reality. The illusion of powerlessness [. . .] I think for me the illusion of powerlessness goes into my leaving my real world behind.

The acceptance of this paradox is indicated by the phrase "power exchange" in the SM community, which is used to describe both the objective and the dynamics of SM interactions. Its meaning is taken for granted, and it is difficult to identify a precise and universally accepted meaning. There is a good deal of agreement that SM is intertwined with power, and that "power exchange" is the objective of most SM play. Leading SM texts that emerge from, and are written for, the community help to frame play as power exchange. In *Different Loving* (Brame et al. 1993), SM is defined as "the willing surrender of sensual control by a submissive to a dominant." Jay Wiseman's *SM 101,* widely recognized as the definitive guidebook for the community, considers SM to be "the knowing use of psychological domination and submission, and/or physical bondage, and/or pain, and/or related practices" (Wiseman 1998, 10). The definition in Patrick Califia's *Sensuous Magic* (2001) is "a temporary, consensual transfer of control from the bottom to the top for the duration of an S/M scene or an S/M relationship. Used as a synonym for S/M."

At its core, the link between SM participants is a quest for a sense of authenticity in experiences of power imbalance. In order to achieve this, participants must suspend belief in their own egalitarian relations for the duration of the scene. When this is successful, the sense of power imbalance *feels* real. This is sought, and is what often occurs, in and through "power exchange."

SM participants seek authenticity in emotional, physical, and psychological *experience,* rather than authenticity in their presentation to others. I use "authenticity" to refer to participants' *feelings and experiences* of relative powerful- or powerless-ness, during and as a consequence of their SM scenes. This achievement of authenticity is *beyond* that of what one might experience when playing a role. In other words, SM participants who, when they play, feel as if they are playing a role (as an actor might) do not achieve the authenticity of players who say that they *feel* afraid, helpless, evil, or invincible during their play. Unlike in improv or other kinds of performance, the authenticity in SM lies in the extent to which SM participants are able to convince themselves, and each other, of the real-ness of the experience. D/s and "straight" SM employ different (but sometimes overlapping) strategies toward the achievement of authentic experiences of power imbalances.

All SM, though, is a carnal experience. It is enacted, performed, processed, lived, and experienced on and through the body. Bodily manifestations and consequences of SM, such as bruises, scratches, and scars, are deeply entwined in ideologies of power. For SM participants, "marks" are indicators of authenticity, as well as visible sites of its accomplishment. Similarly, the spilling of blood (less common in public play but not unusual), is a powerful symbol of authenticity.

> Phoebe stood in the brightly lit conference room beside a small steel table that held supplies for the demonstration. She unwrapped a cotton-looking scalpel pack and laid it beside a bottle of rubbing alcohol, a first aid kit, and a large box of cotton gauze. Aidan, shirtless and in jeans, was lying face down on the table with his arms at his sides. I moved further into the room, closer to the top half of his body. [. . .] When Phoebe cut into the flesh of Aidan's shoulder, he hissed. He came up on his toes, feet flexed and his back muscles visibly rigid. She put her hand on his back and waited a second, while blood trickled from the wound. She continued her work, inserting the tip of the scalpel into his skin and making small slices. Slowly she cut a simple pattern, angled and tribal-looking. Every couple of minutes, she wiped the blood off of the scalpel on a swathe of gauze she kept on the small table. Once or twice she blotted his wound with a fresh piece of gauze (in order to see what she was doing, she later explained). Aidan was quiet throughout, punctuating the silence with only an occasional pained (sounding) moan—soft, deep and brief.

In this demonstration scene, Phoebe is injuring Aidan's body. His blood testifies to her ability and willingness to wound him, and to his mortality. The power exchange—the suspension of belief in egalitarianism—here is assisted by the visibility of Aidan's blood.

In negotiating the tension between the desire for authentic experiences of power imbalance and the aspiration to play safely, SM participants must navigate conceptually muddy waters. Their experiences are constructed and interpreted through a complex, and sometimes competing, set of discursive and social-psychological strategies in the community. Leah said, of the first time that she "got the concept of power exchange":

> He's doing all this really horrible stuff to me. I'm going, "I don't like this." He's going, "I do." And I want you to take five more, seven more, three more, whatever it was, depending on how miserable I looked at the time. [laughs] I don't know where he was fishing his numbers from. But he was going, you know, it was the first time. It was like, okay you have the power. Because you're doing all this nasty stuff. I'm trying to exert what little power I have, going "I don't like it." I'm not safewording, which might be stupid, or might not be, but I really didn't—I didn't want to, and *I don't know why.* [. . .] And it was like okay, well if you want to, and this is going to please you, then that's a good enough reason for me and I guess I can do this, and I'm going to just draw off on the fact that you want to and that's going to make you happy. And I'm just going to draw from that and that'll work for me at some level.

Here Leah constructs an imbalanced relationship by discounting her agency in the scene, recounting the events as if her resistance was genuine. This narrative of helplessness allows submissives to disavow their decision-making, thereby protecting—and arguably constructing—the experience of powerlessness.

The success of a scene depends on the accomplishment of this paradox by the participants. The top must provide the appropriate material cues to the bottom, in order for the performance to succeed. In this sense a scene might be understood in terms of Goffman's team performance—an interaction during which more than one actor contributes to the "staging" of the performance. Again, though, Goffman's "staging" is not intended to convey a façade (at least not any more than all interactions are façades for Goffman), but to indicate the tacit collaboration in social interaction (Goffman 1959b). Here the participants are team performers from one perspective (that of the onlookers), but they are also performers and audience unto themselves, simultaneously. The selves presented are intended to produce effects in the other members of the team, namely experiences of relative power and powerlessness.

Feminist insights into heteronormative eroticism notwithstanding, most people do not conceptualize their sexual activity as being "about" power. Sexual pleasure is located in conventionally defined sexual activity, and provides the motivation to engage in sexual activity. In Caeden, the objective is also pleasure, but the pleasure is linked, *at the conscious level,* to power. This link exists alongside sex in some cases, and instead of sex in others. The common link across all activities and relationships represented in the self-defined SM community is not a sexual context, nor the adoption of roles, but the quest for experiences of imbalanced interpersonal power.

Strategies of Accomplishment

In constructing contexts for experiences of power imbalances, SM participants employ particular strategies, among them the structure of SM scenes, communication during scenes, and identification labels.

NEGOTIATION AND AFTERCARE

Despite a wide range of kinds of SM scenes, most participants adhere to a particular structure in their SM play. This structure itself contributes to the creation and protection of experiences of power imbalance. Because many SM participants are putting themselves into situations in which they "truly could be powerless," to quote Laura, nearly all scenes in Caeden are negotiated beforehand. At its most structured, this may consist of a questionnaire completed by the participants that outlines interests, fears, and limits, which are then discussed before playing. They agree on safewords and safe signals, sometimes carefully selected so as not to disturb the perception of the power imbalance, and outline the kind of scene in which they will engage.

Alternatively, when players know each other well, they may briefly relay the kind of scene in which they are interested (or not interested) and either assume the use of ubiquitous and accepted safewords or rely on conventional communication during play. As play relationships progress, negotiation tends to become less formal, but it remains a visible part of the process in public SM play.

At the symbolic level, the primary objective of negotiation is to allow the bottom to set the parameters outside the scene, so as not to disturb the experiences or illusions of relative powerful- and powerless-ness in scene. During this process, however informal, the bottom determines what cannot and can be done. Typically, and often ideally, the negotiation constitutes, for the bottom, the pinnacle of what is to be his or her power course through the scene.

When the play begins, control of the scene (or the illusion of control) shifts dramatically. In the majority of scenes, the top is *acting upon* the bottom, in one way or another. The top orchestrates and directs the scene. Even when play is not consciously structured around power dynamics, the top usually remains in control on a purely physical level. At minimum, the top is arguably in control by virtue of having a whip (for example) at the moment, when the bottom does not.

The top also determines the end of the scene, by which time the bottom often evidences a shift in mental or emotional state. This condition, similar in appearance to intoxication, is generally attributed to a combination of biochemical responses to intense stimuli (i.e. "endorphin rush") or to psychological responses to physical stimuli or to the psycho-emotional context of the scene. The bottom frequently appears glassy-eyed, unsteady, and intellectually impaired.

In part because of this likelihood, most scenes conclude with "aftercare." The objective of aftercare is to meet the post-scene needs of the bottom (and sometimes, but never only, of the top). Typically this involves caressing, stroking, cuddling with, or rocking the bottom. Although desire for aftercare differs by person as well as by scene, the provision of appropriate aftercare is the responsibility of the top. It is also widely accepted that, because the bottom's judgment and functioning may be impaired to some degree, the top is even more responsible for the welfare of the bottom at this point.

The ways in which scenes are structured and accomplished coalesce to create and preserve perceptions of power imbalances in play. This operates discursively as well; the process includes rather than constitutes what is known in the SM community as the "play," or the "scene." Therefore, the initial stage, in which the bottom defines limitations and outlines desires, is understood as a precursor to play rather than as part of SM "proper." The final stage, in which the bottom is often impaired but the top performs a nurturing service by catering to his or her needs, is similarly omitted from consideration as SM. These experiences are bookends; they are prep work and cleanup, the necessary support for the "big event." Negotiation is framed as information the top needs in order to "make the best decisions," and aftercare as what the top needs to do to be responsible for her or his actions. All of this contributes to a successful front stage (Goffman 1959b), for the top is thus "in charge" when it matters—and what matters are the times when the top is in charge.

The objective of SM—for participants to achieve as total and as authentic a sense of power imbalance as possible within the confines of consent—is ambitious. The negotiation process itself, along with discursive tools through which the bottom's agency is ignored or discounted, helps SM participants accomplish this.

COMMUNICATION IN SCENE

SM play is a dynamic experience. Although negotiation provides parameters, it does not furnish a script for actors to perform. Participants communicate directly in scene, yet this can be confusing when the objective is the construction or performance of power imbalances. A common compromise is to communicate directly first, and rely on safewords as a backup if direct communication is misunderstood.

Though not discussed in public, bottoms deliberately and consciously guide action in a scene through verbal and vocal responses. For example, silence on the part of a bottom (particularly sudden silence) can result in the cessation of a particular activity by the top, while increased volume encourages continuation or intensification. Tops, almost without exception, say that the reaction of the bottom is a prime motivation and objective in their topping. This widely employed metaphor—tops as "reaction junkies"—frames bottoms as providing what the tops need, in order to feed their "addiction" to evidence of their own efficacy. Bottoms, in turn, withdraw the reward when they are no longer satisfied with the situation.

Bottoms develop signals and gestures that acquire meaning between particular play partners, and sometimes throughout the larger community. For example, while play partners may not have negotiated that stomping means that the bottom is at his or her limit, it can quickly become incorporated into the repertoire between players if it predictably precedes a particular response from the bottom. Occasionally, that signal with that bottom becomes common knowledge in the community, leading other bottoms to deploy it toward the same end.

More frequently, however, tops need to learn new signals with new meanings each time they play with a new partner, and it is widely accepted that signals change from one scene to the next. For tops, this can lead to uncertainty in scene; they must read signals quickly and accurately, aware that they differ from one person to the next, maintain the illusion of omnipotence, and still keep the bottom feeling safe. Once, during an early scene with Trey, the stingy pain of the whip was too intense for me, and I asked him to "switch to thuddy." I was surprised when he asked, "Do you *really* want to switch to thuddy, or is what you want for me to make you keep taking stingy?" Having intended no ambiguity, I asked Trey about this later, and learned that, unlike safewords, direct communication in scene cannot always be trusted by tops.

These sets of communicative skills are fundamental to success in the larger SM community. Communication during an SM scene can reinforce or threaten the power dynamic. SM participants make choices regarding their communication that contribute to the accomplishment of their experiences of power and powerlessness.

Whether before play, during play, or outside of play, these practices set the stage for a power differential to be experienced by players without adopting alternate personae. Strategies toward this end extend beyond play-centered discourse and structure, however. The related processes of adopting, presenting, policing, and continuously evaluating SM identification labels is a powerful means of preserving the illusion of a power imbalance between tops and bottoms.

IDENTIFICATION LABELS

The final strategy for accomplishing power performances in Caeden lies in the use of identification labels. Identification labels parallel the hermeneutics of play. Like the distinction between SM and D/s, some use top and bottom as the broadest categories (as I am), but others reserve them to indicate the absence of a D/s dynamic. In simplest form, "dominant" and "submissive" refer to people who play, or seek to play, with explicit power differences in their scenes, while "tops" and "bottoms" may or may not be "playing with power." The terms "sadist" and "masochist," objectionable to some because of their clinical meanings, are rare as stand-alone labels, but are sometimes used to augment an identity (e.g., "a dominant sadist"). Most frequently, they are situational and essentialist, as when one person "brings out the sadist" in another, or a submissive considering playing with pain admits he "has a bit of masochist" in him.

Nonetheless the labels are meaningful to community members. On the practical level, they facilitate the acquisition of play partners. Most of the members of the Caeden community are either single or in polyamorous relationships,[8] making networking for play an important component of the social scene. Misleading labels can be at the root of unproductive flirting, messy or unclear scene negotiations, and, ultimately, bad scenes. Bad scenes, in turn, have the potential to breed bad reputations in the scene, and bad reputations in Caeden can be extremely detrimental to a person who wants to engage in SM play.[9] In addition to these unpleasant experiences for the individuals directly involved in them, all of these things can drive visitors and new members out of the community, which is of much concern among the core members of the scene in Caeden.

In this pansexual SM community, more people identify as dominants and submissives than as tops and bottoms. These identifications carry different sets of assumptions and behaviors even outside of scene. The labels of "dominant" and "submissive" are accompanied by informal but continually policed codes of conduct.

When I began my fieldwork, I intended to bottom rather than top.[10] My options for play were thus limited to people who topped, and I therefore needed to identify as something in order to play. Because the question in the community was most commonly phrased, "Are you a dominant or a submissive?" I identified myself as the latter (and as a researcher). While I was so identified,

I observed several instances of policing submissive identity, a practice that I interpreted (and continue to interpret) as profoundly misogynistic, particularly since they have been most often initiated by dominant-identified men.

The most ubiquitous example posits assertiveness as inconsistent with submission. Once, when I articulated a point in a heated conceptual debate, a member of the group asked me whether I was sure I was a submissive. Another time I asked a companion (a top-identified man) to order my coffee while I went to the restroom, prompting another person at the table to exclaim, "Hey, I thought you were a sub!"

On still another occasion, I went to retrieve my coat from a booth at the club. Catherine was sitting between it and me. When I asked her to let me by so that I could reach it, Hugh (a dominant-identified man) suggested that I crawl under the table for it.

While discussing a scene I had done, both Russ (dominant-identified) and Elliot (switch-identified) were baffled by my approach to play. Russ asked me, "Don't you want to please your top?" Elliot was surprised when he realized that my objective in playing with him was not to make him "happy."

Realizing that "submissive" carried with it a slew of meanings and messages I had not intended, I abandoned the "submissive" identification within three weeks. By then, I was angry about my interactions with many dominant-identified men and deeply troubled by the misogynistic overtones. Interestingly, I was also impatient to begin topping, for the sole purpose of claiming an identification as a switch, thereby ending these particular frustrations.[11]

The differences between these identifications are not merely semantic. They shape interaction both within SM scenes and outside them, in the community at large. In some circles, there are different protocols for speaking to submissives than to dominants, and it is common for dominants to ask one another's permission to speak to "their" submissives. Other lines are drawn less formally, but jokes intended to humiliate, objectify, or silence submissives are normative. One night, early in my fieldwork, I finally met the partner of a woman I'd known for several weeks. Sheila, a submissive woman, had been talking to me about her dominant partner, Pete, since we had met, and when I suddenly realized who Pete was, I said, "Oh! Sheila's Pete!" Pete was visibly perturbed and growled his correction: "It's Pete's Sheila, *not* Sheila's Pete."

SM participants are not merely pretending to be relatively powerful or powerless; they are not donning and stripping these identities as one might change costumes. Rather they are actively constructing experiences in which they can *feel* relatively powerful or powerless, not through their own performances, in the theatrical sense, but through the cooperative performances, in the Goffmanian sense, of all community members.

Most players seek to construct inequality *in* play through front stage performances of dominance and submission before, during, and after a scene, even while decision-making is in the hands of the submissive. Others attempt to construct inequality *through* play, demanding a demonstration of dominance and submission on the body. As I will explore further in chapter 6, these identities (and SM play styles) dovetail with different discourses of pain in the community, in order to construct and achieve authentic experiences of power imbalances.

These identities are not alter egos, but experiences constructed of, by, for, and with selves. The members of the community must work to maintain empowered and disempowered contexts in order for SM to be experienced as transformative. Through play they create, represent, and live selves that are more and less effectual, more and less responsible, and more and less encumbered. SM provides a space for the creation and reinvention of selves more fixed than fleeting identities, and for most, these selves are more nuanced and far-reaching than specifically sexual selves.

Consensual sadomasochism (SM) is a complex and poorly understood social phenomenon. In popular culture, it is commonly represented and understood as either harmless bedroom "kink" or a side sexual interest of serial killers in crime thrillers. Although many SM participants do frame their "play" as having an erotic aspect, the conceptualization of SM as "kinky sex" has obscured a more nuanced understanding of this community and their activities. Unlike most sexual activity, participation in public SM relies on particular public spaces and involves an appreciable learning curve, financial expenditures, and a social network. In the public community built around SM play, SM is better understood as a highly immersive recreational pursuit.

Chapter 4

Fringe Benefits

The Rewards of SM Play

For the first time, I had the chance to wander around the dungeon at leisure. It really was beautifully done—high-quality equipment and great lighting, bright but not institutional. Strands of decorative lights cordoned off "Singletail Alley," where there was ample room for throwing eight-foot whips. An elaborate rope-pulley-cage was set up on one end of the room.

It was packed, and with a lot of well-known people; a lot of serious players. We'd all heard for months about who would be there, and of course I knew the program lineup. Most of them were from elsewhere in the country, and I hadn't met them. It was intimidating—not the crowd in front of which I usually played. I was hopelessly exhausted anyway, and had made no plans for the night.

While I was taking in the scenes, Trey meandered over to me. We chatted for a bit and then he said, "Okay, I'm going to wander around . . . or maybe I'll just come back here and put stripes on you."

He grinned and walked off, but returned just a few minutes later.

"So I have a bag full of floggers and whips and things. Wanna go do something with them?"

It was the first time he asked me directly to play. Usually, he just threw out feelers and danced around them, waiting to be sure I was interested. I was flattered and touched. Bone tired as I was, I was happy to accept his invitation.

There was little available play space anywhere, except right in the middle of the room, on a St. Andrew's cross. Dead center; there would be no avoiding the spotlight there. Unwilling to begin in full view of well over a hundred people, I told Trey I'd be facing the large wooden cross. Trey emptied his toy bag and laid out the floggers he'd brought with him. I counted nine of them. They're large, about two to three feet long, with soft wide leather falls. I untied my backless velvet top, slipped it off, and turned toward the cross. I placed my hands on either side of me, slightly above my head.

He began with Florentine—one flogger in each hand—which I had never seen him do. The floggers landed on my back in rapid succession, dusting my shoulders with the falls and massaging my muscles as he picked up steam. I turned my head to see him; I wouldn't have thought that he'd be so dexterous with them, but he was deft and fast and very impressive.

After a few minutes—maybe fifteen—he checked in with me. Still facing the cross, I said I was good.

The next thing I felt was an enormous thud across my upper back. My face almost smashed into the cross. The blow didn't hurt, but it did make my teeth rattle. I had never felt anything quite like it. In one sense, it felt familiar to me; it was not an uncommon stroke. But that much weight and that much force across my shoulders was a new experience.

I turned to look at him. He had taken all nine of his floggers in his hands, and hit me with them in one blow. Trey is over six feet tall and nearly two hundred pounds. The floggers alone must have weighed thirty pounds.

Kirby and Tammy were standing on the other side of the cross, directly in front of us. Kirby was staring at me wide-eyed. Tammy was looking away, though whether this was out of politeness or indifference I wasn't sure.

I closed my eyes as Trey landed another heavy thump across my upper back. I looked at him again, in time to see him in a batter's stance. I turned my head back to the cross before the next blow landed with a mind-numbing thud, somehow feeling incredibly hard and soft at the same time.

He hit me this way about once every couple of seconds. It was a powerful feeling. It felt like someone was beating me up . . . but "pain" doesn't describe it. And yet I felt a little bit afraid each time he was about to do it again. The act of absorbing the blows was all-encompassing. There was nothing else but the feeling of being hit . . . the weight and the warmth and the softness of the floggers . . . the movement of my body into the cross . . . my breath escaping me in whatever the hell sounds I was making, sounds that felt as if they started somewhere very deep.

At some point, about midway through the scene, Trey switched to a singletail. Each time the whip landed, it burned me—a tiny precise sharp hotness that lasted just a half-second short of unbearable. He threw it fast, slicing my skin with one blow after the other, diagonal down the left shoulder, then the right, then the left—then a shot across the middle of my back. It fucking hurt.

A pause. Then his voice: "How're you doing?" He was beside me, holding out a bottle of water. I nodded, panting, and drank readily, feeling like a boxer in between rounds. I wiped my mouth with the back of my arm and handed him the bottle. He took a swig, set the bottle down, and returned to his spot about six feet behind me to continue.

At one point, I hit the cross with my right hand several times, not particularly hard, but hard enough to sting my palms. I needed an outlet of some sort—I needed to direct some of what I was feeling elsewhere . . . to somehow send the stimulation outside of my body.

A while later, he asked if I was ready to turn around. Having lost all self-consciousness by then, and suddenly interested in protecting my burning back, I turned around and dropped my arms along the cross at my sides, wrapping my hands around each plank.

We'd drawn an audience. About thirty people stood watching us, not close enough to distract us but close enough to see every action and reaction. I didn't know most of them. I fixed my eyes on Trey and watched him as he threw his whip across the narrowest part of my waist, back and forth, cutting a horizontal line just above my belly button.

We played for three hours. When our scene ended, the dungeon was closing and many of the onlookers had gone to their rooms. The ones that remained approached us to compliment us. The next day, several others—complete strangers—sought me out to compliment me on the scene, and Trey confirmed that he'd received his share of accolades as well.

Within the SM community, the euphemism for play, "what it is that we do," suggests that an adequate description of SM is elusive and complex. The community in Caeden can be understood more fully as "serious leisure" (Stebbins 1982): a devotion to the pursuit of an activity that requires specialized skills and resources, and provides particular benefits. The understanding of a recreational activity as serious leisure distinguishes it from "casual leisure," which Robert Stebbins defines as "an immediately, intrinsically rewarding, relatively short-lived pleasurable core activity, requiring little or no special training to enjoy it" (Stebbins 1992, 1997, cited in Stebbins 2008, 38).

Above all else, SM is a recreational activity in the Caeden community. The engagement in SM requires considerable skill and time, and the social circles of participants consist mainly of other participants. Community membership is a central part of the lives of participants, and engagement in SM is central to notions of the self. Understanding SM as a serious leisure pursuit allows for a recognition of the complexity and social richness of SM interaction.[1]

Robert Stebbins's serious-leisure model has undergone multiple adjustments over the past three decades. Several general principles, however, have remained fundamental to the consideration of an activity as serious leisure. In addition to the acquisition of particular skills necessary to participate successfully in the activity, Stebbins emphasizes personal, social, and psychological rewards and benefits provided by participation.[2]

The Making of a Player

Some people enter the scene with a broadly defined interest in SM or D/s. Others come to the community "knowing" their SM identification. It is common, though, for SM interests, and, by extension, identification labels, to change, sometimes multiple times. Often, this change emerges in part from learning to top or bottom; the acquisition of skills co-constructs the desire to practice them. Learning to play is an integral part of becoming a sadomasochist, shaping motivations and forming identities in the process.

For both bottoms and tops, participation in SM involves a substantial learning curve. Even apart from participants' general desires to avoid sustenance and infliction of unintended injury themselves, the community as a whole shares responsibility for recruitment, education, and supervision of SM play. SM is taught, supervised, policed, and regulated in multiple ways.

LEARNING TO TOP

Learning to top involves four distinct processes that each require specialized information sets and modes of practice. The acquisition of technical skills is the most pragmatic of these endeavors, and the one with which most people who top begin. Participants learn to use SM toys almost exclusively from other players. Other players demonstrate how to hold one's arm when throwing a whip laterally and how to tie a "predicament" knot that tightens when pulled. Participants serve as tools for practicing these skills, providing information about the effects of the top's technique itself, as well as a sense of her strength, speed, and range. Learning to top safely also occurs informally; because playing safely is a desirable trait in Caeden, most people are eager to share their safety information, whether modeling a technique, shopping for toys, or casually commenting on a scene.

Tops must learn about safety in SM play as it relates to particular activities but also on the broader level. This frequently occurs in formal settings; a demonstration on the use of a flogger includes a discussion of where one can and cannot strike a person with a flogger without causing injury. Meetings designed for newer participants include basic first-aid information as well as more specialized knowledge such as sensitivity to changes in breathing patterns, the dilation of a bottom's pupils, and how to handle emergencies.

One example, an educational demonstration and workshop, featured Enjo, a well-established veteran member of the scene, teaching community members how to play with fire. Enjo's reputation as a safe, serious, and extreme player preceded her. I had the distinct sense that her presence at the front of the room was somehow more an act of charity than such presentations normally are. She began with a qualifier that there are many approaches to fire play, and that she was going to demonstrate her particular way. Her description of the materials needed for fire play included a fairly lengthy explanation of the differences between isopropyl and ethanol alcohols; apparently, the temperatures at which alcohols burn vary, and ones that burn hotter and faster are safer. She explained the difference between first-, second-, and third-degree burns, and provided an overview of home treatment options (in case of first-degree burns): aloe vera, antibacterial ointment, and bandages. She suggested keeping a spray bottle with water nearby, and said that she likes to keep one hand free in case she needs to extinguish a flame quickly. She also recommended applying Neutrogena lotion onto the skin as part of aftercare. Hair, she said, melts rather than burns, but fire play on clean-shaven skin is safer because hair burns the skin when it melts down. Alcohol on freshly shaven skin is stingy and can be painful, though; if this is not the objective, she said, it is best to wait a day after shaving.

Enjo's "demo bottom" was a boi[3] named CJ who stood, naked and hairless, with his hands clasped behind his back. Enjo informed us, sharply, that she did not take questions during the demonstration because she needed to devote her full attention to the scene. She lit a birthday candle and placed it into a metal cup. Holding that cup in her right hand, she picked up a second cup, which contained a blend of different alcohols. With her left hand, she dipped a chunk of cotton into the alcohol and wiped it in the shape of a large V from CJ's navel to his shoulders.

In one quick move, Enjo dipped her fingers into the alcohol, swept them over the candle to ignite them, and then touched CJ's navel. The flame blazed up his torso in an orange-blue V. It lasted approximately two seconds.

Though the safety precautions of a fire scene exceed those of a flogging scene, the commitment to safety is a part of public SM life in Caeden. Newer players, fresh from SM books or novice groups, often seem eager to demonstrate their knowledge of SM safety to bystanders ("That flogger's a little too close to her spine"), and veteran players generally avail themselves for impromptu lessons, demonstrations, and safety information.

The emphasis on safety is a source of pride and of status. Though occasionally a community member objects that the concern with safety intrudes on the fantasy, safety concerns are not whitewashed nor subsumed under a darker, rawer discourse. Safety is part of SM identity in Caeden, and to contribute to this discourse of safety is to make a statement that one belongs there. Many players—usually tops—carry alcohol wipes for toys, and several also carry rubber gloves and CPR masks. At the local club, safety is generally the domain of the owner, who prohibits blood play and advanced breath play.[4] He also regularly makes rounds throughout the club or sends a trusted employee or associate to do safety checks; I once overheard him tell a staff member to "Go make sure that scream was a good one."

At private parties, or especially large events, hosts post "house safewords"—words that will end the scene at the hands of the hosts or "dungeon monitors," regardless of the top's response. Dungeon monitors take these assignments seriously, and have been known to interrupt scenes out of their own concern for safety, even in the absence of the utterance of a safeword.

The central role of safety in the scene also helps to preserve the perception of power imbalances between participants. Because so much of the responsibility for safety in an SM scene ultimately lies in the hands of the top, the focus on safety is tantamount to a discourse of dependence. The bottom must be accountable for choosing wisely, but that choice is understood as the choice to depend, as entirely as possible, on the abilities and judgment of another.

The concern for safety operates on still another symbolic level. More than any of the other trappings, rituals, and discourses involved in SM play, the efforts devoted to safety keep SM from entirely resembling either role play or sex. The discursive attention to safety and the precautions themselves undermine the view of SM as contrived, scripted, or otherwise "pretend." Safety can be of concern only where the dangers are perceived as real.

Secondly, if heteronormative eroticism is culturally constructed as spontaneous, raw, and passionate, the safety precautions and preparations in SM are decidedly anti-erotic. Rituals and discourses of safety underscore the methodical character of SM play. Contrary to images of "rough sex," a sense of genuine recklessness and chaos is normally undesirable in SM interactions.

Before the start of a meeting one night, I overheard Trey talking to someone about the sensation of a perforated eardrum, which he had apparently acquired in a recent fight scene. In a strange coincidence (since this is not a common injury), I was experiencing similar symptoms, due to a slap that had landed across my ear the previous night. Suddenly concerned that my eardrum was perforated, I asked him to describe his symptoms further. He did, and highly recommended his physician.

After the meeting, Russ approached me and said that he had overheard my conversation with Trey. He was very concerned, and slightly annoyed, about the possibility that I might have been injured, and he wanted to know with whom I had played. Shortly thereafter, Shaun approached me with similar concerns. By the end of the evening, more than five people spoke with me privately, wanting to ensure that I was only playing safely, publicly, and with people who "knew what they were doing."[5]

Evidence of this kind of concern among community members in several other situations suggests that it emerged from a general emphasis on safety, rather than from my role as a researcher. I learned later that Trey's story had elicited responses as well, though because he was a veteran player, top-identified, and a man, the responses were couched in disapproval rather than in concern. Adam, with whom I had played the previous night, deeply regretted the accident, and was worried about me. Aware that this reflected poorly on him, he was also embarrassed, and at least a bit offended, by the suspicion it had aroused in his abilities.

Although the ability to play safely is the most immediate goal in learning to top, it also involves less observable social-psychological processes. Direct communication threatens power performances and handicaps the accomplishment of "pushing limits," a common objective of SM play. Tops must therefore learn to decode communication strategies in play and to recognize signals that the bottom may or may not intend to send. A general tendency among bottoms to safeword only as a last resort makes this an even more important skill. Tops must often decode ambiguous, conflicting, or barely visible signals in order to avoid causing real damage to play partners. This is most effectively learned through playing and discussing the scenes with play partners afterward, though participants offer insight and advice about these matters while watching other scenes or publicly reflecting on their own.

Similarly, tops learn to prepare themselves for potential emotional and psychological reactions of bottoms. One component of this occurs in the negotiation phase (specifically in regard to aftercare), but even more generally, learning about the effects SM play *could* have on *any given* player while bottoming is part of the education of a top.

These four learning processes—acquiring technical skills, ensuring safety, understanding modes of scene communication, and understanding and handling emotional and psychological impacts on the bottom—are necessary in order for tops to acquire, engage in, and secure (future) play. A final part of the learning process is less fixed, but nearly always part of the process nonetheless. At some point—sometimes long before making the decision to top, sometimes after one has gained enough topping experience, and sometimes after a particularly powerful scene—most people who top find themselves wrestling with their performances (and feelings) of sadism and/or dominance. Most tops grapple with feelings of guilt, shame, and fear at some point during their topping careers. This coming-to-terms is usually an informal process; demonstrations on the topic occur sometimes, but they are rare. More commonly, tops process these feelings with their friends in the scene, and turn to other tops for reassurance and support.

LEARNING TO BOTTOM

All SM participants must acquire specialized information and learn challenging skills. For people who bottom, the processes are less obvious. Because tops are charged more fully with maintaining safety in scene, classes and demonstrations focus more frequently on learning how to top. Instructive classes for bottoms tend to focus on submission[6] and service—examples include how to handle the tensions between submission and agency, how to reconcile (female) submission with feminism, and the challenges of submission as a characteristic of a relationship (outside of play). There are few classes specifically for bottoms, though safety information directed at bottoms is a standard component of novice- and safety-oriented meetings.

Most often, learning to bottom involves learning to negotiate the tension between accountability for one's own safety and satisfaction, on the one hand, and the maintenance and preservation of a power imbalance on the other. Thus sometimes bottoms (particularly those who identify as "submissives") learn to give themselves "permission" to recognize and understand their likes, dislikes, and limits, as well as how to communicate those things in scene and out of scene. Further, bottoms learn how to evaluate their limits—"hard" limits that should be left alone, or "soft" limits that may be "pushed" by the top.

Bottoms also learn criteria for playing safely, such as how to choose a play partner wisely and disclose concerns, issues, and health problems. Like tops, many bottoms wrestle with reconciling their activities with identities and senses of self. Finally, bottoms "learn" how to process, navigate, and negotiate pain or unpleasant sensation. Unlike the formalized, technical learning process in becoming a top, this is a meaning-making process. Participants who bottom choose from sometimes competing discourses to contextualize, recast, make sense of, and enjoy the pain, anguish, or subservience of bottoming.

Social-Psychological Rewards of SM

EMPOWERMENT

Both topping and bottoming result in feelings of empowerment, though experiences of bottoming are less often framed this way. Nonetheless, SM players describe the benefits of play as feelings of trust, efficacy, competence, and strength.

Trust

Trust is a central feature of the experience of SM play as well as of the discourse of the community. Participants talk easily and casually about the importance of trust as a prerequisite for play and as an outcome of play, and of play as an indicator of being trusted. For people who top, being trusted is an important component of the experience. Tops, as the initiators of action during the scene, solicit additional, and greater, trust with each risk they take. At the simplest level, each pushed limit, new toy, or higher level of intensity risks (at least) error and rejection, and each acceptance on the part of the bottom evidences and increases his trust in the top. This sense of feeling trusted is often empowering and meaningful, as both Seth and Greg indicate:

> And topping is a lot about—and this is something that we haven't talked about yet, but trust is a huge factor. On both sides. But topping is—it's very much an honor for me, that someone has considered me trustworthy enough that they're willing to put their safety into my hands . . . You put yourself in my hands, trusting my skill, and in exchange, so in that way—our agreement is that we're both doing this for pleasure, and that's our ultimate goal, and you're willing to give up a certain amount of safety and control in exchange for my skill and my taking responsibility for that length of time. (Interview transcript, Seth)

> I have been given this power over you, by you, to allow me to create this [. . .] sensational experience for you. And you're giving me a great gift, in allowing me to do that, and displaying trust. (Interview transcript, Greg)

The connection between trust and SM play is taken for granted in the Caeden community. Play is experienced *as* trust, and this inextricability is rarely questioned. Yet the nature of the trust—defined broadly by Guido Möllering as "a state of favourable expectations regarding other people's actions and intentions" (2001, 404)—is paradoxical in SM play. In a social interaction built around narratives of power inequalities, the notion of "favorable expectations" is exceedingly complicated. Yet in a public SM club, under the often watchful eyes of other community members, and with the knowledge of community-wide safewords, SM participants feel safe when they play. The members of this community express that they are trusting play partners with something profound, yet they are not able to identify or articulate precisely the currencies in an SM scene. Shortly after I began playing with Adam, for example, I realized that I was consistently and unreflectively writing about trust in my field notes about our scenes. This prompted the following musing in my field journal:

> What do I trust him with? I trust him to . . . I don't even know. I don't trust him not to hurt me, because he does. I don't trust him not to harm me, because sometimes it happens . . . it certainly can, theoretically . . . I don't trust him to do what I want him to do. . . . I don't trust him to do only what I'm comfortable with. So why does this feel like trust?
>
> If there were a way to play in which I couldn't stop him if I wanted to . . . if playing without a safeword really meant what it tries to capture . . . would I do it, I wonder?
>
> I might. I just might. . . . I trust him to get me, I think. I trust him to be in my head. That's a whole lot of trust, really—and it came so early . . . I'm probably being foolish.

My attempt to explain my trust in Adam was, as Luhmann's work illustrates, something of an exercise in futility, arguably made more compulsory by my role as a researcher: "Although the one who trusts is never at a loss for reasons and is quite capable of giving an account of why he shows trust in this or that case, the point of such reasons is really to uphold his self-respect and justify him socially. They prevent him from appearing to himself and others as a fool, as an inexperienced man ill-adapted to live, in the event of his trust being abused" (Luhmann 1979, 26).

In Caeden, this inability to account for reasons to trust is accepted; there is little concern about appearing to others, in Luhmann's terms, as "fools" or as "ill-adapted to live." Already on the social margins, SM participants immerse themselves rather readily in the interstitial space that is trust. This space, recognized in Simmel's work (1907), is more recently beginning to be more fully theorized.[7] As Möllering argues, Simmel's understanding of trust "differs radically from conventional trust theories in that it embraces fully the reflexive duality of knowledge . . . and, in doing so, is able to capture the leap of trust as such (which is otherwise taken for granted)" (Möllering 2001). The recognition of the centrality of a "further element" in trust experience allows for a focus on the space in an interaction—the moment—in which prediction ends. SM play is an empirical illustration of Simmel's trust dialectic, constructed around, because of, and to result in feelings of trust. Jack, for example, marveled at the power of this dialectic trust in SM play:

> There's also, especially during, there's trust. You have to have that. It won't work otherwise. It won't work for you otherwise, because you just won't let yourself go if you don't trust the person. You can't believe that you'll ever come back if you don't trust them. And I find it weird that both people go, and yet they both come back. And they both trust the other person to bring them back, but it's really their trust in the person that brings them back, it's not actually them.

Eric also referred to the power of being trusted to "bring back" the bottom:

> You [are] in a trust relationship in which they're saying, "Do whatever you want to me. I trust you to do what is needed. Not necessarily what is correct, what is needed. It may not be safe, it may not be intelligent, but you're the person in charge. I trust you to bring me back.

On the most basic level, "bringing the bottom back" means keeping her alive. More commonly, it refers to ensuring that the bottom returns to a functional cognitive state after the scene. The absence of this guarantee creates the space for trust and imbues the space with emotional and psychological meaning for participants.

SM play requires and evidences trust from tops as well as bottoms. A top must trust that a play partner is not omitting relevant information (such as a heart condition or a tendency to hit back), that the bottom will not later claim that the play was nonconsensual, and that the bottom in fact understands and respects the top's desire to do the things he is preparing to do in scene. Trey, for example, once told me that it took time between when we began talking about playing and when we actually played, because "I had to know *you.* When I felt comfortable with knowing you, I felt comfortable with exposing those elements of *me.* I'm not going to expose those elements of *me* to somebody I don't trust."

Simmel's "further element" is fraught with emotional power; the experience of being trusted, precisely because it is irrational, suggests that the trustee has transcended the level of the ordinary to become someone special and worthy of such an irrational risk. Among SM participants, this recognition can lead to feelings of self-worth and empowerment. SM participants, through play, immerse themselves in trust relationships. These experiences are often empowering and validating. Other implications of these trust relationships will be more fully explored later.

Efficacy

Feelings of efficacy comprise experiences of both topping and bottoming for many SM participants. Feelings of efficacy during topping come from eliciting change in a person. These changes can be manifested physically, in skin color or texture, tears, screams, or blushes. On a very tactile level, topping can be about impacting the body—watching skin yield to one's hand, drawing blood, seeing the emergence of a bruise. Change can also manifest emotionally or psychologically, such as when a bottom does something the top believes she would not have otherwise done.

Feelings of efficacy are not merely rewarding, but often an objective of play, especially given the effort topping demands. Longtime community member Eric categorized one scene as his worst because the effort he expended generated no observable change in the bottom:

> And I started to flog this person. This person, as it turns out, that I didn't know, is known as basically "the wall." In order to make her feel like you hit her, you had to . . . I had to slam her so hard that the next day I could not feel my wrists. That's how numb I was. And I realized that I was set up, it was basically like these people wanted to see me fail, basically. They were setting me up for a joke. She was perfectly happy to go along with it. But it was the worst scene, because basically I had no reason to play with this person. And then it became a matter of pride, you know, I gotta hit them. And I killed myself doing it—I really didn't have to, I could've said lady, I can't do this. Let's put it this way, when I finally slammed her full force, she was like, "Are you doing anything?" She was not being very heavily affected.

Players also feel effectual through submission (as opposed to bottoming in "straight" SM). Submissive-identified bottoms, or bottoms who suddenly "feel submissive" in scene sometimes cast their physical experience as being necessary for the top. In this way they view themselves, or their bodies, as effecting a change in the mental or emotional state of the top. At a meeting entitled "The

Mind of a Submissive: Why We Do What We Do," I was struck by this common theme. The panel members, five in all, couched the appeal of submission in feelings of helpfulness, usefulness, and effectiveness. Georgia said she liked "feeling like you've done something right," and Tony said that he submitted for the same reason he was a paramedic, "to help people."

During our interview, Sophie described a scene in which she understood her submission as meeting a need for her play partner:

> It felt incredibly important to me. This was like probably the first experience that I had that was really about submission. Even though it wasn't what was asked for or whatever. It felt incredibly important to me to give him the outlet to let go of whatever it was that he needed to let go of. And I suspected that if I didn't, he just wasn't going to let go of it. [. . .] It felt really important, it felt important. It felt like more than just play—that there was this serious import, and that if I did not let this continue, I'd be all right, but that was very very important for me, to provide this outlet.

Casting a top's demands as a need, a bottom can view her actions as the only or the best way for the top to meet that need. The bottom eliminates this perceived deficit in the top, thereby drawing feelings of efficacy and empowerment from her acquiescence.

Another component of power performances outside SM play among people who engage in D/s is often to "serve" people who are not part of their D/s dynamic. Though submissives do not usually respond to *expectations* that they will "serve" others, they frequently offer to run errands, bring refreshments, or be otherwise helpful. Because this occurs only in the presence of the sub's dominant, it is not an overarching desire to serve all people, but an extension of their D/s dynamic beyond scene space.

Competence

The skills involved in topping are not easily acquired. They require practice, dexterity, and dedication to their improvement. These skills thus provide a backdrop for feelings of technical, psychological, and emotional competence through play. Because SM play is about doing and being asked to do, it provides opportunities to feel competent on all "sides" of the interaction. Most bottoms describe feelings of competence and success through bottoming, particularly through service. Seth, who switches, captures it well from both "sides" of the SM interaction:

> Topping feeds very much on my need for competency. We've talked about this before. When a scene is going very well, then there's a great deal of—I would say pride, in that fact, in skill well-executed.
>
> There's a mode I get into which is very cooperative and service-oriented when I'm subbing. Cooperative and it's extraordinarily competent and strong. Like, just give me anything that you want me to do, and it will fucking get done.

SM play provides myriad opportunities to feel especially competent. Feelings of competence come not only from the provision of excellent service, but from being able to conduct a stellar sensation scene or a heavy pain scene, from being highly perceptive about one's partner's emotional or psychological state during play, or from managing aspects of a partner's daily life.

Toughness/Strength

Finally, both topping and bottoming provide players with opportunities to revel in their physical strength. Feelings of physical strength come from delivering or withstanding pain or intense sensation. For bottoms, particularly those who engage in straight SM, this can be particularly salient. Some incorporate additional challenges and obstacles to increase this reward. Faye, a retired military officer, said that she prefers to stand free during intense scenes, that she "likes having to control [her]self while giving up control."

PERSONAL GROWTH

The considerable extent to which a top must trust oneself when s/he plays is less a matter of public discussion than it is part of the experience of topping. With the responsibility of the direction of the scene comes the need to know one's own impulses and temptations. Ruminations about this can be unsettling, given the kinds of activities involved in SM play. The process of self-analysis, therefore, sometimes contributes to a stronger sense of self-reliance and self-confidence for tops.

Similarly, players who "stretch" their limits emerge from play with a sense of having triumphed over adversity. In this situation, players (usually, but not always, bottom-identified) having previously cast a limit as a source of fear, discomfort, or anxiety, overcome this concern within and through play, and frame this experience as an accomplishment. For Faye, the trauma of having seen a man flogged to death in an Asian country, while on military duty, had left her deeply disturbed by the idea (and the imagery) of flogging, and so she was consciously working toward becoming comfortable with a flogging scene.

CATHARSIS AND HEALING

As others have noted, SM can be cathartic (Weiss 2006b). Participants are aware of the potential for SM as a space for emotional liberation (though some argue that "anger" is not included in the array of permissible emotions with which to play). A scene from my field notes provides a good example:

> Russ stood behind Janelle and swung the flogger as hard as I'd ever seen anyone swing anything, and it landed on her back with a tremendous thwack. I thought she was going to break in half. She screamed, loudly, and he hit her again. Over and over he hit her that hard, breaking a serious sweat by the fifth swing. And over and over again she screamed, until one—the last one—brought her to her knees. He turned her around, played with her nipples and she dissolved into tears. Russ later told me that this was a formula for them; Janelle's goal was to cry.

The catharsis of play is not always intentional, however. One night, a long and intense scene with Adam ended just as the club was closing. We left immediately (without the usual "come-down" time), and walked to a diner with Sam. As we sat down and opened our menus, I burst into laughter. I was lying on the seat of the booth, gasping for air between gales of unprovoked and uncontrollable laughter. I could not breathe easily, and Adam grew very concerned. I felt out of my mind with giddiness. Adam tried holding me and talking soothingly. When that did not work, he grew serious, but I laughed even harder at his sternness. At one point, he slapped me in the face. Still I laughed.

Regardless of whether catharsis is the objective of a given scene, the physical, emotional, and psychological intensity of SM, combined with its marginalized status, generates emotional responses of an intensity that players often find cathartic. Some participants play with the express purpose of healing from past trauma; among incest survivors, incest play can sometimes be an example of this.

FLOW

In 1990, psychologist Mihály Csíkszentmihályi's treatise on "the psychology of optimal experience" was a national bestseller in the United States. In it he identified optimal experience as autotelic, that which is an end in and of itself, for its own sake. Csíkszentmihályi argued that this state of consciousness, which he called "flow," is the result of attention so intense and all-encompassing that one achieves a sense of order in consciousness, against the default state of psychic entropy. Flow involves challenge and the utilization of skills, intense concentration, an altered sense of time, the loss of self-consciousness, goals, feedback, and the conflation of action with awareness. Elsewhere Csíkszentmihályi described the flow experience as one in which "[t]he ego falls away. Time flies. Every action, movement, and thought follows inevitably from the previous one."[8]

This optimal experience, Csíkszentmihályi argues, can be generated in activities as varied as playing a musical instrument, running, and performing manual labor. For Stebbins, the flow experience is a motivation for the undertaking of various kinds of serious leisure, including mountain climbing, kayaking, and snowboarding (2005). In SM, flow is generated physically and/or psychologically, and through topping or bottoming. Bottoming is more likely than topping to result in observable altered consciousness, but the community is also more highly motivated to recognize altered states in bottoms than in tops. The flow experience for bottoms is most frequently called "subspace" or "bottom space." It has many other descriptors, including loopy, flying, and fried. To the (lesser) extent that the flow experience in topping is recognized discursively, these phrases include "in the zone," "grooving," or "in top space."

Tops achieve flow through mental focus, particularly when engaged in activities that require intense concentration such as knife play, needle play, and advanced bondage. Tops also experience flow through the physical act of topping; the physical and auditory rhythm of flogging, juxtaposed with the concentration required to do so safely, can be meditative. Eric describes his experience as being "in the zone":

> I feel very large. There's an intense sense of space, of infinity, of pure control, of being one with everything. [. . .] I'm not here right now. I've hit that zone. In thirty minutes I'll come out of it and go wow, did I do all that? You know, I remember it but you're totally in the moment in that respect.

At a party one night, I watched Samantha singletail Shaun. She began to "zone" during the scene, and when she ended it, she was very glassy-eyed and seemed intoxicated. Because I had not seen a top look quite so much the way a bottom looks after a scene, I was standing nearby, watching her intently. She saw me and instructed, "Go get me a Pepsi and put it aside." It was not Samantha's custom to speak that way to people, and she had never spoken that way to me. When I did not get her a Pepsi, she "sent" someone else. The next day she did not quite remember the interaction. She apologized to me, explaining that she had been in "top space."

Bottoms experience flow as a result of intense rhythmic sensation, sensation or pain itself, unrelenting focus on a particular task, or concentrated effort to endure a sensation or circumstance. Lawrence said of the first time he experienced the "endorphin rush" of SM play:

> It was a very intense buzz. My body was very light, I didn't feel the weight of my body. I didn't lose awareness of where I was, but my head cleared up completely, which was really wonderful because I'm always thinking. I have a very busy mind and sometimes that gets the better of me. And it was wonderful just to be able to relax and not have to force myself to relax . . . I'd describe it as more as a high than a buzz. The closest thing I can say is that it's like being drunk . . . so it was really amazing at that moment to be—all that I was, was the sum of my five senses. That was the thing that I most relished, being able to use my body to the utmost.

Leah calls her flow experience "the happy place" and frames it as obliteration:

> It actually has a color, it's really strange. 'Cause sometimes it has, sometimes it's really tropical and beachy. And it's just a place where I am so blissed out from whatever is going on that all I can do is pretty much smile and nod and try not to drool. [laughs]

For Kyle, flow is a more classic nirvana:

> **Kyle:** I was at that point notched up so high that they needed to bring me down from that [. . .] and it stimulated every nerve just right, and I just soared. I've never had an experience like that since, where I've just absolutely flown.
> **Me:** What does that mean?
> **Kyle:** Trying to put something like that into words is difficult, because a lot gets lost in translation. But I'll do the best I can. Picture for a moment that you are in a desert. And it's very hot and very uncomfortable and you're dehydrated, and you've been walking for days and your muscles are tired. And you're just about to fall over. And the, all of a sudden, you fall off a cliff and you land in a tropical paradise of an oasis. In the water, but it's drinkable. And it's the perfect temperature and it's very refreshing. And you come out of it and you're clean-shaven automatically, and everything is 100 percent perfect. You went from, really really difficult to deal with and like doing your best just to hang on, to everything's groovy, just like that. That's soaring.

REINVENTION AND REBIRTH

In much the same way as identification shifts create opportunities for the reinvention of the self, immersion in the community facilitates a rebirth process of its own. For most people, immersion leads to a burnout-rebirth process, in which members become temporarily depleted by the scene, decrease their participation or withdraw completely, and return in full swing weeks (sometimes months) later. This phoenix-from-the ashes cycle is so widely accepted as part of the community that it has in recent years become part of the programming for at least one major organization. Thus "burnout" has become part of the community discourse, and how to handle it part of the toolkit one needs to navigate the scene. This commitment to remain involved in the community despite periods of diminishing returns—what Stebbins calls "perseverance"—evidences the centrality of SM identity for the members of this community.

SM identity is important among the members of the Caeden community. This identity is not the same as particular SM identifications (as top, dominant, sadist, bottom, submissive, masochist). These identification labels are not understood as fixed for most participants. For a given individual, they change often, sometimes even day to day.

Identification labels, despite their flexibility, capture a particular "point in the journey" of participants, and, at any given moment, the most current incarnation of what is understood as an SM identity. That identity, in the first place, and the fluidity and flexibility of it in the second, evidences the functions of the community itself in the lives of its members. The possibility of reinvention of the self from week to week—each introduction to the group offers the potential of a declaration of a new identity. Entrenched in meanings that members eschew but uphold through play and non-play interaction, these identity labels shape the way people respond to the bearers. They dictate opportunities for play and friendships, determine their place in community hierarchy, and provide different governing rules for social behavior.

If identification labels in Caeden are mercurial, and play is consistent with these labels, then kinds of play and dynamics of play change as well—from scene to scene as well as day to day. The potential for the reinvention of the self arises not only out of a different self-declaration and therefore out of different social interaction, but also out of play, moment to moment. This is an adventure of the self, a trip to different parts of the self, that may ultimately function to integrate them.

Research on discourses among SM participants in Britain revealed some similar readings of the rewards of SM play, including pleasure, escapism, and transcendence (Taylor and Ussher 2001). Even beyond these direct and specific rewards of topping and bottoming, the engagement in play, in a broader sense, facilitates the achievement of additional rewards in the community.

STATUS

Social status within the Caeden SM community operates on multiple levels. Paths to high status are varied and related to identification labels, and means of status achievement in Caeden are clear to most participants. The highest status is accorded to people who become community leaders. Community leaders are involved in the local, and often the national, SM scene at the organizational level. They are well-networked and serve as liaisons to leather, gay, lesbian, and fetish communities. They are also generally respected in the scene. Though there are several organizations that serve the pansexual SM scene in Caeden, community leaders are concentrated in Horizons.

There are two additional paths to high status: status as a player and status as a volunteer. Those who become community leaders succeed along both of these tracks. Though these paths do not always lead to community leadership, they are necessary in order to become a community leader.

Status as a Volunteer

SM participants in Caeden represent their commitment to their SM identity and community through organizational involvement. This engrossment (Goffman 1974), closely linked to immersion in the community, occurs quickly and easily. Volunteerism is possible for even the newest arrivals in the scene. This is particularly advantageous for people who top. Because of safety concerns, novices who bottom have less difficulty finding play partners than those who top. This results in faster access to status through play for bottoms, but also serves to track tops as volunteers. Volunteerism can result in increased access to play, which helps to mitigate the disadvantage tops face on the path to status in the community. It also contributes to an imbalance between tops and bottoms at the level of community leadership. Because most participants want to play soon after they enter the scene, and because bottoms do not *need* to become involved in order to obtain play, the result is the cultivation of tops as community leaders far more frequently than bottoms.

Entry-level volunteer opportunities include assisting at events with collecting admission fees/tickets and setting up and cleaning up at parties. Although volunteering at this level provides visibility and increased contact in the community, the selection process for these opportunities is nearly indiscriminate. Often, members must therefore become more deeply involved in order to achieve high status. Further involvement means serving on organizational committees or in multiple organizations simultaneously, or volunteering at national SM events.

Status as a Player

The means of status attainment through play also differs by SM identification. In general, being a good player entails achievement in the areas outlined in the previous section, as well as versatility of skill and interest. Play partners confer status as well. For example, submissives, and especially service submissives, can achieve high status by being "trained" (formally or informally) by high-status dominants. Play partners also confer status by virtue of (mainstream) attractiveness. This is especially the case with people who bottom (whether men, women, or queer-identified); tops in particular enjoy a higher status when they play with more attractive bottoms. Overall, though, status as a player in the community seems more tightly interwoven with skill than with conformity to conventional standards of attractiveness.

The achievement and maintenance of a good reputation as a bottom or a top is specific to bottoming and topping. Bottoms earn reputations as good bottoms, and therefore receive more invitations to play, in three distinct ways.

First, because much of the appeal of topping is the sense of efficacy, the observable and immediate response of a bottom contributes significantly to the enjoyment of play by tops. Most tops consider themselves "reaction junkies." A bottom who moans, yelps, screams, laughs, wriggles, and writhes, is thus more desirable than one who is stoic during play, all else being equal. Secondly, bottoms with a high pain tolerance allow for more creativity and less tentativeness on the part of the top. This is often appreciated, though there are tops who play lightly and who therefore prefer to play with bottoms who do not need intense stimulation in order to be satisfied (or responsive). However, bottoms with a high pain tolerance are accorded a high status even by such players; the difference is understood as an incompatibility, but the bottom has a very definite elevated status. Finally, bottoms who are edgy or extreme in their SM activity tend to have higher social status than those who are not. For the same reason as outlined above, bottoms who have fewer limits provide their partners with more possibilities, and often the opportunity to engage in play in which most others are uninterested.

Tops achieve high status in the community foremost through developing their technical skills. Mastery (relative to other tops) of a particular skill, such as throwing a singletail or playing with fire, can confer status, as can proficiency in a wide range of skills.

For the particular people in this particular community, paths to status are meaningful. Marginal identities here do not preclude the attainment of social status. In fact status may be viewed as more achievable given the sources of marginal identity in Caeden. From expertise in Boy Scout knots to meticulous leather care, gadgetry of various kinds is often understood as the domain of geeks. Geekiness is therefore viewed as conducive to the mastery of SM toys.

> I enjoy the cane very much, because of its precision. I enjoy the skill of rope, for both its . . . I enjoy several things about rope. I like the, its sensuality, its physicality of it and also its skill level. I mean, people who are good with rope have *practiced.* And have thought about it. And rope is very . . . it's artistic and it's mathematical and it's complex and it really appeals to the geek in me. (Interview transcript, Seth; italics reflect spoken emphasis)

Fatness does not detract from success in play, and arguably enhances it; larger bodies offer a more imposing presence as tops and the potential for more surfaces and longer scenes as bottoms. The community is rife with opportunities for status, prestige, and even fame in the national scene, often for people whose access to status is more limited elsewhere.

In part because of the romantic view of Caeden as "home," people in the scene are sensitive to, and generous regarding, issues of social status. The reinforcement of good reputations is considered good etiquette rather than poor taste. Participants speak very highly of good players with such frequency that it seems obligatory to do so. For example, although I did not ask questions about other members of the scene in my interviews, most respondents told lengthy stories about other people's scenes and complimented other players, with little provocation and little apparent relevance to their own answers. Further, negative comments about the skills of others are rare; players are very careful about reputation management and normally reserve unflattering remarks for situations in which a concern for safety exists.

SM participants gain a number of social and emotional benefits from play itself and from the community more broadly. These particular rewards are especially meaningful for people with marginal identities, whose life stories are organized around themes of isolation, loss, and trauma.

Despite structuring interaction in ways that create and maintain experiences of inequality among its members, the discursive connections between SM and theater provide vague access to the ideological (and emotional) defense that SM is less than fully real. On another level, for many people in this community, the fantasy element connects SM to other fantasy interests, such as science-fiction novels, films, and role-playing adventure games. From this perspective, SM can be understood as an all-encompassing lifestyle that, in its nurturance of marginal identity, represents liberation from the oppressive plight of the everyman. SM play constitutes "flashes of intense living against the dull background of everyday life" (Csíkszentmihályi 1997).

SM is liberation not just from the mundane, but from the margins of the mundane. Through the acquisition and demonstration of specialized skills, the members of this community achieve social and interpersonal status. The paths to status, moreover, are clear and unambiguous; if members play well and get involved, they are all but guaranteed a high status in the community. In turn, this status confers desirability as a play partner, which is experienced by some as sexual or romantic desirability.

Like other serious leisure pursuits, SM requires a specialized set of skills, provides particular social-psychological rewards, and constructs multiple paths to social status within the community. Framing SM as a serious leisure pursuit shifts the focus away from the ultimately unhelpful questions about whether SM is or is not deviant sex, and allows us to understand SM as, most fundamentally, social behavior.

Chapter 5

Badasses, Servants, and Martyrs
Gender Performances

Two hours before the costume party at the Playground, I still hadn't found an outfit. I'd heard that this was a busy event and I knew I could be meeting a lot of new people. I didn't want to be something cutesy or submissive, but since I was still fairly new to the scene, I also didn't want to stand out.

I rummaged through my closet and chose a copper-colored crinoline ball skirt and a brown lace-up peasant top with poufy sleeves. I folded a white linen sheet, doubled it over the skirt, and fastened it like an apron. I piled my hair on top of my head in a loose curly bun and pulled some strands out. Then I shook my head at my reflection. What were they called, these women? Serving girl . . . bar wench? I sighed, but it would work. When in Rome . . .

When I pulled my car up in front of Casey's place, she was leaning against the building, drawing a deep breath on a cigarette, a la James Dean. She looked incredibly intimidating for a large, almost-forty-year old woman dressed as Minnie Mouse.

Casey and I arrived just moments after the doors opened, and the club was packed. Marty stood near the door, greeting people as they entered. He pointed at my costume and gave me a thumbs-up. I nodded politely and turned away. I heard him call out to someone behind me.

"Hey, she's a tavern wench. Want a beer?" Then, to me, he yelled, "Hey, wench! Two beers! Hey, wench!"

Irritated, I ignored him. I could feel him watching me, and I concentrated on what Casey was saying.

"Two beers, wench!!" he tried again. I did not respond.

Once we finished checking in, we headed into the main room and saw Raven, who was dressed as a vampire. We hugged our hello. Behind Raven stood Russ and Jody, talking with a man I had noticed but not met during my first SM meeting. He was a short, pudgy, cheerful-looking man, thirty-something. He was not in costume. He wore black pants and a black T-shirt that was too tight. The lenses in his thick plastic glasses were badly smudged. He had a moustache, a thick goatee, and an overbite. Russ introduced us, but it was loud and we could hardly hear each other.

He extended his hand. "I'm Liam. I'm sorry, I didn't catch your name?"

"Dakota," I said, shaking his hand.

Liam continued a story he had apparently been telling before I joined them.

"I mean, it's only one word, but it's so clear what they mean . . . 'Women!" He said the last word in faux exasperation and laughed. "And then everyone knows what a man means when he says it. It's pretty offensive, if you think about it. It's just not okay to say it like that!" His voice cracked on the last word. He giggled.

Casey joined us. I was about to introduce her when Liam turned to her and asked, "Do you say 'Men!' the way men say 'Women!?' It's rude, isn't it?" he asked her.

Casey surveyed him coolly. I held my breath, not sure how she was going to take his assumption. It depended on whether she decided she liked him or not.

"No, I don't. But when I say, 'Women!' like that, I mean exactly the same thing that men do."

I grinned and slipped away, as Liam stammered an apology and Casey laughed graciously. In the room next to us, it looked like Doug and Liza were starting a scene, and I wanted to watch them. Liza was bent backwards over a chair, and Doug was using a Wartenberg wheel across her stomach. She made very loud, low-pitched noises that were not quite moans and not quite shrieks. I had never seen a wheel before, but it looked painful. I did not know what to make of her sounds.

While I was watching, Liam approached me and asked me about my research. He wondered whether I was a member of "SCA."

"No, I don't know what that is," I told him.

"Society for Creative Anachronism. I thought maybe, because of the costume . . ." he trailed off. "I like SCA. All that stuff—SCA, fantasy stuff. And computers. Geek stuff. I'm quite a geek." He had a big, warm smile and an infectious giggle.

I laughed. "That's not unusual around here, I'm noticing."

We talked for a bit about geekiness in the scene, and about science fiction fandom. When Doug and Liza's scene caught his attention, he said, "Oooh, a Wartenberg wheel. I love those—it's my favorite toy. The one I have is better than that, though."

After a brief pause, he asked, "Dakota, do you top or bottom?"

I was impressed that he asked it this way. The usual question, "Are you a dominant or a submissive?" is much less comfortable for me. I appreciated the fact that he located scene identities in verbs rather than nouns, and I liked the language he chose.

"I bottom."

He said nothing more. We stood and watched the scene until it ended. I mingled again.

I talked with Russ for a while. He touched my back lightly and commented on the open-ness of my shirt—perfect for flogging, he said. While we were talking, Adam came over and wagged his finger at me, in a "come here" way. I raised my eyebrows at him, but followed without objection.

He stopped at the entrance of the smoking playroom and turned to me.

"So, what's your situation?" he asked, ". . . because my hand's so itchy to spank you."

I bristled at that, for about a dozen reasons. I told him, truthfully, that I didn't generally play with people I hadn't watched in scene.

"You haven't seen me play?" he exclaimed in apparent surprise. I told him that I hadn't, and he marveled at how I could possibly have EVER *been at the club without seeing him play. He was obnoxious, but not offensively so . . . one of those people whose certainty of his own charm somehow doesn't make him any less charming.*

I excused myself and wandered around again. I stopped to watch a special event: "Master George," dressed as a pimp, was supervising a "ho'-flogging." Several women (his "hos") took a turn at being flogged by anyone who was interested, so long as the flogging was limited to the ass.

A few minutes into the scene, Liam was beside me. We started chatting again, and he began to show me his toys. He had an unusual collection—a few he had made himself, including a lanyard flogger. While I was looking at them, he said, "You know, we could find a corner somewhere and I could try them on you."

Having never seen Liam play either, I was noncommittal: "Yeah?" But this sounded casual and experimental to me—as if we'd just fool around with his cool toy collection.

Fifteen minutes later, I still I hadn't decided whether this was a good idea. Liam took a turn at flogging a woman in George's "ho'-flogging" event, providing me with an opportunity to watch him play. He talked during it, to the bottom, and seemed strangely unself-conscious, despite his definite lack of coolness. He seemed so comfortable in his skin.

A little while after that, he asked directly: "So do you want to go try some of these out?"

"Sure," I said, half-surprising myself at the decision.

I followed him to the nook around the corner from the smoking room. I took off my top and stood near the wall. He began by smacking my back repeatedly, in order to warm the skin. The force surprised me; I realized that I had expected his touch to be gentler . . . maybe even tickly. The rhythm of his thump-thump-thump on my back was pleasant, but I was lost in thought.

Perhaps because of that, he seemed antsy. "Come on, back—warm up," he laughed.

Once he was ready (or once he thought I was ready), he turned to his toy bag. The lanyard flogger was what I'd expected: cold and very stingy. A large, thick knotted rope with a quadruple knot at the end—he called it a "thumper"—seemed to reverberate through me when he hit my back and shoulders with it. His home-made "vampire gloves" were black leather gloves lined with pins or tacks: mini-nail beds that he used to scratch and slap my back.

We laughed a lot during the scene. I felt very comfortable, as if we'd known each other for years. After we had tried all of his toys, he led me away from the bench and slowly backed me into the wall beside it. He held my arms up over my head and pinned them to the wall—my cue to struggle.

I started tentatively; I was concerned about making it difficult for him. Though we had not defined the terms, somehow it became clear that this was an arm-strength struggle. I was attempting to break out of his hold, and he was attempting to keep me there, but we only used arms. I exerted enough energy to determine that he was much stronger than I, and then stopped.

"Okay, you win," I laughed.

On the surface, gender does not organize community life or play in Caeden. It is remarkably absent from the discourse of the scene. SM, of course, is deeply gendered, as is community life, but in many ways, the binary between top and bottom replaces the gender dichotomy in the social fabric of the community. Through play, however, gender is performed, mimicked, extended, challenged, and subverted.

Embodiments of Masculinity and Femininity

The term I introduced earlier, "incidental androgyny," implies that "doing" masculinity and femininity are active processes. The (relative) absence of masculinity and femininity markers is simply that: absence. In this analysis, gender becomes an addition, something above and beyond what exists prior to gender performance, and this "incidental" androgyny is less an actively constituted gender than the consequences of not "doing" gender quite so fully or quite so well.

On the level of personal appearance, gender is not done as widely, as consistently, or as successfully as it is outside the community.[1] The social organization of the Caeden community is not especially intertwined with embodiments of masculinity and femininity. Instead, the community is organized around the related but significantly distinct identities built around topping and bottoming.

The social constructionist argument that gender is something that is "done" in the first place is indebted to the ethnomethodological concept of situated action (Garfinkel 1967) and Goffman's interactionist approach to gender display (1976, 1977). West and Zimmerman's subsequent introduction of the concept "doing gender" (1987) shifted the sociological discourse from the occupation of roles to the constitution of social identities.

Incidental androgyny is not a deliberate gender identity project. It is not an attempt to hide biological sex, nor to cross gender boundaries. There are simply fewer explicit attempts to "do" gender; in short, gender is less performed in incidentally androgynous presentations. This naturalness, however, should not be mistaken for the ostensible "naturalness" central to performances of masculinity (Connell 1995; Halberstam 1998; Hole 2003). Successful hegemonic performances of masculinity *imitate* the natural; it is part of the performance. When the natural aspect of a masculine performance fails, it is precisely because performative quality feminizes it. Femininity, though, is inauthentic; it is not only perfectly feminine for one to *apply* one's femininity, but application is a core component of feminity. If gender performance depends on the recognition of others for validation *as* gender performance (the ontological claim at the core of performance theory) then incidental androgyny is the effect produced when femininity is not put on *and* naturalized masculinity is not performed, when the sum total (relative to others) of what is apparent is biological sex.

Topping, Bottoming, and Performance

The conceptual unpacking of gender from sex takes a more radical turn in Judith Butler's work in which gender is constituted through quotidian performance, rather than accomplished by preexisting (gendered) subjects (Butler 1990, 1993, 2004). The performances with which Butler is concerned are constitutive; they are intended to *become* by way of being, and to *be* by way of repeat performance.

Topping and bottoming differ from gender performance in several important regards. Because play occupies a liminal space between authenticity and role play, the performances of topping and bottoming are not quite real and not quite mimicry. They are not performative in the quotidian sense of "girling" (Butler 1993), or in the donning of "naturalized" masculinity that Judith Halberstam describes (1998). A man whipping a woman during an SM scene is a different kind of masculine performance from a man ordering her dinner and from a man rushing into a burning building. It does not conform to a cultural *expectation* of masculinity, but instead symbolizes a (discursively) *unacceptable* masculinity. In this sense, it is a hyperbolic masculinity that is represented—but not constituted—through topping. It is not a presentation or performance of a masculine persona, but the assumption of a hyper-masculine symbolism. Similarly, while bottoming is not a feminine performance in the way that applying lipstick or stripping is, it is symbolically hyper-feminine.

Given the incidentally androgynous presentations common in Caeden, there is a dissonance between what Goffman considers aspects of personal setting in much of SM play in Caeden. Presentations of selves, Goffman suggests, are most effective (and most comfortable) when behaviors (manners) are consistent with appearances (1959). In topping and bottoming, then, as symbolically hyper-masculine and hyper-feminine performances, masculine and feminine *manners* are frequently incongruous with androgynous *appearances.* The symbolically hyper-masculine and hyper-feminine performance is offset by the extent to which gender is *not* being done on the quotidian level.

These symbolic performances are not accompanied by performance in the way that Butler intends it, and they cannot be understood as realism, pretense, or parody. SM play cannot therefore be easily viewed as either accomplishing or performing gender; it is not, in and of itself, a doing of gender on the quotidian level. Instead it is a symbolic performance of gender extremes, engaged in by people who do not live the gender norms. It synthesizes—and blurs—the levels on which gender is "done" *in each moment of each interaction,* often contradictorily. It is a symbolic gender performance over, above, and not necessarily consistent with the repeated quotidian gender performances.

Archetypal Strategies

The symbolism and the practice of topping and bottoming are each intertwined with gender ideology,[2] but the conceptual divide between dominants and submissives in the scene is the most significant hermeneutic distinction. SM identifications have primacy in the community. More than any other identity category, these identifications shape interaction, and despite the close association between SM identification and gender, the former cannot be understood simply as a displacement of the latter.

Community members distinguish between SM activities in which they may engage and the particular identities they choose to adopt or construct. Gender shapes and constrains these choices in important ways. A self-identified male top who sometimes bottoms, for example, is more likely to claim identity as a top than as a switch. A woman with the same inclinations is likelier in Caeden to consider herself a switch. Even within the complex and gendered identity choices made by the members of this community, SM play itself reveals interesting relationships between gender and play.

The strategies in SM play are informed by several gendered archetypes, which illuminate the ways in which gender operates and is negotiated in this pansexual SM community. I frame these archetypes in terms of their use during play, rather than as kinds of players. Most play incorporates at least some aspects of more than one type. It is important to note that topping and bottoming are *not* understood this way in Caeden (or in any SM community, so far as I am aware); these are my own analytic categories, not actual SM identifications.

BADASS TOPPING

If an image of SM exists in mainstream culture that is not pornonormative, badass topping is likely it. Badass topping involves performances of victimizing and personal desire to inflict pain or suffering. During a scene with Adam (months after the night described in the prologue to this chapter), I realized I wanted another sip of water from the bottle I had just bought as he was cuffing my wrists to chains embedded in the concrete wall behind us. I told him that I wanted the water.

"In a minute," he said, and finished cuffing my right wrist. Slightly irritated with him—but hardly any more than I usually was—and curious about where he thought he was going with this, I raised my eyebrows. He laughed.

He started to hit me with the quirt, across my breasts and my stomach. He started slowly at first, but ramped it up very quickly. The quirt sliced back and forth across my waist, hitting the same spot repeatedly. It hurt, I was hot, and I was breathing heavily—and he was still not giving me my water.

I suddenly realized what was going on. He wanted me to ask him for the water, after I was in the cuffs. He wanted me to make the point that I couldn't get it on my own. I laughed.

"Wow—there already?" he asked.

"No. Give me my damned water," I said.

Laughing with me, he put down the quirt and picked up the whip he'd nicknamed "the gray meanie." Only about eight inches long, it's very thin and made of a synthetic material, lighter than leather but softer than nylon. It simultaneously reverberates like a cane—the blow "echoes" through the skin—and slices like a single tail.

He approached me and began whipping my breasts. I writhed and stomped and pulled on the cuffs. After a few minutes, the right cuff started to loosen. I worked it for a while longer, then slipped my hand out and reached for the water, dangling from the other cuff while I did.

Adam got to it first, picked up the bottle and opened the cap. He brought the bottle close to me and tilted it toward my mouth. He looked at me steadily, and threw the water in my face.

Elements of badass topping are found in nearly all topping, for it is most effective at constructing and upholding illusions of power and powerlessness. The more authentic the top's enjoyment of her or his effect on the bottom appears, the more s/he appropriates this archetype. For this reason, badass topping is often closely linked with the willingness to risk taking an action or a course that the bottom may not like.

BENEVOLENT DICTATORSHIP

This strategy involves an exchange of obedience for protectiveness. While the dynamics of obedience and protection appear elsewhere in SM play, these themes occupy a central role here. Topping is understood as simultaneously nurturing and authoritarian. Often the dynamics are not restricted to SM play and are part of a broader D/s relationship:

> Jody bragged about having gotten her clit piercing, which somehow marked her as Russ's, though I don't quite understand why it wasn't just a clit piercing. She said that he arranged it and took her for it, and it was something she'd apparently wanted "from" him and he "finally" consented. As she told the story of the trip, she included a long-winded digression about a strange happening in which she was almost hurt through some bizarre circumstance that Russ thwarted.
>
> Russ interrupted, "Don't I look out for you?"
>
> "Yes," she said.
>
> Russ waited a beat, then repeated, "See, I take care of you."

Russ's reminders, to Jody and to others present for the conversation, served as both a declaration and reinforcement of his benevolent dictatorship topping. Highlighting that Jody did not get hurt and did get her clit piercing, Russ is at once protector, hero, and decision-maker.

SERVICE TOPPING

Though it is almost never critically engaged, service topping is the only archetype that occupies a place in the discourse of the community. It involves either the (arguably courageous) admission of an ultimate desire to please the bottom, or the awareness on the part of the bottom (or sometimes of onlookers) that the top's actions in scene are being determined by the bottom:[3]

> I knew that we'd have good energy if I took on a more dominant role. It wasn't so much "well, I'm going to be dominant because it's going to make her happy." Now, I do have that thought in my mind; I do want to make her happy. But if I did the scene in a more dominant role, I also knew that her reaction would be all the . . . better. And if her reactions were heightened, more vivid, that would make me happier. So it's a wonderful mutual give and take. (Interview transcript, Lawrence)

Because service topping threatens the fantasy of the top's absolute power and the bottom's powerlessness, "service top" is occasionally used as a vaguely pejorative description, by both tops and bottoms. In its purest form, service topping is the antithesis of badass topping, which is borne out in the discourses about topping and in performances of power outside of play.

MARTYRDOM

The relinquishment of accountability for one's "suffering" is a central goal in martyr bottoming. Martyr bottoming therefore involves performances and experiences of helplessness and victimization, but conceptualizes this as a sacrifice for the good of another:

> And even if I was putting myself in a frightening situation, I wanted to do that for him. That was the first time I had this "I'm doing it for you" period. So through the whole thing, I'm thinking, "Can I say the safeword now? Maybe now I should safeword. All right, maaaaybe I should be safewording now. Maybe now's the time I should—Hey, how about that safeword?" But I never said it.

Most accounts of martyr bottoming end without a challenge to the fantasy, leaving undisturbed the conclusion that the bottom "really" did not want to do what she was doing, but was compelled to for the sake of the top. However, Sophie, cognizant of her own martyr script, continued without prompting:

> And I will be honest, it wasn't like this total altruistic experience, because even though I was fearful, (a) the fear was partially a turn-on, and (b) me being this appreciator of sadism, it was also very hot.

Martyrdom bottoming does not rely on the ultimate denial of pleasure, but adherence to a martyr script. Admissions of selfish enjoyment occur, in private and to people other than the top, but are tempered by indicators of secrecy; hence Sophie's declaration that "[I] will be honest," marks the acknowledgement of her own enjoyment as a claim that runs counter to the script.

INDISPENSABLE SERVICE

Service bottoming is often thought of as a kind of submission, though submission often incorporates more than service. Both service and submission seek to meet the needs or fulfill the wishes of the top. Both place high value on approval, skills, commitment, and loyalty; the goal is the successful fulfilling of the expectations of the top:

> There's a thrill in submission. I wanted to be submissive. And there is this thrill in knowing I could cheat and choosing not to do it anyway, in knowing that I could be good. And I *could* be bad, but then I'd be *bad*—I'd be a bad submissive. And I wanted to be a good one. I wanted to do what he wanted. I wanted to please him. (Interview transcript, Lily; italics reflect spoken emphasis)

Service bottoming challenges itself to "goodness." In part, service is an exercise in perceptiveness, and of evidence of familiarity with one's partner; excellent service often requires anticipating the desires of a top before being asked. Unlike martyrdom, the discourse of service is one in which providing pleasure or utility or otherwise being of value is enjoyable for the bottom.

BADASS BOTTOMING

Badass bottoming approaches SM play competitively. It is an explicit dare, either to self or other. It can be internally competitive, in which the bottom seeks to withstand or endure more than ever before or more than the bottom thinks he or she can. It can also, though less commonly, seek to outlast the top or exceed the top's physical or ethical limits:

> Kirby stood with his bare back against the concrete wall. His arms hung limply at his sides. Tammy, at least six inches taller than Kirby and considerably heavier, was standing four feet in front of him, wearing sweat pants and a ratty T-shirt, and holding a singletail.
>
> They locked eyes and laughed.
>
> "You ready?" Tammy asked, grinning affectionately.
>
> "Bring it on," Kirby replied, still smiling.
>
> Tammy checked behind her to make sure she was clear. Then she smiled at Kirby again, and in one smooth motion, she threw the whip horizontally through the air. It landed on his chest and he gasped. She waited, just a beat, and threw it again. Kirby closed his eyes. Tammy got into a rhythm and began whipping him faster, harder, and always across the center of his chest. As the whipping grew more rhythmic, Kirby opened his eyes and kept them on Tammy's face.
>
> Tammy's whipping was serious. It's difficult to see a singletail land, and Kirby has a hairy chest, and it was dark, but I could see how quickly it connected once she threw it, and even in the dim light I could see his skin reddening in places.
>
> Kirby made a lot of hissing whistling sounds—that sharp "ssssssst!" that people tend to make when they feel very precise sorts of pain. He stomped a couple of times and slammed his hand into the wall behind him. Once he fairly screamed and jumped sideways out of her range. She looked at him impatiently, half-smirking, with her eyebrows raised and a challenge in her eyes, and he glared at her as if she'd been the one to jump away. He put himself back against the wall and puffed his chest out. (Field notes)

Similar to service topping, badass bottoming is rarely discussed, for it threatens the powerful-/powerless-ness illusion.[4]

SM and Gender Symbolism

Taken together, these archetypal strategies represent the dynamics of topping and bottoming in the Caeden SM community. SM participants do not take this approach in thinking about play, nor do they limit themselves to one type of topping or bottoming. In the vast majority of SM scenes in Caeden, players move between these types, at least occasionally. Nevertheless this taxonomy is useful in understanding a complex activity from an intersectional perspective. Benefits, rewards, and motivations of SM play differ in accordance with the deployment of these strategies, as do decision-making processes and illusions of power and powerlessness.

It is impossible to understand the archetypes that inspire these strategies outside gender; they are themselves gender stereotypes. Beyond performances of powerful and powerless circumstances, they are active representations of *being* powerful and powerless, or of victimizing and being victimized. Topping and bottoming are both active processes undertaken *to and as* engagement in performances of victimization and power differentials. This is not to claim that these performances are therefore anti-feminist or otherwise philosophically objectionable (a question to which I return in chapter 8). There is, as SM researchers and practitioners have long insisted, an important distinction between victimization and consensual engagement in performances of victimization. Nonetheless, while the latter precludes the former, it is the existence and cultural coding of victimization that gives these performances meaning. In this sense, we can explore these performances within their gendered contexts, yet move away from the categories of "woman" and "man" as the salient hermeneutic constructs. This is important theoretically, but especially so in the case of this community, which comprises multiple sexual, SM, and gender identities.

The objectives of badass topping and benevolent dictatorship mirror common characteristics of hegemonic masculinity (Connell 1987): respectively, physical aggression and risk-taking, and ultimate discretionary power and the provision of protection. These types perform victimization most clearly and at the symbolic level, most unapologetically (though one could argue that the benevolence itself is an apology for what would otherwise be badass topping).

The analogous feminine archetypes of bottoming are martyrdom and service bottoming, though both are, not surprisingly, more complicated. All bottoming constitutes performances of either victimization or powerlessness, but not necessarily both. Martyrdom romanticizes the ideas of both victimization and powerlessness, and actively performs both. It requires the casting of the experience as one of powerlessness, claiming passivity and helplessness, even in the face of evidence to the contrary.

Service bottoming, however, performs powerlessness, but not necessarily (and not usually) victimization. More active than either the martyr or the badass bottom, service bottoming is constructed around principles of approval and competence, and is generally not understood nor performed in terms of helplessness.

The presence of these distinct and varied dynamics in topping and bottoming constructs far more than a community offering of "something for everyone." At the most basic level, of course, they manifest gendered power differentials.

Their relative statuses within each group reflect this; on a continuum of masculinity and femininity, the closer topping moves toward bottoming, the lower its status, and vice versa.

In the cases of service topping and badass bottoming, performances of power differentials are especially interesting. Because the goal of satisfying the bottom is *implicit* in badass topping and benevolent dictatorship, it is performatively and discursively disavowed. In stark contrast, service topping takes the satisfaction of the bottom as its *explicit* goal and is therefore feminized, even as it inflicts pain or performs dominance. In conflating action (masculine) with servitude (feminine) it occupies a lower status than the exclusively masculine archetypes. Not surprisingly, then, service tops are most commonly switches; people who top in badass and benevolent dictatorship are often less likely to bottom or less likely to label their bottoming as such.

Badass bottoming poses a similar theoretical quandary. It epitomizes being done *unto*—the quintessential passivity—but it does not frame these experiences as powerlessness. In fact, badass bottoming refuses to code even extreme performances of victimization as powerlessness. Wrapped tightly around concepts of toughness, strength, and endurance (both physical and emotional), badass bottoming conflates victimization performances at their most extreme (beating, torture, kidnapping, rape) with a masculine commitment to victory through endurance.

Much like service topping, badass bottoms occupy the lowest status among bottoms; terms like "do-me bottom" and "just a masochist" illustrate the perspective that without claims to powerlessness, SM play is less meaningful. As with service topping among tops, badass bottoms are also more likely than other bottoms to be switches. The lower relative status of switches in the scene, then, is not, as is commonly understood, simply about switching itself, but about the challenges that switches pose to the top/bottom–man/woman paradigm that underlies much of SM play.

There is truth in the argument that topping symbolizes (male) dominance and bottoming (female) submission. Most simply understood, topping and bottoming are ways of doing masculinity and femininity, respectively. Even as they symbolically recreate a gendered *system,* however, the complexity within SM play, and play across genders, problematizes the understanding of SM as a categorical reinforcement of gender inequality. If, at the symbolic level, some "doings" of masculinity are more feminine than others, and both men and women are doing masculinity and femininity, alternately as well as simultaneously, then SM is not a simple patriarchal performance. Neither does it simply invert the gender enactments of patriarchal narratives; in complicating our indicators of power, pain, dominance, submission, and surrender, it also troubles the space in which we envision gender relations. Therefore, while it is important to recognize the sources of the symbolism of these performances, it is insufficient to begin and end analysis of SM at the ideological level, as non-empirically based essays about SM have so often done. SM interactions are constructed and constituted by people, through which cultural meaning is not only utilized and thereby reproduced, but potentially reshaped, challenged, and subverted.

The participation of tops and bottoms in these symbolic performances should also not be viewed outside the context of the active performances at the individual level. The view of gender as something to be either accomplished or constituted through quotidian "doings" is not fundamentally incompatible with the argument that gender is performative, for gender operates interpersonally, intrapersonally, and structurally. We can examine the ways in which gender is being accomplished less consciously and deliberately, while also exploring the ways it is, even in the very same individual at the very same moment, performed, signified, and constituted.

These quotidian gender performances change the social space and meaning of this community, and distinguish it from other alternative cultural sites. One of the distinctions between SM and the Goth scene, for example, may be their relationships to gender. Amy Wilkins finds that in one Goth community, Goth is about presenting a highly stylized and feminized self, negotiating gender through the appropriation of stylized clothing and the social positioning of oneself as a spectacle (2008). In the young, northeastern Goth community she studied, men and women place themselves at the center of the public gaze through intense body work and strive for sexual equality in a pornonormative context. In contrast, the SM community in Caeden (not to be confused with the fetish scene, which overlaps with the Goth scene) negotiates gender through its performances of hyper-masculinity and -femininity. In the Caeden SM scene, masculinity and femininity are done at the symbolic level, regardless of the gender of the doers. This is not necessarily an objective; people do not top to "feel like" men or women, on the conscious level. Nonetheless, the engagement in SM is a *symbolic* engagement in masculinity and femininity. These performances occur only within community space—another argument for Hopkins's simulation rather than replication (1994)—and people of all genders can engage in any kinds of gender performance. Both communities can be understood as emerging from gender "challenges," but both also arise in a post-feminist[5] context of gender anomie, where expectations for behavior are less clearly governed by gender membership—and therefore less clear.

Gender in SM play complicates ideas about gender performativity by juxtaposing these symbolic performances against the ways in which participants perform gender at the quotidian level. These negotiations may be gender synthesizing and thereby arguably gender conformist, or gender bending and subversive, and everywhere in between. Not surprisingly, switching, badass bottoming, and service topping are more common (and are higher-status identifications) in subsets of the community in which gender and SM identities are linked less frequently than they are in Caeden. Where SM is queerer, these kinds of play, as sites of gender subversion, proliferate more widely than in the heavily hetersosexual male-top, female-bottom community.

Nonetheless, gender is not policed in the ubiquitous sense in which it is outside of Caeden. In the scene, identity is fluid, and gender is not an exception. Though the transgendered population in Caeden is not especially large, it is growing and supported by the wider community. At the ideological level, of course, SM identifications parallel the masculine/feminine dualism. In this way, gender regulation is replaced by SM-identity regulation in Caeden.

This can be read as gender-subversive in two ways. Most basically, because of the ways in which topping and bottoming have primacy over gender, the space for men to bottom and women to top constitutes a space to defy gender expectations.[6] Though top and bottom identifications do reinforce the gender binary, this link is troubled by cross-gender engagements in topping and bottoming, as well as by the "switch" identity. Secondly, the range of dynamics of topping and bottoming facilitates sites of conflation of masculinities and femininities in SM, as is clear in the cases of badass bottoming and service topping.

Because the community regulates identity through the SM dualism instead of through gender, the relative prevalence of male topping and female submission is less important than the fact that these identities confer no greater status than their cross-gender counterparts; a man who tops is no more a top than a woman who tops.[7] Additionally, the conceptualization of SM as a "journey" reflects and contributes to a fluidity in both SM and gender identities, and therefore to challenges to gender as an organizing category of social life.

SM provides a space for constructions and constitutions of gendered and (hetero)sexed experience. These joint collaborations in the creation of the illusion and experience of powerless and powerful (and thereby of masculine and feminine), symbolize masculinity and femininity to varying degrees, but can involve gender accomplishment as either ends *or* means. The plethora of motivations and objectives in SM and of gender signification *during* these symbolic performances allow SM play to challenge gender essentialism and problematize the male/female dualism itself. In this way, SM creates a space in which participants achieve a gendered experience; the participants inhabit gender paradoxes of action and service, passivity and strength, powerfulness and powerlessness, but these paradoxes are linked neither to biological sex nor to gender identity.

SM is constructed around conquest and defeat, dominance and submission, and power and powerlessness. Power differences (whether lived, performed, or fantasized) lie at the core of all SM interaction. Based on this quest for inegalitarian experience, SM is not subversive at the level of gender ideology. Gender is about power, and SM builds on, draws from, romanticizes, and eroticizes power differentials between actors. If the feminist agenda depends upon attacking inegalitarianism at the sites of all its manifestations, it follows that SM should be under assault.

If, however, it can be feminist to disentangle inegalitarian dynamics and realities both from sex and from gender at the level of everyday life, then there is room for another feminist perspective on SM. SM explicitly rejects gender as an organizing category of social life, often subverts gender roles as normative and sex-based, and contains the potential for further and more extreme subversion. That is, SM often extricates power differentials from genitals and gendered presentations. Further, for many players, this subversion is a conscious objective of SM.

Moreover, even entirely apart from SM, (heteronormative) eroticism itself cannot be disengaged from questions of power (MacKinnon 1989; Dworkin 1997; Hardy 2000). The process by which we have come to understand and experience the erotic as such is inseparable from gendered power relations, so that all understandings and experiences of eroticism, are, on the ground, currently gendered. A feminist perspective on sexuality, as MacKinnon (1989) argues, is one that recognizes not only this legacy, but also the masculinist imperative of the eroticism of dominance and submission and explores sexuality "as a dimension along which gender pervasively occurs and through which gender is socially constructed" (1989, 318). The fact that hegemonic, heteronormative (and therefore masculinist) sexuality is a dimension on which gender inequality is played out does not mean that the former causes the latter.

Relatedly, the subversive possibilities of SM exist also in the risks it takes. SM functions as a space in which women engage in risk-taking behaviors on levels, in ways, and for reasons that have conventionally been the domains of men. The ways in which erotic life is gendered is intertwined also with the ways in which risk is gendered. SM challenges relationships between gender and risk. SM functions also as a space in which people enact different and diverging masculinities and femininities. SM play allows for the discursive, physical, and sexual positioning of selves in different relationships to gender. While gender is too oppressive and constraining a regime to allow for simple adoption of different positions from one interaction to the next, the cultural space of SM can be viewed as a corollary to the theoretical space of R. W. Connell's concept of hegemonic masculinities; SM participants "dodge among multiple meanings according to their interactional needs" (Connell and Messerschmidt 2005, 841).

Not all SM play is subversive of gender roles, and not all SM participants understand it as such. Many do, however, and their intellectual engagements with issues of gender inequality warrant further study. The consideration of intersections of gender performances at the levels of the everyday, symbolic, and meta-performance may offer an answer to Judith Butler's provocative call: "[W]hat kind of gender performance will enact and reveal the performativity of gender itself in a way that destabilizes the naturalized categories of identity and desire?" (Butler 1990, 177).

Part 3. Edges

Chapter 6

Reconcilable Differences

Pain, Eroticism, and Violence

I was sitting cross-legged on a couch in the back of the dungeon, with a paper cup of water in one hand and a rich fistful of Shaun's long, soft hair in the other. As we chatted casually about the success of the party, I tugged gently on his hair from time to time. His eyes were closed, but he looked at me longingly when I yanked his head backward to expose his throat. He moaned. I ran my hand around the base of his throat. I was wondering how he would respond if I laid my hand across his mouth and nose, when Trey approached.

Trey squeezed onto the couch on the other side of me and put his arm around my shoulders. Shaun opened his eyes and asked Trey how many paid admissions we'd had thus far. I gathered more of his hair into my hand and pulled it, hard, drawing from him a deeply satisfying hiss.

Trey didn't know about the attendance and changed the subject to something about a moving brownie—a "brownie in motion." Shaun chuckled. Trey put his hand in my hair. I put my head on his shoulder.

"I have something for you," he said suddenly.

"What?"

"Close your eyes."

I did. I felt him shift; his arm hung heavier on my shoulders as his other hand dug into his pocket.

Something hard pushed into my breastbone, driving a sharp pain deep into my chest. I gasped and released Shaun's hair.

"Hey . . ." Shaun objected, to Trey.

I opened my eyes and laid a hand against Shaun's cheek. He closed his eyes.

"You might want to get your face away from her hand," Trey advised, as he jammed the whatever-the-fuck-it-was into my temple.

I can't find the word for the sound I made when I felt that pain. It was quieter than a scream, louder than a whimper, and much higher-pitched than a moan. The hurt seared me, scared me—it was a panicky, desperate hurt.

"Jesus! What IS *that?" I panted.*

He ignored my question. He lifted the thing from my temple. I tried to see it, but his hand closed over it quickly. Holding my head firmly, he pointed it into the empty-seeming space where the jawbone meets the skin of the neck. He pressed it into my flesh.

I couldn't even understand what was happening. It was so tiny, that one spot, and yet it took over my entire body. All at once, it shot up into my head, seared straight through to my back, and slammed my body into his. My eyes welled with tears.

"I can't . . . I can't . . ." I whispered. I closed my eyes.

"Sure you can," Trey replied. "Here, look. It's called a fid."

It had a name, the thing. Trey held it up for me to see. It was made out of either wood or a very hard plastic, about six inches long. It was brown and tan, and tapered from one end to the other, but both ends were blunt. It was a sailing tool, he explained, used to untie knots in heavy rope.

I looked at him, incredulous. He grinned. I had never heard of a fid. I had never heard of being poked with anything as part of SM play. He placed the fid on my shirt, directly in the center of my breastbone, and pushed it into me.

I gasped. "But it hurts . . . oh god, it really hurts."

I was amazed by the pain, by its precision and its intensity. It was so . . . big, somehow. I couldn't understand it. It went so deep. It was sharp at first, then more diffuse as it seemed to plow through layers and layers of skin and bone—of me. I was amazed that so much feeling could come so quickly and easily.

He placed the fid in the crease above my upper lip. Weird, I thought—what a weird place to put something. But when he pressed it into my face, it was . . . crazy. Everything was crazy. I felt my eyes fluttering, rolling back in to my head, closing, opening, welling up, rolling back. My fingers dug into his leg, clutching him out of some emotionally unintelligible mélange of desperation and frenzy and anger. The cup of water in my hand had long since been crushed and dropped. He used the fid on all sorts of spots—pressure points, he later told me. I heard myself making sounds that I didn't particularly want to be making . . . my fists were clenched and a couple of times I shivered or shuddered or shook my head suddenly, trying to regain control.

When he stopped, I took a deep, grounding breath. When next I looked at him, he had a knife in his hand. It was different; the handle and the blade were all the same material, the same dimension; the handle simply curved into the blade.

He pulled my hair to stand me up, and guided me against the wall beside the couch. He tilted my head back, exposing my neck to him. He put the blade to my throat, just under my jaw, and murmured something to me about the position of the knife. His playfulness had disappeared completely; things suddenly felt more serious.

His fingers were close to the tip of the knife, nearly touching my skin. He watched the blade as he dragged it slowly along the sides of my neck and across my throat. I began to tremble. He put his arm around my shoulders and held me very firmly. Keeping the point pressed into my neck, he moved the knife under my chin, across my jawbone and down the other side of my neck.

My trembling intensified. It wasn't fear, though, exactly; whatever fear there perhaps should have been was lost in the experience of being overwhelmed. I felt the trembling as a result of general sensory and psychological overload, not a fear specifically.

He whispered directly into my ear. It didn't sound at all like him. When he whispers he is less familiar to me even as it seems more intimate.

"Do you feel how sharp this is?"

The knife was at my throat, just under my jaw; I felt it push into me as I started to nod.

"Yes," I said—said, breathed, panted, whatever; my lips were dry and I wasn't really able to speak. But it didn't occur to me to do anything but answer him.

He slid the point up the left side of my face, stopping at my temple. He pushed it into my head. It scared me. I yanked my head away. He slid the blade upward. I felt it scratch my skin as he dragged it across my forehead. Slowly he brought the blade down to my eye. He rested the point directly at the outside corner of my eye, where the top lash meets the bottom lash.

I looked at him. He looked at me. My heart pounded; he was no longer looking at the knife, which was awfully *close to my eye. I tried not to breathe. He held the blade steady as he looked me in the eyes for what felt like a very, very long time.*

I closed my eyes.

"Open," he whispered.

When I did, he dragged the knife just along my lower lid, from the outside corner to the inside corner, tracing the shape with sharp side of the blade. He dragged it down my cheek, and across my mouth. The blade skipped and caught on my dry lips. I tasted blood.

He put the knife into my mouth and, using the very tip, pinned my tongue to the bottom of my mouth. I closed my eyes and tried to keep still.

Moments passed. I don't know how long we stood like that.

Then, with a sudden, horrifying quickness, he put the knife to my neck and drew it horizontally across my throat.

The lightning-brief terror sent me reeling. My eyes closed, or rolled back, I'm not sure which, but I suddenly didn't see anything. I slumped onto the floor. The fact that it had been the dull end of the blade did not fully register until a few seconds later.

The Erotic-Violent Dualism

In her deconstruction of the feminist reconceptualization of rape as violence rather than sex, Catharine MacKinnon (1989) argues that this position maintains the ideological and conceptual distinction between sex and violence: "Whatever is sex, cannot be violent; whatever is violent, cannot be sex" (1989, 323). Her underlying objection in this argument, of course, is to the ideological preservation of "the 'sex is good' norm," rather than to the implications of its corollary, "violence is bad." Regardless of the moral position of her argument, MacKinnon's point is important; violence and eroticism are positioned in diametric opposition to one another. Where overlap is suspected or identified, it is pathologized, legislated, or reconceptualized as not "really" one or the other. A conscious and deliberate relationship between the erotic and the violent is ethically unacceptable. In the context of powerful feminist critiques of (hetero)sexuality over the past three decades, the conflation is especially problematic.

While the conceptualization of SM as an alternative kind of sex is reductionist, SM is, for most people in Caeden, sexualized, at least to some extent. SM is almost always presented and performed as having erotic meaning. It is normative to pay attention of one kind or another to the breasts, buttocks, and genitals of bottoms. The bottom is often dressed in conventionally sexually provocative or exhibitionist clothing. Most of my respondents considered SM a part of—or entirely—their "sexual identity," and themselves members of a sexual community. For some, the recollections of SM scenes serve as masturbatory fantasy. Though SM interaction is not simply, solely, or always experienced as sexual, it is nonetheless linked to eroticism.

Yet the relationship between sex and SM is problematic for participants. The link is difficult to identify and even more difficult for participants to articulate. The eroticism of SM is not quite the same experience as the eroticism of sexual arousal. Physically and psychologically, SM differs from conventional sexual experience, leaving participants grappling for language:

> When I play with somebody, casual play in the club, I'm getting something out of it. I'm getting turned on, but it's not from a standpoint—like, I know no sex is coming. It's not that kind of thing. It's still something—don't have a word yet. Don't know what that word would be. But it's something, it's a turn on, it's exciting, it's fulfilling—it's definitely fulfilling some need, whatever that need can be defined as. (Interview transcript, Laura)

Kyle explained that for him, SM and sex "are separated, for the most part, and were, early on, separated. For me, when I was doing SM, it was about SM, it was about endorphin rush." Although he said that they were "separated," he did not say that SM was one and not the other. When pushed to explain further the relationship, if any, he clarified:

> It'd be kind of like reading the fantasy book prior to masturbation. You don't necessarily get hard at the time because you're busy concentrating, but certainly when you're done, it was like, wow.

Even when SM is not understood as sex, it is *sexually relevant* for participants. It matters in and for the sexual understandings and experiences of most (but not all) players. It is also linked to power and to violence. The connection between SM and violence is often deeply problematic for SM participants as much as it is for social (and particularly feminist) theory. In their illumination of the important relationships between heteronormative sexuality and ideologies of domination and violence, feminist analyses[1] have helped to transform an ideological objection to the conflation of the erotic with the violent into a theoretical and conceptual limitation. As Pat Califia pointed out, "Anybody who questioned [the anti-pornography activists'] definition of porn or violence was accused of having bad consciousness about violence against women" (1981, 256–57). Violence, then, could not be problematized; conflated with violent crime, "violence" is intrinsically morally problematic.

SM participants do not generally use "violent" as an adjective to describe their play. Most would, understandably, vociferously object to its categorization as violence, as Carol Truscott did: "Consensual sadomasochism has nothing to do with violence. Consensual sadomasochism is about safely enacting sexual fantasies with a consenting partner. Violence is the epitome of nonconsensuality, an act perpetrated by a predator on a victim. Consensual sadomasochism neither perpetuates violence nor serves as catharsis of the violent in the human spirit" (Truscott 1991, 30). Yet transgressions of the boundary between eroticism and violence are fundamental in SM play. In the scene described in the prologue to this chapter, Trey and I were undeniably engaging with fictions of violence—of murder in particular. His sudden flip of the blade to draw it quickly across my throat was intended precisely to overwhelm me with the idea that he could, might, or had slit my throat. While this is an extreme illustration of the symbolic violence of SM, most play is practiced around and predicated on either actual or symbolic violence. Beyond the obvious connections between violence and injurious treatment of the body during SM play, the rhetoric of SM in Caeden is the rhetoric of violence. Many SM participants speak with pleasure of "getting beat," or share that they "bloodied her back" or "pummeled the hell out of him." Toys are sometimes referred to as "arsenal," and impact play, including spanking, is often called "beating." SM play is profoundly and significantly different from nonconsensual interactions in nonconsensual contexts, but it is nonetheless a performance of violence. Whether these dynamics are constructed at the level of the psychological (e.g., service) or the physical (e.g., pain) or some combination, playing with hierarchies, exploitation, and dominance and submission *is* playing, if only symbolically, with violence.

In Caeden, this occurs in a particular context: between men and women, long after the peak of second-wave feminism, and among people for whom feminist arguments are familiar, meaningful, and even resonant. The intersection of eroticism and violence thus poses a challenge for participants themselves. The language of eroticism is an obstacle to the articulations of their experiences in a meaningful way. If desire feels sexual—that is, it manifests itself in bodily understandings, such that one can "feel" it in one's body, but the site is not in genitalia (or other "erogenous zones"), what do we call this? What if the desire—desire that is understood in the same essentialist terms as normative eroticism (ache, hunger, want)—is for pain or tears or blood? And what do we make of circumstances in which people orgasm from blows to the back or being kept in a cage? While psychological perspectives, and psychoanalytical approaches in particular, offer entry points into exploring these conflations, they do so in the wake and shadow of essentialist models that themselves pathologize intersections of eroticism and violence. Further, if we wish to understand these experiences as socially situated and constituted, we need to explore these dynamics as they are produced within and understood through the interaction in which they occur.

The sociological literature of violence presents its own challenges to understanding the intersection of eroticism and violence in a productive way. Randall Collins's recent powerhouse of a monograph on violence (2009) provides a complex and nuanced perspective on violence at the microsociological level, but consensual activities cannot be understood as violence within his framework. For Collins, violence is "a set of pathways around confrontational tension and fear." Injury to the body in the absence of confrontational tension and fear does not qualify as violence. Despite, for example, the "patterned violence of slamming body against body under shared control" (2009, 279) in slam-dancing, Collins excludes the mosh pit from consideration as a violent situation. Thus boxing merely "pretends to be a real fight" (2009, 286). These inflictions of physical harm on the body of another become what Collins calls "pseudo-violence," given that participants and bystanders are not necessarily tense and fearful. Violence, then, cannot be that which is welcomed. This assertion, alongside Elaine Scarry's premise that pain can be defined as such only if the person in pain feels averse to it (1985), informs us that SM does not hurt, and it is not violent. Pain and violence are, from these perspectives, fundamentally *bad;* Collins writes that there is "no single remedy for the ills of violence. Different mechanisms of violence need to be headed off in different ways" (2009, 466). Yet if we use a definition of violence framed by assumptions that violence is inherently undesirable, antagonistic, or otherwise bad, we obscure not only the ways in which SM resembles violence, but countless other sites of intersections between violence and everyday life. Alternatively, we reject the premise that these sites of intersection are sociological phenomena, and (continue to) relegate their study to psychology and theology.

In his analysis of Lonnie Athens's work (1992) on socialization into violent acts ("violentization"), Ian O'Donnell recognizes the importance of theorizing a multitude of social contexts for violence. Acknowledging that violentization may be a useful way to understand displays of extreme violence for some people, O'Donnell maintains that for others violent displays result "from obedience to a higher authority, conformity to a social role, adherence to a code of conduct or the search for pleasure. To think of violence as largely the preserve of the violentized is to constrain our search for understanding" (O'Donnell 2003, 766–67).

Hamstrung by the moral heft attached to the word, the sociology of violence remains what Mary Jackman calls a "conceptual quagmire" of issues concerning intent, complicity, intention, and context. Recognizing that our (often competing) conceptions of violence are "biased and morally charged," Jackman proposes an understanding of violence that extricates it from its moral tether: "Actions that inflict, threaten, or cause injury. Actions may be corporal, written or verbal. Injuries may be corporal, psychological, material, or social" (2002, 405). Violence here is not defined by the intention of the actor, nor by the judgment of the recipient. Most importantly, it is not inherently aggressive, hostile, unwanted, or otherwise negative. It does not conflate violence with domination, but recognizes it as a component of social interaction. Under Jackman's concise and logically inclusive definition, SM can be usefully understood as violence, without its accompanying and limiting moral position.

The adoption of this definition is of course problematic. The violence of SM is constructed, performed, and enacted specifically toward the achievement of objectives that are consciously intertwined with the *symbolism* of violence. To dilute the conceptual potency of violence by including SM in its definition is understandably ideologically troubling, as would be (yet another) contribution to the criminalization of SM. This is not an argument that SM is tantamount to *that which we generally understand* as violence, but a recognition of violence as such despite the contextual complexity. Lacking adequate vocabulary, the foray into SM studies has had little recourse other than to try to render SM more palatable and graspable by pretending that it is merely kinky sex. Jackman's crucial recognition that "without the full population of violent actions held coherently in view, we impoverish the quest to understand the place of violence in social life" (2002, 415) urges us to accept an understanding of SM as violence, even as it avoids condemning it for being so. The violence of SM is thus *not* simulated, as Hopkins claims when he maintains that "SM scenes gut the behaviors they simulate of their violent, patriarchal, defining features" (Hopkins 1994). The conflation of violence with badness muddies Hopkins' argument; while it is true that in SM, "core features of real patriarchal violence, coercive violence, are absent" (Hopkins 1994, 123), and that "what makes events like rape, kidnapping, slavery and bondage evil in the first place is the fact that they cause harm, limit freedom, terrify, scar, destroy and coerce" (Hopkins 1994, 124), none of this makes SM (at least some of it) any less violent. Violence in SM is often authentic as well as symbolic—yet not coercive, antagonistic, or evil.

The conceptual tension between sex and violence shapes the discourse, meaning-making, and strategies surrounding SM play in Caeden. My efforts to understand how participants made sexual (or nonsexual) sense of their activities were consistently frustrated, as community members struggled to negotiate a discursive space in which the conflation of the erotic and the violent was not pathological. Few of them succeeded in this endeavor, ultimately choosing instead to accept the binary and disavow one "side" or the other of the SM experience.

Strategies of Resolution

DISAVOWAL AND DETACHMENT

Of the conceptual extrication of sex from rape, MacKinnon charges, "Aside from failing to answer the rather obvious question, if it's violence not sex why didn't he just hit her, this approach made it impossible to see that violence is sex when it is practiced as sex" (MacKinnon 1989, 323). Again SM poses an interesting turnabout: what is it if he often *does* "just hit her?" The "rather obvious" question implies that the hitting itself cannot be sex, in which case we would be left to conclude that SM is *only* violence, since it is not being "practiced" as sex.

For—and regarding—the SM community, this conclusion makes little sense. First, though SM is not sex, it is sexualized, and for many participants, it is an erotic experience. Similarly, while SM should not be confused with nonconsensual interactions in nonconsensual contexts, it makes little sense to ignore the ways in which it is violent.

Most of us, though, are not working with Jackman's definition. We accept instead the underlying assumptions of Randall Collins's perspective when he explains that "in slam-dancing, any sexual connotation is consciously negated by the violent tone, similar to the forearm bashes, mock punches, and butt-slaps that express solidarity among athletes" (Collins 2009, 279). The erotic is negated by the presence of violence, and otherwise-violent acts become non-violent when they express solidarity. Since SM cannot be both erotic and violent without also being pathological, the members of Caeden must divorce the two, in practice, discourse, or meaning-making, in order to understand their experiences. Violence is thus defined in accordance with its contextual meaning rather than its action.

Discursively, this reconceptualization hinges on consent. Consent serves as the mediator between violence and eroticism, rendering SM *not* violence. It revokes violence's claim to authenticity, setting it apart from nonconsensual violence (a term that then becomes redundant). Creating a distinction between violence itself and the performance of violence, the notion of consent problematizes the authenticity of the violence among SM participants.

The use of consent as the intercessor between violence and eroticism is evident in multiple places in the community, including in the ways in which many of my respondents qualified their descriptions of their identities and activities:

> A sadist to me is very pure—I believe in the dictionary definition [. . .] someone who derives pleasure from causing pain, inflicting pain on someone. Note in the definition it does not say consensual or nonconsensual. It just says inflicting pain, period. A masochist is someone who derives pleasure from receiving pain. Period. I identify myself as a sadist. I do enjoy inflicting pain. I do get turned on, and sometimes get hard, seeing someone in pain. Knowing that I caused it. It just so happens I [also] have a kink for consensuality. Well, maybe not a kink for consensuality; I say that kind of figuratively. (Interview transcript, Frank)

Frank emphasized the word "kink" in his last sentence above to indicate that this did not quite capture the role of consent in his play. Regardless, the statement is a testament to the importance of the role of consent, and serves to reconcile his sadism with his erotic response. This conceptual and discursive rendering of SM as categorically nonviolent by way of consent legitimizes his erotic experience. It does not succeed in neutralizing the violence of SM entirely. It does not eliminate the experiences of pain and powerlessness in SM, and it does not address the erotic response to, or the desire for, the concept-elsewhere-known-as-violence. It does not, in other words, succeed in recasting SM as "kinky sex."

There were many examples of the incongruity between violence and eroticism during my interviews, but the tension between them in SM crystallized for me during a casual conversation. Justin, who identifies as a dominant and who has a reputation as a particularly affectionate play partner, talked to me about his reluctance to bring (consensual) violence into his play despite the extent of his sadistic desire in erotic fantasy. He shared his sense that he has "become more of a sadist" over time, as indicated by his inability to reach orgasm with either vanilla or standard SM pornography. Instead, he uses "severely sadistic stuff," in which people are badly beaten. There is a disjunction for him between what he likes on one erotic level, and his comfort level in play. Trying to reconcile being "a nice guy" and being a sadist, he waffled back and forth in his characterization, alternating between using dramatic sadistic language ("I mean, I could throw you against the fucking wall," he said while explaining himself to me) and lamenting this disinclination to play that way, given his inability to find "nice guy" material erotic.

The difficulty that Justin had in reconciling violence with eroticism even within his own SM play underscores their culturally embedded moral opposition to one another. Despite the violence of his fantasies, Justin's SM play often seemed more like kinky sex than a safe space for the intersection of eroticism and violence. When violence and eroticism are linked at the level of social behavior, the result is not only more morally problematic than either on its own, but more conceptually problematic.

In other cases, the violence of SM is disavowed entirely, and the erotic significance becomes central to the understandings and the descriptions of play. Bobby, a dominant, indicated that eroticism is not only integral in his play, but both the motive and the objective. He maintains that he does not eroticize hurting women. Therefore, he views his desire to bind and torture women as entirely sexual, in both origin and outcome:

> You can tease someone sexually the same way. Where you can get to a point, slowly, slowly build up, where they just are screaming and can't stand it and they can't sit still anymore. Well, if they're restrained, you can take them past that point. And—well, tears, screaming, crying—and bring them to a higher level of endorphin rush than they could otherwise have achieved. And then, you know, that's—they come back looking for more. The restraint is not there to hurt—it's not the endorphins that shoot the pain to the endorphin rush; it is direct, it's done for long, extended periods of sustained stimulation.

When I asked Bobby if this is erotic to him, he responded affirmatively. But he was careful to point out:

> Nothing deflates me faster than if she's hurting. And really hurting. I mean, I'm talking about if this is distress pain, "I'm being hurt and I'm being panicked."

It was important to him, both in the community and during our interview, to make it well known that he does not like to hurt women. Yet he also told me:

> I've dealt out some pretty, you know, severe switchings, canings, stuff like that, if this is what—you know, we've worked to that level and I know she can take it [. . .] As far as fantasy play, anything goes, any dress and level of bondage and restraint, as long as it's being watched. I've done breath play. That can be very dangerous, but it's like a swimming pool. You hold your breath and you go underwater.

For Bobby, play is about captivity and controlling sexual pleasure, rather than pain as its own end. This avoidance of pain play or its recognition as such, combined with drawing on a discourse of the conventionally erotic (his arousal and her orgasm) mitigates the violence of his play.

Because the pain in SM is inflicted, it is a symbol of violence. Accidents aside, when pain occurs in SM play, it is the result of violence. Even if we reject Jackman's conceptualization of violence, pain remains necessarily the result of performances of violence. Yet most of the members of this community deny pain, as either a goal or an experience. This disavowal emerges from this relationship to violence. The renouncement of pain, combined with the important issue of consent, provides the foundation for an understanding of SM as not violence.

Most SM participants do not view pain as integral to their play or to their identities. Pain, in and of itself, was not a thematic focus of my interviews. Because meanings surrounding pain were so varied, I did not identify it as an especially salient concept across the community. Later analysis of interview transcripts and field notes, however, revealed that pain was central for the community, even when it was being resisted, disavowed, refused, or ignored.

DISCOURSES OF PAIN

The members of this community draw on four different discourses in framing and understanding pain. Three of these discourses—which I call "transformed pain," "sacrificial pain," and "investment pain"—reproduce pain as inherently negative. The fourth, which I term "autotelic pain"—is uncommon and stigmatized.

While some SM participants are comfortable with the verb "hurt" to describe their actions and their experiences, many people reject this in favor of "giving pain" or "receiving pain." During my fieldwork period, this distinction had such a stronghold in the social scripts of the community that it was rare to hear the word "hurt" in this context without the subsequent objection. A brief (and formulaic) discussion normally followed. Some, however, saw no need for discussion; one person forcefully corrected an assumption I made during conversation: "I don't like to be hurt. I like to receive pain."

In this formulation, pain is not something that is happening to her, but something provided to her, something she can accept if she so chooses. While both views are equally passive, and therefore equally effective in maintaining the belief in a power differential, she is not a victim of pain in her reconceptualization of it. If she is not a victim, this cannot be violence. *Being hurt* indicates that violence is occurring; *receiving pain* does not. This discursive twist provides the foundation for "transformed pain."

Transformed Pain: Turning Pain into Pleasure

The transformed pain discourse centers on a disavowal of pain as such. SM participants who frame pain this way tend to engage in mild to moderate pain play, but when pain is experienced, it is understood as *not hurting.* Instead, pain is "transformed into pleasure." This transformation occurs almost instantly, usually in a process that is understood as conscious, though barely. Viewed this way, would-be painful situations are not experienced as hurt. This relies on a conceptualization of pain as an objective stimulus, which may or may not result in the *feeling* of hurt. During a conversation at a restaurant one night, Faye captured this idea; she said that she "can convert pain to pleasure . . . make my body produce chemicals" by changing the context in her conscious experience.

This "processing" of pain sensations as pleasurable, within seconds or less, fuels a discourse in which pain can be *real* but not *bad.* For bottoms, this discourse reconciles masochism with rational thought; if pain does not "really" hurt, it is de-pathologized and therefore its enjoyment is unproblematic. Tops engage in the same discourse, potentially mitigating some of the struggles with guilt that often accompany topping, particularly for newer players. When I asked Seth about a scene I had watched, in which it seemed to me he had caused Stephanie a good deal of (intended and desired) pain, I again used the word "hurt." Seth was quick to correct me:

> **Seth:** No. I want to provide the sensation of pleasure. If that pleasure is pain transmogrified into pleasure, I'm very happy to provide it.
> **Me:** What if it's not?
> **Seth:** I don't want to beat somebody who wants to be beaten so that they feel something. I'll beat somebody—I'll flog somebody or I'll cane somebody who is enjoying the sensation of being caned. The experience. It's having a good time. That's what I'm there for. [. . .] If they're going, "Fuck, that hurts!" Generally, my agreement is—what I say to people is, for me, if you say "Ow," in a way that indicates that you don't like it, I'm going to yellow.[2] I'm gonna yellow on our scene and I'm going to slow down or do something else. I use "Ow" as a safeword. My default position is "Ow" is bad. Generally when someone says "Ow," it's something that they don't like.

Seth's sense was that his play partners' experience of pain is "I like pain; pain feels like pleasure," rather than "I like to be *hurt.*" His definition of SM hinges on this distinction:

> SM is the seeking of pleasure, I think, in a way, by people who can translate pain into pleasure, and by people who can translate the act of giving pain . . . or seeing that the other person . . . is having pleasure. I think a

good sadist is somebody who is really empathic—somebody who really can feel what the other person is feeling, and take joy in that.

By recasting pain as something other than hurt, Seth, like other participants for whom this frame resonates, does not draw explicitly on discourses of violence and victimization. Pain becomes a gift, a gesture of affection; there is therefore nothing "violent" about it.

For Bobby, the presence of anger threatens the context of his infliction of pain, which he finds enjoyable only if he interprets it as pleasurable for the bottom. In the context of punishment or discipline, pain is experienced and performed as pain. During our interview, I found it challenging to address pain in its own right, divorced from pleasure. I tried rather doggedly to talk about pain, resulting in the following exchange about his enjoyment of caning:

Bobby: It's from her reaction. And not in—from seeing the rear end getting a strike, but the end that I prefer to watch is the front end. Watching her eyes, and her reaction to what's going on.
Me: If it hurts—?
Bobby: Yeah, the pain, the reaction—or the pleasure of being in pain. That's what has to be there.
Me: It has to look like pleasure . . . ?
Bobby: Oh, she can be grimacing and yelping and so forth, but I will also check and make sure that's something that she wants. But I have a young lady who's playing with me, and she's hanging up naked by her ankles on the front stage of the Playground. [. . .] My favorite place is to be holding her head in my hand. And watching her and headspacing her. But she's under control; it's a male control, while the body is being [makes snapping sound] by an expert if the pain is being inflicted on the other side. But that's my favorite place to be is in her face, watching the eyes.
Me: But if it just looks like it hurts, then it doesn't do anything for you?
Bobby: Not—that's fantasy, yes, but in real life, no. In real life, no.

Although Bobby is interested in power-imbalanced experiences, this particular construction of imbalance is uncomfortable for him. In the transformed pain discourse, "hurt" is a negative word, and an undesirable experience for all involved. This perspective reflects a wider cultural understanding of the desire to hurt or be hurt as ethically problematic and/or individually pathological. Thus it draws a binary distinction between the active and intimate "hurting," on one side, and the abstract, nebulous, and passive provision of "the sensation of pain" on the other.

This recasting of pain as transformed frames the pain in accordance with the hegemonic views of pain, but modifies the pain (and the narrative) by turning it into *not* pain. The participant who modifies pain is actively changing the sensation, working to claim it and process it differently, toward an eventual understanding of the pain *as* pleasure.

Sacrificial Pain: For a Greater Good

In a definitive contrast, pain is framed as undesirable sensation that *remains* an undesirable sensation throughout (as in, for example, punishment and discipline). In this conceptual move, pain does not transform into pleasurable sensation. Pain is, and must remain, *suffering,* for the suffering is a sacrifice on the part of the bottom. This sacrifice is conceptualized as being for the benefit or desires of the top. Pain hurts, and the bottom derives no pleasure from it. It is a gift in the other direction; the bottom gives her experience of pain willingly, a token to the top of her affection or devotion. Still, then, for people who draw on this discourse, the pain is not an indicator of violence.

This is significantly distinct from transformed pain; when pain is cast as pleasurable, bottoms do not view themselves as victims and tops do not view themselves as victimizing, in scene space.

In Caeden, the discourse of sacrificial pain is more commonly deployed by women who bottom, particularly those who identify as "submissive," than by other participants. The authenticity is bolstered in part through the identity of the "submissive," distinguishing it from role play by its emphasis on the "realness" of the hierarchical relationship between players.

Interestingly, the transformed pain discourse is also sometimes given voice within the larger frame of sacrificial pain. Here the bottom is understood as pain-averse because she or he (usually she) does not have the "ability" to transform pain into pleasure. This at times mimics a deeply gendered fairy-tale narrative; the bottom lacks the ability until a particular moment in a particular scene in which the connection between play partners bestows this transformative power on the bottom.

Although there are exceptions, transformed and sacrificial pain discourses tend to be more commonly utilized among people who engage in D/s. D/s players participate also in performances of power outside of the space of SM play itself. The emphasis on dominance and submission also helps these participants navigate this challenging moral territory. By imbuing SM play with significance above and beyond the realm of the physical, SM participants shift the focus of the activity from both eroticism and violence to power, thereby sidestepping the conflation of the erotic with the violent. The discursive role of dominance and submission in the community facilitates not only the experience of scenes in this context, but also the reading of SM scenes in this context by spectators. It thereby reinforces the sublimation of the sensory experience to the psycho-emotional context of the scene. While this provides a context that renders the sensory experiences less important, it does not resolve the dissonance between eroticism and violence for them.

Investment Pain: Pain Payoffs

In contrast, the investment pain discourse draws heavily on hyper-masculine narratives of pain ("No pain, no gain"). This discourse frames pain as an unpleasant stimulus that promises future rewards. Not surprisingly, men, whether bottoming or topping, frame pain this way more often than women do.

Sociologists of sport find that pain is often framed as an investment toward a greater reward. Pain is understood not merely as an unfortunate byproduct, but as a means to a particular end. While the hurting is not the goal, in and of itself, it is rewarding for both what it evidences and what it produces. Greg Downey finds, for example, that participants in no-holds-barred fighting "must steel their wills against pain so that they can venture further and further into suffering without dissolution . . . fighters must learn from pain and, in some sense, are legitimated by it" (Downey 2007, 217). Because this suffering is not for the sake of another, it is uniquely masculine. It is competitive—a challenge to the self—an investment given of free will, and, more importantly, framed as such.

Describing a hook-suspension scene, Kyle, for example, did not romanticize the pain itself, but wanted it for what it could provide him, physiologically:

> After I got over the pain of it, and I was—you know, with any sort of play in the scene, there's a time early on where it just hurts. And then after awhile, the endorphins kinda build up and it doesn't hurt anymore. That's kinda how this was too. Once I got past the pain of it and I could really pull back, and really pull, and have the hooks pull forward . . . at one point, early on, when that happened, I stopped caring about the pain of it and just wanted the experience.

Pain is not sought, appreciated, or eroticized. Its infliction is a means to an end, its value derived from and located in the body of the bottom. It is impersonal, experienced not as an assault but as a desired catalyst toward another end. The violence of its infliction disappears in the higher value of its physiological provisions.

Autotelic Pain: Liking the Hurting

These three discourses maintain and reproduce the conceptualization of pain as aversive. Most people in the Caeden SM community draw on one or more of these discourses, in which pain is something to be withstood, endured, altered, or conquered. To be able to do so provides rewards, but pain is still, in and of itself, negative. The infliction of pain, however, is not violent; a complex set of strategies ensures the experience of infliction as not violence. Most importantly, SM play is understood, at least to some extent, as erotic experience. This discourse provides SM participants with permission to find SM erotic precisely *because* it is not violent. It is not violent because the pain is either a gift, an investment, or ultimately pleasure rather than pain.

In contrast, the terms "sadist" and "masochist" are used to describe people who frame their relationships to pain in positive terms. These identity labels are somewhat stigmatic in the community. In some instances, these are self-identifications. They are also attributed to people who do not appear to rely on strategies to achieve authentic experiences of power imbalance. Participants who transform or provide pain, for example, distinguish themselves from masochists, who they believe "like the pain," and also from sadists, who "like to hurt people." Interestingly, the only discourse in the SM community in which pain appears as an (almost) unqualified "good" thing is the least common.

The foundation of this discourse is fairly simple for those who draw on it: the pain hurts, but the hurt also feels good. Participants who frame pain this way have an extraordinarily difficult time articulating their experience of pain. They generally distinguish between kinds of pain that they do like and kinds of pain that they do not like; the particular kind of pain, rather than the context, determines whether the response is favorable.

At times, the autotelic pain discourse is also used publicly to represent pain as positive. For example, during an educational presentation on the use of canes, the following occurred:

> At some point a woman in the audience . . . asked what to do if you're playing with someone who can't leave with marks. Jamie talked a bit about how to avoid marks even with a cane, but then someone in the audience else offered an alternative solution: there's something in Chinese-herbal type stores to get rid of bruises. He said that it needs to be rubbed in and he warned that it was "exceedingly painful—more painful than the scene."
>
> Chelsea, who was sitting beside him, said, very loudly, "That's not a bad thing . . . how is that a bad thing??!" Everyone laughed.

The idea that the pain would be welcome even after the scene suggests that the "play" context is not necessary for the enjoyment of pain. The pain is its own end. Kevin, for example, said that he sought the SM community after pledging a fraternity in college. The twelve-week hazing period included physical beatings of various degrees. Kevin said that when the hazing was over, he "realized that there was some part of me that found it pleasurable."

This extrication of pain from the context of the cordoned-off SM interaction is a slippery slope. The widely held and passionately defended position (to outsiders, for it is not usually challenged within the community) is that SM participants simply would not enjoy pain in a nonconsensual situation.

Autotelic pain is experienced, valued, and appreciated as pain. Bottoms who frame pain this way say that it hurts and that they like it *anyway.* Unlike those who frame pain as transformed, those who view pain as autotelic do not feel that they engage in a conversion process; the hurting itself feels good, instantly and without work. For tops, this discourse casts them as villainous, drawing on a romantic, Sadean concept of the seductive evildoer. Tops who frame pain this way are often desired as play partners precisely because of their sadism; the stronger the belief that the top enjoys the actual infliction of pain, the more authentic the scene becomes for bottoms.

Tops and bottoms who identify as wanting pain, for its own sake and to its own ends, are in the minority in the community. The autotelic pain discourse rejects conventional conceptualizations of pain as undesirable and, by extension, pain-seeking as pathological. Most SM participants actively employ strategies to disavow, minimize, or rationalize their engagement with pain, perhaps precisely to avoid understanding their activities in the pathological terms of sadism and masochism.

Ultimately, this discourse appears to disentangle the enjoyment of pain from the understanding of pain as bad. While the end result of transformed pain is pleasure, it becomes, post-transformation, pleasure *instead* of pain. Autotelic pain begins as pain, ends as pain, and is enjoyable nonetheless. However, the overarching context must remain one of inflictor/inflictee. Sadists and masochists, self-defined and other-identified, do not appear to enjoy pain in other, solo contexts (such as medical pain, accidental harm, or self-injury). Nonetheless they claim to enjoy pain in and of itself, extricated from contexts of power and control.

Yet among these participants, *eroticism* is often denied or recast. Most of the people who say they like to hurt or be hurt also say that SM is not sexual for them. And those who do use the word "hurt" draw their line between "hurt" and "harm," with the distinction being largely temporal; harm is lasting. In this case, pain becomes symbolic not of violence but of power. Power and violence are thus extricated from one another, allowing for the eroticization of power, so long as violence has been excluded from the equation. This dualism mirrors the scholarship on pain, which is heavily concentrated in medical literature and the sociology of sport. In the former, pain is an involuntary condition of life, and in the latter it is a byproduct of a recreational or professional pursuit. In both cases, pain is experienced as not having been an intended outcome; in the case of medicine, there is no actor to inflict the pain, and in sport, when there is, the actor has inflicted pain toward another end, such as the securing of the ball. In either case, the pain itself is not the primary experience, objective, or tool; it is not processed or perceived as a provision unto itself. Theoretically interesting questions focus on the impact of cultural, social, psychological, and emotional conditions on pain (Zborowski 1969; Aldrich and Eccleston 2000). Activities in which pain might be viewed as an end—boxing and fight clubs, for example—have not been explored with a focus on the bodily experience of pain. Where the experience of *inflicted* pain might be observed—such as in studies of victims of violent crime, abuse, and torture—the focus is on psychological and emotional rather than sensory experience. There are few spaces in which to understand the infliction of pain, and the social contexts of infliction are therefore often ignored.

Unofficially, then, a criterion for the consideration of pain as such is its undesirability. Any instances of its reconceptualization, recasting, or enjoyment simply cease to be painful, much as consensual violence ceases to be violence. The issue in both is intent. If pain is not deliberate, then there is no cause to consider the pain as a positive experience. If is inflicted, it is either undesirable or not really pain. It is mired in the same dualism as sex and violence, and its relationship to violence is tautological: pain is undesirable because it evidences violence, and violence is undesirable because its consequences are painful.

The subjective experiences of inflictors of pain—the feelings, motivations, and understandings of people who inflict pain in noncriminal contexts—are similarly absent from the literature. Experiences of infliction might be understood through examination of the experiences of, for example, emergency medical professionals who perform excruciating procedures on unanesthetized people and boxers whose objective is to cause pain to the point of unconsciousness. In the endeavor to make sense of pain, whether as social-psychological experience or an existential reality, if context matters then it is crucial to explore the motivations and experiences of people who cause pain.

This negation of pain does not occur in other narratives of the body; childbirth is romanticized and glorified even as its pain is recognized as such. The pain of childbirth is "worth it," as is the pain of contact sports when victory is at stake. For SM participants, the pain of SM is "worth it" in submission; submission becomes the higher cause and the pain necessary to withstand. Bottoms who "like" the pain, however, do not borrow this rationale, and are left with no understanding other than the pathological. This theoretical parallel of the previously unchallenged assumptions about risk in the scholarly literature can be similarly addressed. When risk was intrinsically undesirable, voluntary risk-taking was paradoxical, and the examination of risk among people who seek it leads to a fuller understanding of risk as a social phenomenon. No less socially constructed, the meaning-making of pain can be similarly explored.

Similarly, we are willing to apply the term "violence" to other consensual situations; sports are considered violent when they require aggression and physical contact, so consent is not the issue. The presence of women also fails to explain the disinclination to consider SM violent; women's contact sports (rugby, for example) are not exempt from the consideration as violence. Generally, though, we understand participants in violent sports to be "only playing."

SM is different. Jackman attributes some of the acceptance of violence in sports to voluntarism in sport, but this not the only, or perhaps even the most relevant, issue. We can understand that athletes are "only playing" because first, the infliction of pain is not perceived as the goal of the sport, and second, we do not understand the sport to be a sexual experience. Critics of SM have often directed their outrage at the *eroticization* of violence (Nichols et al. 1982; Stoltenberg 1982; Wagner 1982). The implication is that violence on its own is terrible enough, but when it meets the realm of the erotic, it is especially disturbing. The spoken prelude to each episode of the long-running crime drama *Law and Order: SVU* captures this perspective: "In the criminal justice system, sexually based offenses are considered especially heinous."

Violence, Eroticism, and the Infliction of Pain

There is therefore a tendency in Caeden for participants to speak of their play in terms that might be plotted on a continuum between eroticism and violence, and the further one moves toward one end, the less likely one is to draw, discursively, on the concept at the other end. Despite the fact that they are nonconformist in many ways and that SM play negotiates multiple boundaries, their play is constructed and processed through and alongside cultural filters that compel conceptual acrobatics in order to make sense of their experiences and their enjoyment of them.

In the first of these conceptual moves, the sublimation of the carnal experience of SM to an ostensibly nobler experience (the quest to gain or relinquish power) legitimizes their satisfaction. Secondly, in the absence of a non-pathologized conceptual frame in which eroticism and violence might be reconciled, SM participants define their satisfaction as one or the other, thereby disavowing the conflation that lies at the core of SM. Far from having successfully merged the concepts of sex and violence, many members of this community seek ways to understand—or at least to render discursively—SM as one or the other; even for people engaging in SM, it simply cannot be both.

Whether SM participants would seek to merge the erotic with the violent at all if a theoretical reconciliation were easily reached is an interesting question, but one that cannot be answered using the current frameworks for violence and eroticism. Moreover, nonconsensual sites of intersection between the two—including sexual assault, rape, serial homicide, and kidnapping—will continue to be relegated to the fringe of sociological understanding if we cannot make sense of these relationships. A broader, cleaner focus on the social criteria for, and construction of, both violence and eroticism is necessary to understand these relationships far beyond consensual sadomasochism.

In the quest to understand social-sexual behavior, conceptualizations of the erotic need to be extricated from their moral underpinnings. We must recognize the similarities between experiences of serial homicide, spousal abuse, sadomasochism, animal cruelty, cosmetic surgery, consensual bloodletting, and spiritual body suspension (hanging by hooks through the skin), in our efforts to make sense of their differences.

Even more importantly, when we confront the discursive inaccessibility of the coalescence of eroticism and violence, the function of this limitation as a mechanism for the social control of sexuality becomes staggeringly clear. As Foucault has illustrated, the linguistic and conceptual limits of discourse are also very much a part of its regulation (1978). The inadequacy of our language in the discussion of experiences of desirable violence anchors SM to its marginal position, both in society at large and in academic work.

Chapter 7

Collaborating the Edge
Feminism and Edgework

I paced the room nervously, uncharacteristically tidying things that weren't mine and looking for people who weren't there. Perhaps it was the bed; it was strange that I was about to play in a room with a bed. In fact, I realized as I looked around, it seemed likely I was going to play on *the bed, since there wasn't much free wall space.*

Perhaps it was the fact that we'd just been watching Law and Order *reruns and eating Chinese takeout. Or maybe it was the fact that I was wearing sweat pants and a T-shirt; it had seemed silly to get dressed in order to hang out in an apartment.*

He walked into the bedroom. I wondered how scenes even begin in a private space. What are the cues? Where are the cuffs? Who's going to laugh with us when funny things happen? Just us?

I followed him into the bedroom.

"It's weird," I said.

"What is?"

"Being here, playing in private. You don't think it's weird?"

"It's different. Where's the light bulb?"

I'd forgotten he was supposed to replace the light bulb—our payment for borrowing the apartment from a friend. I found it on her dresser, handed it to him, and sat on the bed while he climbed up to reach it. When he finished, he stepped down and looked around the room.

"Guess it's the bed," he said as he walked into the living room and picked up his toy bag.

While he set up his toys, I sent my "I'm okay" text message. The confirmation—"Message sent"—flooded me with guilt. Trey knew who to call if something went wrong. And I trusted him enough to be here in the first place.

He sat down and guided me backward. I knew at once that I was about a thousand times more comfortable standing against a concrete wall.

He knelt over me, straddling my waist, and laid a thick, rubbery cord across my throat. By itself, it was just uncomfortable. Then he placed his hands at each end of the cord and leaned into it, pinning my throat to the bed.

I began to gasp for air. My hands flew to his hands; I tried to pry his fingers off the cord. He pressed harder into the base of my throat. I was slightly dizzy and although I felt that I couldn't breathe, I was actually breathing, at least a little bit. Without loosening his hold across my neck, he told me to tap his shoulder if I felt I was going to pass out. I nodded.

For a moment, I marveled at the feeling, wondering how it was that I could be breathing and still losing consciousness. I looked into his eyes; he was watching my expression intently. Weak and lightheaded, it suddenly hit me that he had not told me to tap him if *I felt I would pass out . . . he had said* "when." *He wasn't going to stop until I tapped him.*

I also realized that I had not really known him very long . . . that no one else was here . . . that stranger things have happened. For the first time since beginning my research, I felt a quick flash of real and unambivalent panic.

The room began to spin. It grew darker. My hands found his shoulder. I tapped. He released me instantly.

My heart racing, I lay there and tried to shake it off. I felt strange, slightly removed from myself, heady but vigilant. He straightened up, watching my face, waiting for my breathing to slow. When it did, he lifted his arm to the side as though he were going to slap me. Trey's slaps were always rigid and forceful. I braced myself for it.

Instead, he bent his arm across his chest and swung out, away from his body. The back of his hand smashed across my face. I cried out, as much from surprise as pain. He hit me again, hard enough to knock my head aside, into the bed. This time I cried out purely in pain. His knuckles bore into skin and bone.

He backhanded me repeatedly, and quickly, switching from one arm to the other. I lifted my arms in a vague motion to stop him. With one arm he brought my hands down over my head. He closed the other hand into a fist. Holding it above my eyes, he studied me for a moment. He brought his fist down slowly and landed it on the side of my face.

He mock-punched me in the face several times, almost lazily, as if he didn't yet feel like a full punch, but he was thinking about it. I wondered if he was.

He opened his hand and moved it over my nose and mouth. He pinched my nose closed and drove his hand into my face. I tried to inhale. Usually, I can find a crack between his fingers, or by moving my mouth around, I can shift his hand to find air. This time there was no crack and no shifting. There was no space for breathing. Not even a little.

I looked up at him. His eyes assured me that he knew the difference. I was not entirely sure whether this was better or worse.

"Sssshhhhh," he said. I hadn't heard myself until then, but I was making noise—the same stifled, wordless protests one expects to hear when someone's air supply is cut off—the stuff of crime dramas. About a dozen misogynistic cultural scripts flashed through my mind, vying for my attention.

He released my nose and mouth. Gasping, I sat up. I think I blinked repeatedly, shaking my head from side to side, trying to get my bearings. He stood silently and leaned across the nightstand. When he sat down beside me, he pressed a blade to my cheek.

I didn't recognize the feeling; it wasn't a knife. It was paper thin, and not pointy. Trying to see what it was, I tentatively turned my face toward it. I felt its sharpness immediately; it sliced a teeny tiny tear into my flesh. I froze.

He smiled as he dragged it horizontally down my face, scraping my skin. Then I felt its precise sharpness again, at the corner of my mouth . . . then across my lips. It was lightweight—it didn't have the heft of a knife. Again I tried to see, but his hand blocked my view. I pulled back toward the wall, away from his hand, suddenly desperate to identify the blade. He put his hand in my hair and tugged my head backward. I waited. He brought his other hand into my view and brandished the straight-edged razor blade in front of my eyes. He held it for a moment, between his thumb and forefinger, before bringing it again to my lips. His fingers opened my mouth. He set the blade on my tongue. His hand closed my mouth and clamped my jaw shut.

The credo of the SM community is SSC—Safe, Sane, and Consensual. For participants, SSC is what differentiates SM from other (allegedly less moral and more criminal) activities, such as assault and rape. Though the three concepts are subjective, most of the community is in consensus about their use and meaning. The criteria for "sane" are most ambiguous. Generally, "sane" is understood as having full awareness of the risks involved; activities are considered sane when participants are informed of the risks and in full control of their faculties when making the decision to take them.

SSC serves as the basis for internal policing of play. It is also a tool for community outreach. For the community, there is much at stake politically in the adherence to (or abandonment of) SSC. It is used to allay the fears of concerned family members, to convince hotels and catering halls to allow SM events, and in legal defenses of community members as evidence of their upstanding citizenship. On these levels, SSC is a much-needed conceptual tool for achieving understanding and acceptance.

SSC also functions as a social-psychological security blanket, a moral barometer against which participants can judge the acceptability, within the community, of their actions, experiences, and responses. "Safe, sane, and consensual" is what makes SM morally acceptable. The concept thus has come to constitute SM; what is not safe and sane and consensual is not SM, and therefore does not belong in the community.

The margins of the SM community, then, are marked by the activities and participants that straddle these lines. "Edgeplay" is about playing on the boundaries of SSC—between safe and unsafe, sane and insane, consensual and nonconsensual. Edgeplay threatens the efforts of SM activists toward social and legal tolerance and recognition of SM, and is therefore controversial in Caeden. Emerging from related debates over the subjectivity of "safe" and "sane," parts of the community have argued to adopt an alternative to SSC: RACK—Risk Aware Consensual Kink. RACK (which appears to have been posited as a half-serious, frustrated response to a heated email discussion) eliminates these more nebulous concepts, but keeps SM ensconced in the discourse of sex. In part because of the potency of SSC as a political concept, RACK has not gained much ground in the community.

Though all SM is concerned with boundaries, edgeplay is about negotiating *internal* boundaries—boundaries set within, for, and by SM community members. In practice—that is, beyond the rhetoric of SSC—these boundaries end up being those between consent and nonconsent, consciousness and unconsciousness, ethical and unethical, temporary versus permanent, and life and death.

Edgeplayers occupy a marginal role in the scene. From the perspective of the rest of the community, edgeplayers play on the boundary between SM and assault. They represent the outer limits of what can be called SM, and the most salient threat to the political safety of the community. Edgeplayers are the rogue members, the outlaws of the scene; they are alternately reigned in, policed, and excluded from consideration. Despite the high value placed on "pushing" limits, "stretching," "growing," edgeplayers are those who go the furthest—who push limits that too few people are comfortable pushing.

Edgeplayers also enjoy the notoriety of outlaws. Their names are spoken with an uneasy mix of reverence and disapproval. Edgeplayers are "feared"—the idea of playing with them elicits displays of nervousness or awe. The status of edgeplayers, though tainted, is generally high; because they play on edges, they are considered extremely skilled and safe (as tops) and particularly tough and strong (as bottoms). Despite the "fear" of edgeplayers, then, they have little difficulty finding play partners.

There are no criteria for edgeplay per se, and community members generally identify it intuitively; "We know it when we see it." I identify five particular edges, or boundaries, on which play constitutes edgeplay for the members of this community.

The Edges

ETHICAL AND UNETHICAL

Because of the physical and psychological risks involved, the responses of onlookers, and the need for control of space in order to ensure safety, most edgeplay is limited to special events and private parties. Edgeplay along ethical lines is the most regularly visible in public play spaces, the most readily discussed, and for many, the least controversial. Given that SM itself, to many outsiders, is understood as transgressing ethical boundaries, this is not surprising.

Like the 1973 Supreme Court ruling that "community standards" determine obscenity (upheld in 1997), this kind of edgeplay is recognizable by the extent to which it offends the community on moral grounds. Some role play is included here, such as incest play (as illustrated in Weiss 2006b), rape scenes, and race play. Extreme pain scenes can also be understood this way, as well as symbolically unethical transgressions, such as hitting in the face (particularly when man-to-woman). Though bestiality is generally not considered SM, the idea is sometimes invoked in the context of humiliation or degradation. Should such a scene actually occur in this context, it would likely fall into this category.

CONSCIOUSNESS AND UNCONSCIOUSNESS

Risking unconsciousness in scene is generally considered edgeplay. These activities include extended bondage (and particular kinds of bondage), knife play, breath play, blood play, or pain intense enough to result in fainting. Edgeplay is not defined by the actual fainting, however; bottoms sometimes lose consciousness because of low blood sugar, unintended psychological trauma, or weakness. These (uncommon) occurrences are viewed as unfortunate accidents. Because they are considered preventable, these unintended circumstances do not confer edgeplayer status. Accidents are more likely to occur among new players, and edgeplayers tend to be veterans in the scene. Therefore, what is generally understood as resulting from inexperience or negligence detracts from the reputation as a player for both tops and bottoms.

TEMPORARY AND PERMANENT

The temporal boundary in SM refers to physical, emotional, or psychological effects of play on players. It overlaps with other boundaries, particularly the lines between consciousness and unconsciousness, and ethical and unethical. Community members make distinctions on these grounds often enough that it warrants separate consideration, however. Body modification is one example; although branding, piercing, and cutting also play with the boundaries of consciousness and unconsciousness, it is the permanence of the effect on which the play is judged. Similarly, catharsis scenes—those in which players engage with past trauma in order to work through them—run a risk of leaving lasting psychological damage, and as such are edgy on both ethical grounds and temporal grounds.

LIFE AND DEATH

SM play that deliberately negotiates the boundary between life and death is relatively rare in public SM play, but engaged in privately by some members of the community. Edgeplay along this boundary involves a riskier version of other kinds; namely, advanced play with breath control, blades, guns, blood, and fire. This is the edgeplay most frequently considered "not sane."

CONSENT AND NONCONSENT

Criteria for sanity being nebulous as they are, the most serious of the boundaries with which to play, from the perspective of the community, is not the line between life and death, but the edge between consent and nonconsent. In the consciousness of the community, deference for a sharply drawn line here separates SM from criminal behavior, though this is not always the case legally. When edgeplayers play here, however, they play *on* this boundary; though factions of the community might argue otherwise, most edgeplayers concern themselves with these questions and continually evaluate their actions in these contexts.

Scenes along this boundary include those in which tops attempt to defy negotiated limits in an in-progress scene, take a non-negotiated action that cannot be revoked once taken, or begin a scene during a moment or in a place that is not understood by the bottom as "scene space." However, in much the same way as unintended unconsciousness signifies incompetence rather than edgeplay, casual attitudes toward consent are breaches of moral obligation instead of edgeplay. The boundaries negotiated by edgeplay are, in this sense, privileges of veteran players (at least veteran tops). They are not simply the boundaries between consciousness and unconsciousness, consent and nonconsent, but these boundaries contextualized in paradigm of power and powerlessness, and in the negotiations of morality in which SM participants regularly engage. The constructions of power differentials both justify and reinforce particular instances of edgeplay, rendering it understandable to the rest of the community.

Negotiating Risk

Edgeplayers negotiate these boundaries repeatedly, with play partners who are willing to play this way. Tops who simply ignore limits or push boundaries in the absence of a relationship in which this kind of behavior is permissible are not considered edgeplayers; this crosses the boundary on which edgeplayers play. Further, the consideration of these actions as edgeplay is restricted by community standards of edge; if a top plays with a bottom whose range is narrow and limits are many, her pushing of those limits will not be regarded as edgeplay.

Edgeplay is not recklessness. SM participants play the edges because they are trusted to do so. The perception of heightened risk increases the salience of the experience of being trusted. The limit-pushing of edgeplay becomes a way of ensuring repeated engagements with trust, by consistently increasing the severity or perceptions of the likelihood of potential consequences. This continual ramping-up of risk, or "crowding the edge" (Lyng 1990) in SM maintains trust as active and emotionally potent. Actual risk, though, can sometimes be less relevant than perceptions of risk. Eric, for example, said that breath play can be (merely) "a mindfuck." When I asked for elaboration, Eric replied:

> Yeah, I'll tape it [the bag] shut. But the point is that you can tape it shut or you can pull it down. The point is that there's a lot of air in the bag. Even though you tape a bag shut, you're not actually cutting off air, it's not an air pipe. I'm being distinct about it because even though I may have used the word "mindfuck," it's a dangerous thing to people, in their minds this is "Danger Will Robinson."[1]

Eric implies that danger and risk are contextual and relational. The very concept of "mindfuck" in SM seeks to capitalize on this relativist aspect of risk experience; a player sometimes seek to understand the risks as dangers, thus necessitating and constructing a greater level of trust.

When Kyle mentioned to me that he plays with a partner without a safeword, he couched it in terms of the extraordinary trust that this takes.

Me: What are you trusting her with, to play without a safeword?
Kyle: Trusting her not to damage me. No matter how painful something gets, that it's not going to cause damage. Trusting her not to violate any of the limits that [we agreed on], which are things like pedophilia, bestiality, things like that. Like, intense bad things. What I consider to be intense bad things. Like not sexy bad things.
Me: And if she violated a limit, you would safeword?
Kyle: I would say "Hey, remember [our agreement]," or something like that.

For Kyle and his partner, the idea of the safeword increases the sense of trust. The agreement to play this way evidences and constructs a deeper sense of trust. It feels riskier, for even though Kyle's reminder about the agreement might, on the surface, serve the same function as a safeword, his partner is under no "obligation" to stop when he tells her to stop. This increases the perception of risk and his actual risk, while playing privately. In public, however, the utterance of a safeword will likely result in intervention by other community members.

Policing the Edge

The interruption of another player's scene is a severe breach of etiquette in Caeden. Members generally avoid speaking too loudly while watching a scene, and keep their distance during aftercare, waiting for a signal from one of the participants before approaching to talk. Hosts of parties or events that utilize "dungeon monitors" (DMs) to ensure event safety provide instruction and training and select people who will be cautious about even covert distraction from play, and judicious about interruption.

Much of this is an economic issue; clubs exist for profit, and parties are hosted by organizations who need party attendees to stay afloat and scene members who wish to have more parties. The interruption of a scene is disturbing enough for SM participants that it threatens event attendance. The interruption of scenes is rare.[2] The most common impetus is that a DM, or sometimes an onlooker, sees a danger the top *does not,* such as a loose bolt in the wall (to which the bottom is attached) or a nonresponsive bottom. In this case the observer normally attempts to get the top's attention without speaking, but will speak if s/he must. If it is clear that the top also sees the danger, experienced

DMs and onlookers will usually assume that the risk has been calculated or that the top is making adjustments. It is far more common for an observer or DM to ask for a second opinion than to interrupt a scene. In the following case, the players were not part of the Caeden scene, but visitors from a nearby city, and familiar enough to the club's owner and veteran scene members.

> A large, solidly built but big-bellied, relatively handsome Hell's Angel–looking man was standing in the front of the room flogging a very overweight woman, who was standing above him on the stage and wearing only underwear. He was wearing jeans and a leather vest, and had a lot of tattoos, long hair in a ponytail, a full beard, and blue eyes. They must have been doing something else before then; I vaguely remember seeing them set up, but they were on my radar clearly when the flogging became intense. He was very skilled, and used a two-handed florentine, mostly on her ass, though he hit her back occasionally. She made a lot of noise throughout the flogging, which may have been what caught my attention in the first place. He appeared to be completely immersed in what he was doing and did not seem to notice anyone around him.
>
> The flogging continued for a bit, and I directed my attention elsewhere. When I looked back, he was inserting small needles into her back. Josephine had come out from behind the soda counter and was watching closely; I assumed that James (the owner) had sent her. She stood about three feet away, with her arms crossed and her eyes focused intently.
>
> He threaded each needle vertically, under her skin and then out again. He was wearing latex gloves and I noticed that she was standing on a blanket on the stage; I thought it had been there before.
>
> The needles were about two inches long and had green plastic tips at one end. He worked very methodically, threading the needles into her skin. He began at her left shoulder blade and traveled down the middle of her back, down to her waist. A second line of needles mirrored this pattern on her right shoulder blade, and then he placed several needles across the middle that didn't really belong to a row. (He may have been making a letter, but I couldn't tell.) In the end, there were about twenty needles in her back.
>
> She didn't make any noise while he was doing this. I tried to watch her face . . . she seemed not to be reacting much. At one point, I thought she was smiling, though I couldn't see her very well.
>
> Once the needles were all in place, the top affixed a birthday-sized candle to a needle on her lower back. He did this with three more candles

> across her lower back. I watched in fascination as he lit each candle and then stood back and watched them burn. He didn't touch her, he didn't talk; he just stood there and watched silently as the dripping wax intermingled with tiny trickles of blood on her skin.
>
> Josephine shook her head in apparent disapproval, but she left them alone. Several people were visibly freaked out, wincing at the needles as he inserted them, or raising eyebrows at the candles. It looked as if this was not something most people there would do. Gladys and Adam each commented to me that they did not see the appeal. Some people would watch for a few minutes, react negatively but politely, and then walk away as if they couldn't bear to watch more. The top seemed unconcerned with anyone else's reaction. (Field notes)

Regular members of the Caeden community would not likely have engaged in this scene during a regular night at the club. The use of needles plays with boundaries between temporary and permanent, and the potentiality of blood navigates the space between ethical and unethical. Given this, the sheer quantity of needles caused *onlookers* to feel faint, negotiating at least projected boundaries between consciousness and unconsciousness. At the most basic level, the general impression was that the club's owner didn't like blood play. Still, James—via Josephine—allowed the scene to continue. The players may have discussed the scene with James beforehand, which is the custom when one plans an edgy scene in a public space. The top was clearly skilled, had taken all the necessary safety precautions, and few in the community would disagree that they were playing safely. The owner allowed the scene to continue, though not without a disapproving response, however polite, from the onlookers.

On another night, a group of people engaged in similar play were stopped and asked to leave the club. It was during a citywide fetish weekend (that night in particular, the club attracted people from different Caeden communities and different cities), and a group of three people in their twenties, heavily tattooed and with multiple piercings, began a needle play scene, also focusing on the upper back. They were not wearing gloves or using a drop cloth, and they were playing in a poorly lit, high-traffic area. When James asked them to stop the scene, they refused. He insisted that they leave the club.

In terms of reputation and status in the community, playing—and policing—the edge is a precarious endeavor. The interruption of a scene, at least when undertaken by an experienced member of the community, is not only an insult, but a public declaration of a loss of control, poor decision-making, or both. The interrupter runs the risk of being labeled "a safety Nazi," and the interrupted must choose between casting the event as an irrational persecution of edgeplayers or accepting that the scene was problematic.

Edgeplayers, then, threaten SSC, and hence the safety of the community on both a political and an emotional level, as well as the harmony of the community. While the community discourse accepts and encourages narratives of edgeplay and the expertise of edgeplayers, participants are often less comfortable with edgeplay in public spaces. By continually challenging the rules and the role of the community in their enforcement, edgeplayers call into question issues of social status and authority. These are salient issues in the lives of community members, and closely intertwined with participation in this SM community.

Edgework

Research on risk has conventionally focused on risk taken for a particular, distinct objective—the risk of contracting an STD for the sake of enjoying unprotected sex, for example. These considerations—for example, as calculations in decision-making in modern life (Beck 1992; Giddens 1992; Luhmann 1993) are limited to the sphere of risk as a condition, and risk-taking as the decision to enter into that otherwise undesirable condition. This posits risk as a phenomenon to be explained; as Donnelly notes, "Implicit in this view is the value-laden assumption that no one would take a voluntary risk if he or she were not driven to it by circumstances" (2004, 43). The objectives of social scientists in risk studies are often to understand why, when, and for what purpose actors take risks (Lupton 1999). Only within the past two decades has work on risk begun to consider instances in which risk *is* part of the cognitive and phenomenological value of particular experience.

In sociology, the perspective on risk as an objective in its own right has emerged in the related studies of sport and deviance. An alternative to the frame of risk as an unfortunate necessity in achieving certain goals, this recognizes risk-taking as an end—though not the only end—unto itself. Stephen Lyng's seminal work (1990) shifted the conceptualization of risk from means to ends. Borrowing the term "edgework" from journalist Hunter S. Thompson, who used it to describe the quest for extreme experience (most frequently and famously through drug use), Lyng's model for understanding voluntary risk-taking as a social process in and of itself, hinges on one common aspect of all edgework experiences: "they all involve a clearly observable threat to one's physical or mental well-being or one's sense of an ordered existence" (1990, 857). For Lyng, these boundaries can be constituted by the lines between life and death, consciousness and unconsciousness, sanity and insanity, and order and chaos, of self and environment.

Lyng's framework has since been widely applied, mainly to extreme sports and criminal behavior.[3] As the first explicit treatment of risk-taking as voluntary, it has come to subsume risk-taking as part of the motive itself.

That Lyng's edgework is gendered, raced, and classed, broadly speaking, has been noted elsewhere (Miller 1991; Lyng 1991, 2005; Laurendeau 2008). In these critiques, the problem has often been understood as the gendered nature of participation in these risk-taking endeavors. The idea of edgework is gendered because edgework *is* gendered. Attempts to rectify this problem have thus included the consideration of dangerous but feminized activities as edgework (Gailey 2009), focusing on the emotional dimensions of edgework (Lois 2001) and considering the factors that shape gendered participation in edgework (Laurendeau 2007).

The problem with the edgework concept, however, is not that women do not engage in these activities to the same extent as men. While this certainly appears to be true, the more fundamental problem is one of theory and application. Lyng's concept theorizes the edge itself from a (hyper-)masculinist perspective, thereby limiting its usefulness to edges that resonate for masculinity. Laurendeau's attempt to shift the analytical focus from different (gendered) ways of doing edgework to gender differences in whether or how people engage in edgework suffers from the same problem: one overarching perspective on what edgework looks like, or more specifically, which edges being negotiated "count" as edgework.

Edgework is rooted in a masculinist perspective on three levels. Its framing of the boundaries being negotiated reflects the romanticism of conquest of the natural world, particularly through a reliance on a combination of technology and skill. The edgeworker successfully negotiates the edge through his skill and technological superiority, and in so doing, defeats it.

Secondly, the risk itself in edgework studies is limited to bodily risk; what is most risky is that which threatens physical safety. A broader perspective recognizes that the negotiation of boundaries between being in control and out of control can be a meaningful experience only for those who are accustomed to being in control. Similarly, gambling with one's physical safety can be edgework only for people who do not perceive themselves as making that gamble in everyday life, outside their edgeworking. Although Lyng's original model incorporates the flexibility for emotional and psychological risk, this has not been the standard application of his framework.

Lastly, in studies of edgework thus far, risk-taking is a solitary endeavor. Though the risks may occur in social groups and have a social component (Lois 2003; Laurendeau 2006), the risks themselves appear to be selected, undertaken, and negotiated independently. The underlying assumption is that edgeworkers come together in order to add a social component to their edgework (Lyng 2005; Ferrell 1996, 2005; Miller 2005).

Lyng's original writing on edgework explicitly excludes risk-taking in which the risk is perceived as in the control of others; roller-coaster riding, for example, however thrill-seeking, is not edgework. In this perspective, edgework is about not only conquering, but conquering alone; dependence on the roller-coaster operators, engineers, or maintenance workers hardly affirms the rugged self-reliance intrinsic to Lyng's edgework. Though interdependence is a likely aspect of what might otherwise be considered edgework (rock-climbing and mountain rescue work come to mind), the literature has not explored joint negotiations of the edge.

Edgework, then, as it was originally conceived of by Lyng and as it is currently most commonly used, emerges from and reinforces the romanticization of the man-versus-nature narrative. Although Lyng recognizes the ways in which the engagement of edgework is classed, raced, and gendered, the application of the model thus far is *itself* classed, raced, and gendered. This does not make it less useful in studying some kinds of edgework; not surprisingly, edgeplayers in Caeden are mostly white, middle-class men. Lyng's model, however, only implicitly assumes these masculinist principles; they are not intrinsic to the edgework concept. The idea of the edge is sufficiently fluid so as to understand differently understood and defined edges.

Edgeplay as (Masculinist) Edgework

Because the boundaries on which edgeplayers play are extreme, and often physical, edgeplay offers the clearest example of edgework in SM. In a voluntary and recreational context, tying plastic bags over a partner's head engages in the thrill-seeking risk of life and limb that has generally been regarded as edgework. One challenge, though, from the perspective of Lyng's original paradigm, is to identify which is the edgeworker. Only the bottom is risking her life, and only the top is risking a prison sentence[4] (and a life of psychological torment, should the bottom die). Peter Donnelly observes the complexity of the philosophical question about responsibility in risk-taking and notes the social pressures for women not to risk (2004). Edgeplay in SM complicates this question further; at least according to the way the edgework paradigm has been applied thus far, it is not immediately clear whether the top or the bottom is the edgeworker.

Both participants in an edgeplay scene are playing at the same edge. Neither could be negotiating this boundary (between life and death, consciousness and unconsciousness, control and loss of control) without the other. Both are, together, exploring the lines between chaos and order, sanity and insanity, and sometimes life and death. The edgework of the top is no less "embodied," in the sense that Lyng means when he notes that "the emotions and sensations [of edgework] are produced through a process in which the 'knowings' and the skills of the body organize action in the absence of the social mind" (2004, 360). Even outside edgeplay, sadistic experience (i.e., the experience of topping) is as embodied as all aspects of SM. The discourse of topping is the language of embodied experience: desires, for example, to hear whimpers and feel the heat of welted skin.

Nonetheless, tops in edgeplay are engaging in threats to their mental well-being and ordered sense of self and environment (and more, if imprisonment can be understood as a threat to one's physical well-being). On one level, the risks to the top emerge from the fact that he is the one who needs to stay "in control." As with skydivers and BASE jumpers, this includes technical control; a top cannot afford to forget to secure a knot in a suspension bondage scene, or fumble with one in a breath play scene. The risks of edgeplay inform decision-making and the emotional experiences of risk in the scene. Eric illustrates:

> I'm not going to risk my life [. . .] What if I do take it that far and somebody dies? I don't know this person. I mean, this is like, what the fuck am I doing here? At that point, I'm in serious fucking trouble. The element is—you're playing with somebody, there's a risk element which is part of that relationship. But at the same time, you're not stupid.

On another level, SM play depends heavily on the psychological and emotional self-control of the top. In intense circumstances involving extreme pain, anguish, and the aspiration to extreme indicators of power, the risk of a top "losing control" is real for participants.

A scene between Sophie and Ari provides a good example. When I watched it, their play was familiar to me. I knew Sophie fairly well, and Ari and I were friends. Still, as I watched the scene he seemed unfamiliar to me, and as it progressed he seemed to grow less and less "recognizable" to me. The scene was pivotal for Ari; during it he had allowed himself to "go someplace" that was new for him. Sometime later, Sophie described her experience of the scene to me:

> He said something that almost sounded—I don't remember the words now, but if anyone else had heard it, it wouldn't have sounded like a warning, but he meant it as a warning and I heard it as a warning. And I responded in some way that signified like I get it, and I'll come along for the ride. So then he stood up, he dragged me across the room, threw me to the ground. So then he restrains me to some piece of apparatus and he's singletailing my back [. . .] Then he turns me around. So several things were going on, one of which is that he's going to be singletailing me in the front, which I had just said that's not going to happen. So I'm thinking, okay. He's never done this to anyone before, and he doesn't have all that experience with me doing it to my back, and there's a lot more here, you know, my boobies *and* my face, and do I really feel safe about this, from a purely technical point of view? Then because I was turned around I could also see his face. Which had completely changed. It was the first time I had ever seen him look like that. And to hear him talk about it afterward, to a certain extent, the first time he said he let that [side of him] out. And it really—it was like watching somebody be possessed. It did not look like the same person anymore. And I started thinking to myself, Oh my God. How well do I know this guy, and what is he going through right now, and does he have the capacity to hold it together, or is so . . . altered by whatever is going on in his head that I should stop? And I was absolutely petrified through the entire scene. [. . .]
>
> I called him afterward and said I was really worried through the whole time that you were actually going to lose it. I said I wasn't sure how much control you had, just because you looked so transported, that I really didn't know whether you were still in control of yourself. I really wasn't sure. And he said, "I was in complete control the whole time." I honestly will never know how true that was [. . .] I don't know if at that point, when he was experiencing it in that way for the first time, he really was completely in control of it or not.

The edges here are boundaries of edgework as it has been most commonly understood. Importantly, though, the edgework of SM is jointly undertaken and jointly accomplished. Participants *need* each other along two distinct axes in SM play. They need each other in order to play on these boundaries, for the boundaries are social and interpersonal. They also *represent* the boundaries for one another. An edgeplaying top's line between sane and insane, ethical and unethical, temporary and permanent, in control and loss of control, citizen and criminal, *is* the bottom; the two are inextricable, for in the scene, the bottom exists to constitute this boundary. The bottom's line—between temporary and permanent, consciousness and unconsciousness, life and death, *is* the top.

The chaos and order are not only physical, but social; the boundaries between the body and other (access to the body), violence and nonviolence, and safety and harm are socially defined and regulated limits. Precisely because it involves risks at the hands of others, edgeplay explores the boundary between social regulation and anarchy. In edgeplay, the chaos and order extend beyond the realm of the physical to play on the limits of social experiential meaning.

Not all SM is edgeplay, and thus cannot be understood as "edgework" in the precise way it has most often been understood and applied. If, however, we expand edgework beyond its masculinist underpinnings, then all SM can be usefully understood as edgework.

(Feminist) Edgework

COLLABORATING THE EDGE

In her critique of the edgework model as masculinist, Eleanor Miller asks: "If men have a skill orientation toward the environment, what do women have?" (1991,1532). It is true that narratives of womanhood are not bound in control over the natural world through skill, and true that the edgework model has peered through only this lens. An expansion of edgework beyond its masculinist frame requires a challenge to its emphases on particular masculinist skills, as well as on the masculinist values of independence, physical risk, and control and conquest. However, to move away from the utilization of skill sets as a criterion for consideration of an activity as edgework in order to include women, as some have attempted (Rajah 2006), is also problematic. Lyng's edgework, skill-based, intense, and deeply fulfilling, *is* a particular social phenomenon, and one that warrants attention. If we apply "edgework" to all risky behaviors, all emotionally intense situations, or all coping strategies in dangerous situations, we lose the value of edgework, which lies in its framing of voluntary risk-taking endeavors as a leisure activity—that is, for enjoyment. The charge for a feminist edgework is not, as I see it, to recast all of women's risk-taking behaviors as edgework, nor to find evidence of rushes or empowerment that may come from surviving victimization. A feminist edgework model needs to move beyond the particular masculinist conceptualizations of "the edge" and of "skill," while preserving its fundamental core: skill-based, voluntary risk-taking that seeks to (and does) negotiate extreme boundaries between chaos and order.

The case of SM poses these challenges, inspiring a feminist model for the use of edgework as an analytic category. The consideration of what I call "collaborative edgework" is one step. Activities in which edgeworkers depend on each other for successful boundary negotiation reveal the potential of edgework as an interactive social process. This extension of edgework to *shared transcendence* of existential boundaries allows for a broader and less gendered lens on voluntary risk-taking.

A second step is to contextualize risk in the lived experiences and social positions of women. Because risk—actual risk as well as what is experienced as risk—is shaped by broader forces and structures, voluntary risk-taking needs to be understood in relation to what is (and what is not) risky for the particular risk-takers involved.

Finally, understanding of control and conquest can be shifted to the realm of the emotional without sacrificing the theoretical value of the concept of edgework. "Edgework involves not only activity-specific skills but also a general ability to maintain control *of* a situation that verges on total chaos, a situation most people would regard as entirely uncontrollable. . . . [M]ost edgeworkers regard this skill as essentially cognitive in nature, and refer to it as a special form of 'mental toughness'" (Lyng 1990, 871, emphasis added).

If "total chaos" includes emotional chaos (for example, overwhelming rage or fear, nervous breakdowns, or other instances of "freaking out"), then control of one's emotions and of one's actions is the source of the "order" at the other boundary. Viewed this way—in which "order" is control of the self—the boundary between order and chaos is negotiated in any situation in which most people would regard these feelings as so intense as to be uncontrollable. Edgework thus becomes applicable to the realm of the emotional and psychological. The inclusion of emotional and psychological risks allows for a broader view of edgework and edgeworkers. This expansion is important not simply for the sake of it, but to understand the experiences of people who develop and acquire particular skills in order to voluntarily negotiate extreme emotional and psychological boundaries.

The shift away from a masculinist understanding of what the edge is and what it means would allow for a shift from control *of* a situation to control *in* a situation. In practice, this has at times been the case. Jennifer Lois's work, for example, is not about control of mountain rescue situations so much as control of emotions during high-risk, intense crises. If edgework refers to control of situations as well as self-control in situations that verge on "total chaos," then it moves a step away from its masculinist perspective, as the quest for control moves away from others to self.

Still, a consideration of emotion management in edgework situations is not necessarily a feminist perspective on edgework. By focusing on the emotional dimensions of edgework, Lois brings a feminist component to edgework. The paradigm itself, however, remains masculinist; Lois's work studies the emotional aspects of masculine edgework. A feminist framework needs to be useful for kinds of edgework that are not rooted so entirely in hegemonic masculine ideals. One possibility for a feminist direction for edgework is to look for examples of "emotional edgework"—that is, not emotional aspects of edgework, but edgework that negotiates *emotional edges.*

EMOTIONAL EDGEWORK

All SM is about risk. While some kinds of play (such as fire, knife, and breath play) are inherently riskier than others, most SM play is not inherently physically dangerous (e.g., spanking, flogging, and role play). However, SM is often laden with other kinds of risk. In each scene, players take the risks that normally accompany self-disclosure, uncertain how a particular action or response will be received. The Caeden community is small, the national community is well-linked, and community status is meaningful to participants. Further, both tops and bottoms risk the experience of liking or wanting something they feel they should not, each time they play. These recognitions are common in Caeden, and additionally, the recognition process is rarely private.

In SM scenes, trust can be violated at three distinct levels. First, the bottom trusts the top technically; she trusts his competence and his ability. The top also trusts in the bottom's competence; he might trust her, for example, to know not to grab his hand if he is holding a knife. They trust that neither player will make poor judgments that will lead to serious harm, and that neither will "miss" the mark. This is not trust that there will never be accidents, but trust that accidents will not be severely detrimental. The cost of violating trust here is minimal. Accidents are, most often, forgiven; as was the case with Adam's injurious slap to my ear, the bottom does not generally *feel* deeply violated by minor accidents. The sense of trust that accompanies play in which accidents are likely to be more serious is therefore heightened, as Bobby explained:

> **Bobby:** I've done breath play. That can be very dangerous, but it's like a swimming pool. You hold your breath and you go underwater. You don't leave anyone unaccompanied, you don't leave anyone alone, but the idea of having a plastic bag over the gal's head and sealed around the neck and she's starting to, you know, [makes gestures of panic].
> **Me:** Panic—
> **Bobby:** Yeah. And unable to—her life is literally in your hands is a big charge. [. . .] That's something, when she's able to trust me to that level. And a lot of women have.

Bobby here values not only the experience of trustworthiness, but being trusted "to that level"; the greater potential for harm imbues the trust with more meaning.

A second level of implicit trust is that, should accidents occur, the members involved will take the incident seriously, express remorse, and perhaps be informed by the situation. A member of the community once shared with me a story of an accident in-scene for which s/he was responsible. The speaker appeared devastated by having failed to maintain control and safety of the scene. No one was severely hurt, and the speaker insisted that the details remain private—not because s/he was embarrassed, but to spare the bottom from public knowledge that trust appeared to have been misplaced. In SM play, things sometimes go awry; a mistimed throw of the whip can slash the skin, or an utterance can trigger a difficult emotional or psychological reaction. The trust, at this level, is that if something should happen, the people involved will direct their efforts toward improving the situation. Had Adam laughed when he realized that he had slapped me, or shrugged his shoulders and said that I moved, or told me to shake it off, the consequences of the accident would have been more substantial.

SM players also trust one another's integrity, or goodwill. They trust that neither will *intentionally* harm the other. In my time in the field, I never witnessed, nor even heard of, a violation of trust at this level. There were, however, one or two members of the community that did not play because they were not trusted. Andy, for example, was a visible and involved member of the community who very rarely played. During the four years that I was in the scene, if newcomers expressed interest in playing with Andy, veteran participants cautioned them against it. This was not because Andy had explicitly violated trust in any known scene, but because his broader ineptitude with boundaries cast doubt on his intentions. By most members of the scene, though, he was viewed not as a poor decision-maker, but as lecherous and untrustworthy. I had also heard, on several occasions, a tale of a participant who had violated a safeword years before I had entered the scene; his play partner was having a severe emotional reaction and safeworded, and he continued to hit her. I had already heard of him on discussion lists with an entirely different SM demographic; he had, the story went, been immediately blacklisted at the national level for failing to stop the scene. The cost of violation at this level is high; most obviously, SM play can result in death or severe psycho-emotional trauma induced not only by the physical experience, but from the betrayal of trust itself.

All risk, of course, is not edgework. For example, flogging (limited in SM to muscular areas of the body) is not a particularly dangerous activity in and of itself, but for Faye,[5] flogging scenes were emotionally and psychologically threatening. From a feminist perspective, though, all SM is edgework. Even when SM is not edgeplay, it is "emotional edgework." It exists on and *for* the edges of what people should and should not feel in given situations. This is distinct from the emotional culture of edgework that Lois explores among rescue workers. This emotional edgework is not about the emotions that come with edgework or their management, but about the risk in emotional experiences. Emotional edgework explores the line between emotional chaos and emotional order, between emotional form and emotional formlessness, between the self and the obliteration of the self. SM, at its most fundamental, and therefore even when it is not edgeplay, is emotional edgework, seeking heights of emotional experience. On the symbolic level, SM transgresses normative boundaries and separates the acceptable from the unacceptable and the moral from the immoral. The boundary between violence and nonviolence is the boundary between chaos and order, transposed onto the social realm. SM negotiates social and cultural boundaries between chaos and order.

SM play is the joint boundary transgression of personal boundaries between people, of hegemonic social and ethical boundaries, and often of physical and physiological boundaries. This distinguishes it from solo boundary play, as well as from risk-taking and from escape from self. It changes the edge experience into a social one, achieved in and constituted through social interaction. It is intrinsically and necessarily *collaborative.* Unlike even partnered edgework, in which people may require each other's assistance in the safe exploration of the boundary, SM requires another person in order to first *create* the bounded situation and then to transgress it.

The authenticity of the edges in SM is less clear. SM is entirely a consensual *social* interaction; the thrill of the edge is neither the rescue of participants who presumably would rather not be part of this edgework situation, nor victory over natural elements (e.g., wind, mountains, water). The transgression of boundaries in SM depends almost entirely on the social interaction. Even in SM that explores the boundary between life and death, the rush, the victory, comes from the interaction itself—it lies in the *doing to,* and being *done to by,* another person. SM is therefore both collaborative and performative in a way that Lyng's edgework is not.

As a stigmatized social activity and a reputation as a deviant sexuality, SM transgresses normative boundaries of interaction and sexual behavior. Beyond that, because one of the overarching objectives is to stretch limits and to push one another further, either emotionally, physically, or psychologically, it transgresses personal—and interpersonal—boundaries. Further still, SM is inherently transgressive at the ideological-conceptual level, and normally crosses physical-physiological edges as well.

Viewed this way, edgework retains its fundamental tenets of voluntary risk-taking that negotiates boundaries between chaos and order, control and lack of control, life and death. Moreover, the autonomy of edgework is not necessarily sacrificed in the shift of edgework from a solo endeavor to a joint one, as Sophie illustrates:

> I guess it was just having a boundary pushed that was not a fun boundary to have pushed, and not having that acknowledged until it was really too late. Like until it had clearly gone very, very badly. Now that's part of the risk I like to take, because I always say to the person who I'm playing with, "Don't set my limits for me." And I want to have the responsibility to say, enough. And so I would say okay, so then the other really bad scene is, when I should've said, enough, and didn't. And so it was too late. And I don't put the blame on the other person at all.

SM occurs at the point of intersection of physical, fixed boundaries, social, normative boundaries, and boundaries of self and other, in real and consequential ways. For Lyng, edgework involves "an effort to define the performance limits of some form or object, and in the process, explore the line between form and formlessness" (1993, 111). By extending "form" beyond the body to include notions of identity and the self, all SM explores this line, seeking as it does to negotiate the boundaries of violence and nonviolence carnally and symbolically. Order and chaos and form and formlessness, viewed this way, are negotiated also along the lines between self and other.

This extension provides us with a more feminist model for the application of edgework as it moves away from masculinist emphases on physical control, strength, and independence. Secondly, this feminist model allows us to understand SM as edgework, which in turn allows us to understand the experience of SM play as voluntary risk-taking and transgressive.

The inclusion of emotional and psychological risks allows for a broader view of edgework and edgeworkers. This expansion is important in understanding the experiences of people who develop and acquire particular skills in order to voluntarily negotiate extreme emotional and psychological boundaries. There are two aspects to feminist edgework in the extension I propose: collaborating the edge, and *voluntarily undertaking* emotional risks as emotional edgework. While these aspects can be explored separately, they intersect in SM in ways that help illustrate how we might expand edgework beyond its current constraints. The development of a feminist perspective on edgework might proceed from this attention to the ways in which edges are defined and understood by women. It also requires additional steps toward the fuller consideration of the gendered social contexts of risk-taking.

Chapter 8

"What It Is That We Do"

Intimate Edgework

There was something going on with him tonight, I thought; the look in his eyes was different somehow. One minute we were smiling and laughing as he cuffed me to the wall, and in the very next he smashed me across the face with his open hand.

He picked up the quirt. I hate the quirt. I really hate it. I used to wonder, when bottoms said they hated a particular toy, why they used it. It didn't make any sense. If you don't like it, I thought, don't use it . . . yet there I was, playing with the quirt again. I swear I hate it. But I love to hate it—it's becoming symbolic now—of contest, of strength, of antagonism, and of the play relationship itself. It's not something I can't take. It doesn't bother me philosophically and it doesn't cause me any harm. And still I say that I hate it.

My back was on fire. I was raw and chafed. He must've drawn blood—it felt like my back was a complete mess. I spun myself away from him, giving him my side instead of my back. Usually, he stops and waits for my back—waits for me to be ready for the next blow. Tonight it didn't matter in the least. He wasn't letting up. He was going to keep swinging, and it would land wherever it landed.

When he put the quirt down, I took a deep breath. My panting subsided a bit. He moved closer to me, took my nipples in his hand, and pinched. HARD. *Obnoxious. His hands were sweaty and cruel. I threw my weight forward, knocking him off kilter a bit, but he pinched harder. I spun back around and banged his hands into the wall to which I was chained, trying to force him to let go by hurting his hand.*

"Oh . . . so *close . . . ," he taunted.*

His hand closed around my throat. Something happened to me. I forgot that I had agreed to this. I forgot that this was research. I forgot that he was not going to harm me, that we were in a club filled with people, that I could stop him with a single word.

With my arms chained to the wall and my neck suddenly pinned by his hand, I kicked him, hard, with my right leg. It caught him off-guard and he doubled over, releasing my throat. I stood still, watching him with satisfaction, wondering who the hell he thought he was.

"You kicked me. You fucking kicked me." Disbelief.

He walked over to me, and stood very close. Quietly, in a voice I hadn't heard before, he said, "Don't do that again. You understand?"

We were chest to chest, nose to nose—he's not that tall and I was in boots with two-inch stack heels. Something about his swagger, his cockiness—the very things that often made our play what it was—tonight made me want to kill him. I swung my elbow around to the side of his face and at the same time drove my knee into his stomach.

He ducked my elbow, but my knee caught him.

"You bitch. *You want to fight? Is that what you want? You think you can take me. Let's go. Let's see what you've got."*

In a flash, he uncuffed my wrists.

I threw a punch. He sidestepped me and grabbed my arms. I wrenched one arm free and punched him in the back. He grabbed it again and we wrestled for control of my arms.

He wrapped my arms in his, behind my back. My face pressed against the rough concrete wall, cold against the heat of my skin. He was panting. I bent my knees and spun around, breaking his grasp on my arms and knocking him off balance with my shoulder. He reached for my hair and yanked my head back. He bent me backward, so far that I was almost on my knees.

I was not going to hit my knees.

At 4:00 in the morning, we'd been playing for over two hours. We were exhausted, drenched in sweat, and emotionally spent. The club was, technically, closed.

A puff came over the loudspeaker, then the owner's voice.

"Adam, stop hurting that poor girl and get the hell out of the club."

We laughed. For a long moment, we looked at each other. Then Adam walked away from me and plucked my shirt from the table near our play space. He spun around and threw it at me.

The shirt landed on the floor in front of me. Suddenly, I began to cry. I did not sob and I did not reach out to him. I just stood immobile for a moment, tears streaming down my cheeks. I didn't quite know why. I found the gesture ugly and hurtful and I felt confused.

I bent to pick up the shirt, but Adam got to it first. Without a word, he picked it up and shook it . . . as if it had even had the chance to get dusty. He held it against his chest and smoothed it. He folded it neatly and handed it to me. Once I pulled it over my head, he put his arms around me and held me close.

SM is paradoxical. It is subversive and conformist, liberating and constraining, performative and authentic, and misogynistic and feminist. Most fundamentally, though, it is about intimacy. Through play SM participants construct deep feelings of intimate connection. Because it challenges our assumptions about intimacy, its examination contributes to theorizing intimacy on a broader level: what we mean when we call an experience intimate, and in what processes we engage in order to achieve and construct it.

The etiological root of the word "intimacy"—the Latin "intimus," for innermost—translated to and for the social world is the revelation of that which is innermost to another actor. Theories regarding intimacy and intimate relationships take this perspective as a foundation, but move in vastly different directions, resulting in, as Register and Henley note, "a disturbing divergence in the scope and nature" of its conceptualization (1992, 468).

Most theoretical and empirical treatments of the concept of intimacy occur in the fields of psychology and social psychology. Erik Erikson's highly influential positing of the intimacy-versus-identity crisis stage frames each as necessary for the other, but sets personal identity in conflict with the achievement of intimacy, the one threatening to overwhelm the other (Erikson 1950, 1968). Intimacy becomes one side of a binary, the diametric opposition to personal identity; too much self-disclosure is unhealthy and undesirable. Since then, much of the work in psychology has proceeded from an assumption of the nature of intimacy as intrinsically a positive, healthy, good feeling.[1]

Part of the difficulty in the study of intimacy is the conflation of the emotional experience of "intimacy" with the characteristics and benefits of "intimate relationships." Taking an "intimate relationship" as the unit of analysis frames intimacy as a characteristic embedded within or produced by that relationship. Intimacy is also most often understood, within these literatures, as inextricably linked to feelings of closeness and connectedness. The assumption of intimacy as a close, connected, and healthy characteristic of an "intimate relationship" precludes an understanding of intimate experiences that may fall outside the margins of social acceptability and our paradigms of psychological wellness. It means also that intimacy, at the conceptual level, is trapped in a circular logic; intimacy is the closeness that arises in intimate relationships, and intimate relationships are those that are especially close. Intimacy can instead be viewed as a social situation, with a focus on the moments in, through, and by which people construct intimate experience, regardless of the nature of the relationship, or of the emotional experience of the intimacy.

Sociological approaches to intimacy suffer from the same limiting assumptions, from Nelson Foote's consideration of intimacy as "a social-psychological achievement . . . the acme of communication and exposure of self" (1954, 162), to more contemporary work.[2] Particularly in research on exotic dancing and prostitution, the widely used notion of "counterfeit intimacy" or "feigned intimacy"[3] refers to an implicit promise of closeness in a relationship (usually romantic or sexual) that does not exist and will not likely occur. The notion of counterfeit intimacy rests upon the assumption of a "true intimacy," of a particular kind—good, honest, reciprocal, and, as Katherine Frank observes, not commodified (2007). It also, though, conflates the moment of intimate experience with the nature of the relationship between actors.

Anthony Giddens's widely reviewed *The Transformation of Intimacy* proceeds from the well-established view of intimacy as self-disclosure. Following a psychological model, Giddens understands intimacy as a healthy and desirable condition of a relationship, fueled by open but bounded communication between partners. Giddens's work is not an epistemological or phenomenological engagement with the experience of "intimacy," but a procession from this unquestioned assumption toward an exploration of the changes in sexual and family lives in modern society. As Lynn Jamieson points out, Giddens "draws relatively uncritically on therapeutic literature" (Jamieson 1999); the conceptualization of intimacy in Giddens's treatise is drawn from a 1988 self-help book entitled *Intimacy: Strategies for Successful Relationships*.[4] Thus Giddens explains the importance of boundaries in "intimacy," in a quote that warrants including at length:

> Clear boundaries within a relationship are obviously important for confluent love and the sustaining of intimacy. Intimacy is not being absorbed by the other, but knowing his or her characteristics and making available one's own. Opening out to the other, paradoxically, requires personal boundaries, because it is a communicative phenomenon; it also requires sensitivity and tact, because it is not the same as living with no private thoughts at all. The balance of openness, vulnerability and trust developed in a relationship governs whether or not personal boundaries become divisions which obstruct rather than encourage such communications. (Giddens 1992, 94)

From this perspective, intimacy is the disclosure of some otherwise-private aspects of self without disclosing so many that intimacy is destroyed. It is a fragile social condition that requires planning and tentativeness (as well as sensitivity and tact) to maintain. Moreover, it should be maintained. Giddens's intimacy thus contains a cautionary tale; people who disclose too much in their intimate endeavors become "codependent," an unhealthy condition in which boundaries are blurred to the point of conflations with self and other (1992, 94).

Giddens's aim in this macrosociological analysis is not to unpack the notion of intimacy at the level of interaction. For Giddens, intimacy is not an experience nor an emotion, but a social obligation, "a cluster of prerogatives and responsibilities" into which people enter under particular (but not quite clear) conditions (1992, 190). He writes not of the transformation of intimacy as a social process or situation, but of the transformation of intimate relationships, of the social sphere to which we refer as intimate. Consequently, he draws on a particular understanding of intimacy that mirrors patriarchal ideals of sexuality, monogamous marriage, and, by extension, social control (particularly of women). Yet elsewhere he writes that "[i]ntimacy means the disclosure of emotions and actions which the individual is unlikely to hold up to a wider public gaze. Indeed, the disclosure of what is kept from other people is one of the main psychological markers likely to call forth trust from the other and to be sought after in return" (1991, 138).

Georg Simmel's view of intimacy also depends on self-disclosure, but is less concerned with the goodness of intimacy, and more concerned with positing a working conceptualization of the experience:

> The "intimate" character of certain relations seems to me to derive from the individual's inclination to consider that which distinguishes him from others, that which is individual in a qualitative sense, as the core, value, and chief matter of his existence. . . . The peculiar color of intimacy exists . . . if its whole affective structure is based on what each of other two participants gives or shows only to the one other person and to nobody else. (1950, 126–27)

Intimacy, in Simmel, is not bounded by the requirement of moderation, nor that of psychological or emotional health. Although Simmel cautions that this extensive intimacy can threaten a relationship, he does not consider the destruction of the relationship to be synonymous with the destruction of intimacy. Simmel's recognition of the absoluteness of this self-disclosure is clear: "even material property should be common to friends" when friendship "aims at an absolute psychological intimacy" (1950, 325). For Simmel, the elimination of limits is central to intimacy; the refusal to draw a boundary at the sharing of material property for the sake of intimacy constitutes a limitless sharing of the self and of its extensions.

Following Simmel, then, intimacy is most fundamentally about *access.* It is constituted by and through access to another's secrets, another's private or new expressions of self, and another's resources. Intimacy is not necessarily about love, sex, or tenderness, but about *access* to emotional and physical experiences of others that we consider inaccessible to most people.

Intimacy therefore depends on the cultivation of a belief in the privacy of a particular experience. What is intimate is that which is normally not apparent, accessible, or available. It is therefore always dependent on whether the access is perceived as commonly available or highly guarded.

In *Unlimited Intimacy,* Tim Dean proceeds, though implicitly, from this understanding of intimacy. His exploration of intimacy in the acts of barebacking and bug-chasing extricates it from the moral backdrop against which intimacy is so often understood.[5] The title of Dean's book is one barebacker's description of unprotected anal sex; regarding the phrase, Dean quotes documentary pornographer Paul Morris: "you can take unlimited intimacy to mean either something that is in itself unsafe, or something that's just basically physically and emotionally open" (quoted in Dean 2009, 45). The relationship between intimacy and freedom from constraint is part of the fabric of the book, and of the lives of barebackers. In his deconstruction of an anal fisting scene in a pornographic essay, Dean writes: "The sexual act of fisting brings one man so far inside another as to temporarily obliterate the boundaries that conventionally separate persons. By occupying exactly the same physical space simultaneously, the men in this fantasy have become in some sense beyond individuation" (2009, 46).

The view of intimacy as accessing what is innermost approaches literal manifestation in fisting. In one sense, fisting, of course, parallels sexual intercourse (anus-penis and vagina-penis) in its construction of the occupation of shared physical space (penetration) as intimate. In another sense, it moves beyond the transgression of this particular boundary through the additional transgressions of cultural lines that separate the erotic and the mundane, dirt from cleanliness, and sex from violence. Fisting crosses, also collaboratively, social, ethical, and sexual limits as it simultaneously "obliterates" the boundary between self and other. The intimacy of fisting (which is also practiced in the SM community, though less so in public spaces) derives from the access to another self that it grants and provides.

What is experienced as intimacy is what is understood as somehow *distinguishing the relationship from others.* As ideas about what is protected and private change, the experience—and quest—for intimacy also changes. The (potential) transformation of intimacy lies not in the places where intimacy newly appears, but in the processes through which it is created. It lies not necessarily in marriage, disclosure, or sex, but anywhere that people experience each other *differently enough* than other people experience them.

The achievement of intimacy is therefore also an inherently competitive process. It rests on the notion that one actor possesses special experiential information about another—information that is not readily available or not easily presented. It is always an attempt to gain access to something otherwise restricted, and to be the only one to gain it. However it is constructed or achieved, intimacy represents conquest; the experience of intimacy is always a victory.

Intimacy in SM Play

It is a basic assumption in Caeden that participants "access" each other through play in ways that others do not. Even the observation of play is understood as revelatory; the statement "I've seen you play" is a common means of claiming intimate knowledge, euphemistic in Caeden for "I know you." Although intimacy is assumed to be greatest between people playing together, SM scenes generate feelings of intimacy even among onlookers through their access to the intimate experience.

The relationship between boundary transgressions and feelings of knowing another was articulated rather clearly in the Web blog of a longtime member of the Caeden community:

> But . . . there is a deeper, more significant drive to why I play.
>
> The reason is that I love people. I am fascinated with them, love to be around them. I constantly seek out new connections, new friends, and dive head first into kinky social situations. Even more importantly, I love to see the REAL person underneath the layers. The human being is an amazing creature, but we are too often guarded by walls. Walls of our own creation and for our protection, sure, but walls none the same.
>
> I find SM to be an amazing method to get glimpses of the real person underneath. The pain sheds the layers. Endorphins fly out, bringing with them the very essence of the person out to be enjoyed and marveled. Joy

> and sadness and pain and catharsis all leap out of the body in a world of trust, honesty, and safety.
>
> I played with someone this weekend who is known far more for her sexual energy than her SM bottoming. [. . .]
>
> This round, she instantly stated how badly she wanted to fuck, and expressed remorse about my inability to do so (more on that in another post). I replied that I didn't want her cunt, but that I wanted her soul. I wanted to see the REAL girl behind the veil—what lives beyond her drive to have sex. She was scared . . . warned me that I wouldn't want to see it.
>
> I did want to, and I did see it.
>
> Through a singletail, she shook, she gasped, she moaned, she cried, she screamed. And in all that shaking the real person came to view. The rawness of humanity came to vision . . . I looked into her eyes and could see everything. There was connection. There was oneness. There was the very essence of being. She was alive, and I was the conduit.
>
> I love to play because I love to see what is deep within each of us. I long to embrace the part of all of our souls that makes us whole. To connect with the animalistic part of our beings. (2006, reprinted with permission of author)

The word "intimacy" is not part of the discourse of the Caeden community; rather, words such as "connection" and "energy" are used to describe the experience that I am calling intimacy. These narratives focus on access—on knowing others in ways that they are not normally known, and on feeling known in ways that one usually does not. These experiences are assumed to be a part of SM play, and are highly valued in the Caeden community:

> A good scene to me is more than just a sadistic, masochistic element. There's also a connection between the person . . . it's the energy I have with that person, it's where we let our minds go, it's how much that person gives themself over to me at the time, whether physically, mentally, or emotionally. (Interview transcript, Frank)

For SM participants, "connection" and "energy" are better tools for describing intimate moments than "intimacy." Jack's discussion of intimacy illuminates the tension between intimacy as an authentically good and long-lasting condition of a relationship and intimacy as a social situation:

> But either verbally or nonverbally, or both, you definitely share a huge part of yourself, and a huge very personal part of yourself, with people.

> And many people. And people you don't know so well. People you only know certain parts about. And it's not the foundation of anything long-lasting. Anything long-lasting has to be based in something that is at least a proven substance, I mean there has to be something there. And if you just met the person a couple of parties ago, for example, you're not going to know them, really. You don't know what kind of foods they like and what their favorite color is, or shit like that. Or, maybe that's all you know. And so what ends up happening is that a lot of people will get very naked with each other and think that they're very personally involved with these people, with these other people. Which [. . .] creates this immense feeling of false intimacy, well, of intimacy, which when you actually take a look at it, turns out to crumble under any close inspection at all.

By calling into question the authenticity of intimacy of SM play, Jack questions its meaning. As with Giddens, if intimacy is something healthy and positive that must hold up under scrutiny, then Jack's feelings must be something else. Jack's account vacillates between an intimacy linked to meaningful disclosure and one that privileges experiences in interaction; that the latter does not necessarily mean the former leads him to posit that the intimacy is "false."

Immediately, though, Jack corrects himself. His sense of intimate experience is betrayed by the absence of conventional and accepted forms of disclosure. Ultimately he refuses to disavow the intimate nature of SM. He reconciles this tension by considering it authentic but short-lived; the intimacy is not false, only fleeting. This passage is mired in the very same positive and retrospective view of intimacy: if we are later betrayed, then we conclude that the intimacy was inauthentic; we were fooled by our feelings. Nonetheless, in the moment, the access to otherwise unknown parts of people—the transgressive metaphoric nakedness—creates a sense, whether justifiable later or not, of intimacy.

Intimacy, Eroticism, and Violence

The understanding of intimacy as the moderate and healthy space between too little and too much disclosure in personal relationships obscures the extent to which intimate experience amounts to gaining access. The challenges in understanding intimacy parallel the problems in conceptualizing violence, pain, and eroticism. Trapped in moral frameworks and tethered to political agendas, these ideas are rarely deconstructed. SM forces us to confront the apparent inconsistencies and paradoxes contained within them. In so doing, we can trace conceptual links between intimacy, eroticism, and violence that move beyond psychological models of innate drives and pathologies.

Heteronormative sexuality, of course, has been constructed around restricting access. As Foucault illustrated so powerfully, sexuality as we understand it is built upon issues and questions of access; we can barely think about it apart from concerning ourselves with who gets to do what, where, to whom, for what reasons, and with what consequences. Heteronormative eroticism is inextricable from ideas about, and experiences of, interpersonal access; the parts of the body we eroticize are the parts that we guard. Monogamy and virginity are systems of meaning (and power) built around access to women's bodies. Eroticism is rooted in access and intimacy is achieved through access; eroticism and intimacy are linked through their emphasis on access to particular aspects of others. Non-normative eroticism is similarly rooted in issues of access—voyeurism, exhibitionism, frotteurism, and even foot fetishism all eroticize the granting or gaining of access to the normally inaccessible.

As regulatory (and thereby disciplinary) forces regarding sexuality are challenged and sexual practices and identities change, other aspects of self acquire the potential to supplant sexuality as a highly protected aspect of self. As Giddens argues, the portrait of what has conventionally been understood as "intimate" life is changing (Giddens 1992). He does not argue that what is understood and experienced as intimacy—that the very notion of what is and what is not intimate—is undergoing a transformation. Intimacy is culturally and socially situated; hence sex becomes less intimate as it becomes less protected. This may be a function not of a "purer" relationship in the context of gender egalitarianism, as Giddens assumes, but of changing, and perhaps increasing, avenues and realms of disclosure in social life. Changes in intimacy are directly impacted by changes in the importance of notions of privacy.

As sex becomes less protected and less guarded, sexual experiences no longer represent the specialized access they may once have. Other aspects of self—more guarded aspects of self—become understood as more difficult to access; they replace the naked body as the metaphor and means for the knowing of another. Because intimacy is constituted through and by experiences of others that are normally restricted, the quest for intimacy becomes the effort to find aspects of selves that are more restricted than sexuality.

Understanding intimacy as the experience of achieving access to protected aspects of others' selves provides a theoretical framework for understanding the intimacy of interpersonal violence. Nonconsensual violence (what most people mean when they say "real violence") transgresses physical, social, emotional, and ethical boundaries between actors. Perpetrators of interpersonal violence gain access to experiences of others that most do not. The "sneaky thrills" that Jack Katz finds among thieves are intimate thrills (1988). The sexual metaphor he uncovers in the narratives of the thieves follows, for the thrill in both heteronormative eroticism and theft lies in gaining access. To violate, and to be violated, are intimate experiences. If we cease to reserve the word "intimate" for situations that are desirable or healthy, we can see, for example, the intimacy of violent crime. Rape, which many of us would shudder to consider "intimacy," is so heinous precisely *because* it is so intimate.

The social situation of murder,[6] from this perspective, becomes the most intimate act imaginable. Murder not only transgresses all social, moral, and personal boundaries, but it facilitates and provides access to the experience of death. For the murderer, the infliction of death grants access to an experience that cannot be replicated in another moment, or with another person; no one else has ever witnessed the same expression on the victim's face, heard him draw his last breath, or watched the life leave her eyes. Simultaneously, the murderer eliminates the potential for future access to any other aspects of self; no one will see any expression on the victim's face again. Murder grants the murderer the ultimate access to the self of another, in very same moment in which it is destroyed.

The victim shares with her killer the same intimacy; a particular experience she can have only once, with only the person (or people) present in this moment, and after which she will have no other. Her murder grants her access to the self of the murderer that is normally restricted—even in the case of serial killers, the vast majority of people do not know this aspect of the murderer's self and do not see him in these moments. Those who have seen him in these moments are likely no longer alive; the victim is the only person alive with direct, lived, felt access to these aspects of the murderer's self.

In sharp contrast with most intimacy research, particularly in social psychology and in psychology, this perspective does not treat intimacy as, inherently, an experience of closeness and connectedness, but as the experience of accessing in another that which is normally thought inaccessible. This is not to draw a qualitative or ethical parallel between violent crime and SM, in which intimacy *is* a reciprocal and positive experience. The intimacy of SM play illustrates the limitations of current thinking about intimacy. My aim here is to explore the process of the construction of intimacy in SM toward a reconceptualization of intimacy more broadly, and to illustrate the potential implications of this rethinking. Understanding intimacy as a phenomenological experience that may not result in feelings of mutual closeness and connectedness is important in understanding a range of social phenomena from pedophilia to murder.

In the analysis of intimacy as, ultimately, interpersonal access, intimacy cuts across all kinds of social interaction. It is created through social experiences of disclosure and of boundary transgression, and through sites of potential trust violations. At the root of the pathologization of intersections of violence and the erotic as social processes and judgments is what they have in common. Because both provide access to the body in ways that are normally protected; both can, and often do, construct intimate experience. The various conditions under which access is gained, under which disclosure occurs, constitute different paths to intimacy. While experiences of intimacy are different when access is consensual and reciprocal than when it is not, it does not cease to be intimate simply because it is unwanted, unpleasant, or violent. For the concept of "intimacy" to be of more analytic and theoretical value, it needs to be extricated from the conceptual mire of sex, love, and romance.

SM, Intimacy, and Trust

Intimate experiences are always created through interpersonal access. The emotional dimensions of intimacy are qualitatively different across different situations. The intimacy of SM is not the same as the intimacy of violent crime. On the most obvious level, this is because SM is a consensual activity and violent crime is not. Debates about SM have raged around the issue of consent; SM defenders use consent to argue that SM should not be understood as coercive, as violent, or as a mechanism of oppression. Anti-SM activists have objected to this on the grounds that it obscures the false consciousness that accompanies oppression.[7] These conversations often begin and end with the idea of consent, though, neglecting to unpack the ways in which emotional and psychological experiences *change* with consent—specifically, experiences of trust and of violation.

In nonconsensual violence, access is experienced as violation. We use the phrase "I feel violated" to describe the sense that a boundary has been crossed and we do not like the way we feel. It may be felt as a violation of the body or of personhood, but nonconsensual violence is a violation also of trust. It is a violation of our trust in humanity, or in a particular person, in our own ability to assess situations, to judge others correctly, to prevent the violation or to escape from it.

When any of these trusts is breached in the gaining of access to some aspect of our lives, selves, or identities, we feel violated. The violator, however, has still gained access to this normally restricted experience. Because of this, the *positive* experience of intimacy—the warm, positive feeling of connectedness that has come to characterize all intimacy—is not reciprocal. A rapist may feel that a rape was intimate, but the victim does not. When access is gained without consent, the subsequent distancing is a rejection of the intimacy, a refusal to condone the intimacy of the violation. Nonconsensual access, in this view, is in a sense, cheating; it circumvents the role of trust, obtaining access by force rather than consent.

To be violated is an intimate experience, yet violation changes intimacy. It is the feeling of unwelcome intimate experience, but there is no being violated without feelings of intimacy. The warm, positive feeling that people mean when they speak of "intimacy" is the state of *appreciation* of that transgression. If we do not appreciate the transgression—if the transgression has been violative—this does not necessarily render the experience less intimate, conceptually. It only makes it undesirable and unacceptable. This feeling of violation that arises from trust having been breached, characteristic of nonconsensual violence, causes a reluctance to consider violence intimate.

SM play is fundamentally based on trust. It is not violative, but it is potentially so, always and deliberately. It plays with the dialectic relationship between trust and risk. SM is about plunging repeatedly into a risk-trust cycle, one that revels in the risks of betrayal and harm and incompetence, to emerge from them without having been betrayed, harmed, or found incompetent. Through this cycle, SM participants achieve a sense of understanding another and of being understood that cannot be created elsewhere. The "connection" of which SM participants speak exists in this space—it is the feeling of riding on the suspension, the thrill of the unknown and the risk of the violation.

It is here, in this unknown, risky space, that intimate experience is constructed and understood as such. This space of potential violation—the risk-trust cycle—carves a space in which this vulnerability is performed and lived and felt. Participation in this cycle thus constitutes an experience of access to one another that cannot occur outside these spaces of potential violation. Through transgressing interpersonal boundaries, access is granted. Through immersing oneself in the potential for violations of trust and body and mind, still other access is granted—through this access, intimacy is constructed.

If intimacy is access to pieces of the self that are otherwise inaccessible, then even the threat of violation is an inherently intimate space. Violations of the body that do not explicitly violate trust grant access to the body and to carnal responses that are normally unavailable—and thus these violations are intimate. The granting of trust and the being trusted for these violations of flesh alone are intimate experiences. The potential, however, for that trust to be violated results in feelings of intimacy on still another level. The cost of a trust violation exceeds the cost of a carnal violation; a trust violation not only shatters trust, but injures the body in unanticipated and undesired ways. Through play, participants engage in practices of trust, and thus in risking violation.

In reveling in a trust-risk-access cycle, participants feel knowing of, and knowable to, another. When the scene fails, this intimacy fails; in SM, when the outcomes are unfavorable, participants feel like strangers to one another. Trust, on this level, is the trust that players deeply understand one another; it is destroyed when participants in a scene feel like strangers.

Stories of failed SM scenes illustrate this. Sophie, for example, had been engaged in a long and intimate play relationship with Carl, a friend whom she deeply trusted. During the scene she recounts below, Carl changed his approach, and Sophie subsequently felt that Carl was somehow not quite himself. Sophie and Carl never quite recovered from the incident; though they remained friends and tried to play again, it was, according to Sophie, never the same.

> He was very much a rope top. That was his big thing, was bondage. And he was excellent at bondage. And our dynamic was always—I mean, yes, he would absolutely hurt me when the time came for that, but there was also always this element—even when he was hurting me, it was done in this incredibly, like, touchingly caring way. And especially when he was tying me up, it was this soothing, wonderful thing.
>
> So one day, Ari and I are over at Carl and Sasha's, and the plan was to play later in the evening, if we decide we feel like it, which we do. Carl starts a scene with me. Carl has decided in his head, from all the things that he's heard me say about how I play with Ari, that that's what I really want from an interaction, in order for it to be the most gratifying and valuable. So we proceeded to have a scene where Carl was not Carl. And I didn't stop it because it was so like, I couldn't understand what was going on. I couldn't understand why it felt so horrible. And it wasn't that I didn't trust him, because I trust him completely. [. . .] I just couldn't figure out what the problem is, I felt horrible through the whole thing. And he was so out of touch with me that he wasn't even aware of how horrible I was feeling. The scene went on for some time. It ended with him putting a rope noose around my neck, and then knocking me off-balance. It was just the most jarring, horrible [. . .] and the second it was over, I just like burst

> into tears. I was just, like, you know, traumatized. And he was like, "Oh my God, what's wrong?" [and] he carried me into the other room. I said something like, "Where did my Carly go?" and then he started to cry. [. . .] He's like, "I was trying to give you this sadistic experience."

In Sophie's story, Carl's risk backfires. His efforts led Sophie to feel that she did not *know him* so well as she had previously felt, and, because he had made this particular decision in the first place, that he "knew" her less well also. The risks were unsuccessful; each ended up emotionally distraught and distant. Ultimately, they sacrificed the relationship.

The risk-trust cycle in which SM participants immerse themselves constructs spaces for potential violations, thereby constituting the ultimate emotional edge of SM play. This potentially violative space is itself transgressive; it negotiates social, ethical, and interpersonal boundaries. It grants access to aspects of participants' selves that are otherwise inaccessible. The vulnerability of play is the access to one's own experience of opening oneself up to potential violations on physical, psychological, and emotional levels.

Intimacy and Edgework

The SM community in Caeden is built around SM as a recreational endeavor. It is a serious leisure pursuit through which intimacy is constructed. More specifically, it can be best understood as edgework. Like Jennifer Lois's rescue workers with their victims, SM players grant each other access to presentations of emotions that they do not feel, let alone grant access to, under normal circumstances. It is in this access to emotion, the condition of being privy to self-disclosure, where intimacy is created and experienced. Lois argues that the intimacy she finds among rescue workers is born of access to "aspects of the self that can only be constructed through an intense interaction with another" (Lois 2003, 172). Because these unprecedented selves transpire in the circumstances in which they are constructed, the sharing of the circumstances creates the sense of knowing, and of being known to, each other.

To the extent that SM scenes involve the transgression of bodily boundaries, access creates intimacy. Even beyond that, though, because SM scenes often involve altered states, normal mechanisms of self-presentation are sometimes unavailable. Because these presentations are sometimes unpredictable and less intended for public consumption, access to this back-stage information also contributes to experiences of intimacy. Importantly, this is the case not only for those granted access, but also for those whose presentations have been, in a sense, compromised by the altered behavior.

The boundaries that are transgressed in SM range in severity and in consequence, but the opportunities for boundary transgression, and therefore for intimacy, are always mutually created rather than seized. Through these constructed transgressive experiences, which grant players emotional and physical access not normally granted, SM play actively creates the sense of knowing another and of being known. SM results in feelings of intimacy because it creates intimate experience. Rather than exploring edges together, SM players are *defining* their edges together, creating the space in which the edges can be explored, and then responding to one another in the very ways that *constitute* the edges themselves.

These experiences of self-revelation and self-disclosure, and of access to the same in others, are transgressive in means, in kind, and in form. In the presence of others and, indeed through interacting with others, these experiences of intimacy stem from the transgression of interpersonal boundaries. The public nature of SM scenes does not, then, detract from the intimacy created through boundary transgression; rather, it widens the circle of intimate relations to people who watch the interaction. The revelation and disclosure accessible to onlookers is passive, but they are still accessible, and still not normally disclosed or revealed. A sense of group intimacy is created through this public transgressive experience and the revelations and disclosures that emerge.

Beyond that, however, SM scenes themselves are sites of boundary transgression. Because violence and eroticism do not comfortably converge elsewhere, the site of its confluence *itself* becomes transgressive; most people do not disclose to most other people what is disclosed in and through SM play. Normative boundaries between accepted and unaccepted social interaction, assault and consent, violence and sex, masculine and feminine, sane and insane, safe and unsafe, power and powerlessness, and dominance and submission are explored through SM play, as well as (sometimes) physical boundaries between consciousness and unconsciousness and life and death.

At least part of the goal in all edgework is the risk experience itself. Collaborative edgework seeks the added thrill of depending on one another for the success of the risk-taking. All collaborative edgework requires and constructs trust (and therefore risk) in order to transgress social and interpersonal boundaries. These transgressions also construct intimacy as they grant particular and unique access. This particular kind of collaborative edgework—that which constructs intimate experience through the joint transgression of interpersonal and social boundaries—is also therefore "intimate edgework."

The Feminist Question

SM revels in the space of potential (and multi-layered) violations. Through these repeated trusts and risks, SM play is a path to victory in the competition for intimate access to another. This is, on one level, easily read as consistent with heteronormative eroticism. Women in Caeden are more likely to bottom to men than to top them; men clamor to access them, and they are accessed only when they risk being hurt. Men who top can become successful clamorers, gaining access to intimate moments through repeated assurances that they can simultaneously violate women and keep them safe.

Even aside from the potential to invert hegemonic gender roles by allowing women to clamor for access to men, the parallel of SM to the dominant structure of heteronormative eroticism is not as simple as this. The long-debated and highly contentious questions surrounding women's engagement in SM can be framed differently if we understand SM as edgework. For example, tops risk much more than would-be seducers do. The otherwise-inaccessible aspects of selves to which tops grant bottoms access are confessions of sadism—manifestations of cruelty and aspirations to superiority. These are socially dangerous confessions, and their practice can be physically and emotionally dangerous as well. Additionally, the empowerment of bottoming is complicated and seems paradoxical; SM blurs distinctions between active and passive and subject and object.

This trust-risk-intimacy cycle draws on age-old binaries, including good/evil, safety/danger, clean/dirty, and sacred/profane. It also challenges these binaries—from moment to moment and scene to scene, player to player, deploying meanings and performances of masculinity and femininity. Men, women, and queer-identified people inhabit, perform, and construct good and evil in different relationships to each other. These questions are too complex to be reduced to the eroticization of male dominance that feminist theorists have illustrated lies at the crux of patriarchal power.[8] They are intertwined also with notions of risk-taking. Social contexts not only determine which risks are socially acceptable and for whom, but also define what is (and is not) risky. Risk-taking is shaped, as Sandra Walklate notes, by fear, and fear is gendered; risk-taking behaviors acquire meaning in the context of gendered relationships to fear (Walklate 1997).

As Elizabeth Stanko has argued, the space for potential violation is the space in which women live their everyday lives. The continued immersion in cycles of potential violations of body and mind, viewed from the radical feminist perspective, is a ritualistic engagement in women's oppression, the repeated enjoyment of the playing out dynamics of male violence on the body. These cycles, though, are not merely cycles of violence and potential violation, but cycles of *trust.* From this same perspective, trust, in regard to the safety and strength of the body, is *not* part of the space in which women live their everyday lives. In Stanko's analysis, women's fear of violence translates to women's fear of men; women move through the world afraid for their physical and sexual safety and men do not—even when men are at higher risk of assault (Stanko 1987). Chan and Rigakos elaborate, "Women negotiate the risk of personal harm in the context of knowing that their assailant will most probably be a man" (2002, 743). What Stanko calls the "bravado" of men is the sense of being able to handle risk, of being able to withstand whatever attack may occur (1987). Men move through their worlds with trust, if not that they will not be assaulted, then at least that they will emerge intact.

The immersion in spaces of potential violation, then, may constitute and construct women's own bravado. Through bottoming, women confront and withstand and symbolically survive male violence. Women work the edge in SM of their everyday fears of violation, flirting, challenging, daring their would-be violators. These women are not *celebrating* violation, but actively defying the cultural proscription to live in fear of it. Chan and Rigakos's contention that the "thrill-seeking aspect of edgework is less present in women's involvement in risky behaviours" underestimates the thrill of the space for violation. In much the same way that skydivers (Lyng 1990; Laurendeau 2006) prove their ability to control or defeat the natural world in the face of the threat to (masculine) order, women prove their ability to defeat men in the face of the threat to their order—safety and caution. Chan and Rigakos recognize this as edgework in their analysis of gendered risk, but they neglect to explore the *thrill* of the metaphoric victory. An edgeworker who revels in the sense of control over the natural world relishes the rush of power that comes with having ascended the mountain (albeit with a rope tied around his waist). The rush of power that accompanies having survived a knife to the throat or a bag over one's head (albeit with a man who is not "supposed" to kill her) facilitates a similar sense of control. Viewed this way, SM play for women negotiates the edge of everyday fears and affirms their ability to confront the ultimate threat: the hands of a man, literally and metaphorically. A woman in an SM scene can stare into the eyes of a man who *looks* as if he could rape or kill her, and feel as if she is daring him to try. Whether women are topping men or bottoming to them, the potential for men to "snap," to overpower them, to lay claim to women's bodies, and to violate their trust is part of the chaotic edge. This edge for women may be no less thrilling than the edge of the cliff that threatens the rock-climber's sense of order through its reminder of his mortality. From the top or from the bottom, by playing with intersections of violence and eroticism with men, women are also asserting control over the uncontrollable—trusting men whom they "should" not trust not to take advantage of them. Elizabeth Stanko illustrates that for women, risk is "about misogyny and the continued perpetration of women's oppression through fear of crime and blame for their situation" (1997, 492). SM play is a space in which *women* can insist, "I will not be hurt . . . even if I put myself in harm's way." It is a path to feelings of invincibility to which only men have historically been privy, in a particular and deeply gendered context.

On still another level, this reveling in fear constitutes emotional edgework. The moment in which a bottom feels compelled to safeword but does not is the journey to the emotional edge. These are also the moments in which the top's desire to hear cries and see blood feels visceral, and she almost says, "Never mind—I don't want to feel this way. This is not good." This emotional edgework is not the attempt to maintain control over emotions that threaten to overwhelm (and thereby jeopardize the success of physical edgework), but the negotiation of the boundary between emotional chaos and emotional order. Emotional edgework travels between metaphoric life and death, between emotional awareness ("I know what I'm feeling and it makes sense to me") and emotional unintelligibility. Emotional edgework, framed this way, is not about the management of emotions during intense moments, but about actively seeking the lines between emotional control and the loss of emotional control.

This is not an argument that women engage in SM as a conscious (or even subconscious) strategy for coping with oppression or the pervasiveness of male violence. Framing women's voluntary risk-taking in SM (or elsewhere) as responses to patriarchal oppression while simultaneously dismissing the thrill of the risk reproduces the limitations of conceptualizations that Peter Donnelly (2004) calls "risk response" theories. We can simultaneously recognize the social contexts in which risk-taking acquires meaning and reject the notion that risk-taking is always a coping mechanism with some (ostensibly unfortunate) social condition.

Marginality and Intimacy

In Caeden, experiences of marginality inform and shape quests for what is experienced as superlative intimacy. Among people who view themselves as having spent much of their lives in peripheral positions, this intimate edgework seeks to know and be known to another; it grants and achieves access to presentations of the self not otherwise presented. The community thus becomes both a means and the consequence of intimate edgework, and as such its meaning in the lives of its members is constituted as "home," a metaphor for a sense of belonging, safety—and a network of intimate relationships. If intimacy is both highly valued and inherently competitive, then it is likely that we seek it, but differ in how well equipped we are for this quest. Among people who are navigating the multiple stigmas common in this community, access to intimacy may be particularly challenging. Cultural capital in the intimacy market includes social skills, good hygiene, a healthy weight, and conformity to gender norms—signifiers to the world that we are worthy of being known. Without this capital, paths to intimacy are traveled differently.

I wish here to be especially clear: I am *not* contending that social marginality leaves SM participants with little choice but to turn to SM as the sole path to intimacy. The social marginality among people in Caeden is multi-leveled and complex, and it emerges at least in part from extraordinary creativity, intelligence, and nontraditional choices in all realms. If intimacy can be understood as access through boundary transgression, it must be noted that SM play transgresses more interpersonal boundaries in number, by more extreme and riskier measures, than conventional paths to intimacy. It is one among many nonconformist choices for the people in Caeden.

The incidental androgyny in the Caeden community provides a backdrop for gender performances in members' SM play. These performances, however, occur also in a social context in which gender expectations are less clear and arguably less rigid than any time in recent history. I do not share Anthony Giddens's optimism that the pure relationship is empirical evidence of a changing gender order, nor do I believe that SM, by itself, is a mechanism for wider structural change. Lynn Jamieson maintains that "the creative energies of many social actors are still engaged in coping with or actively sustaining old inequalities rather than transforming them" (1999, 491). On one level, this is certainly the case, but I do not view this as an either/or proposition. The irreconcilable tensions that have so long plagued feminist theory emerge precisely from viewing the power problematic as an either/or proposition.

Intimate Edgework

Much more than it is about sex, SM is about intimacy. That sex is also often about intimacy does not mean that SM should be understood as an alternative kind of sex. SM is about constructing intimacy through social interaction. It is about obtaining access, securing it, granting it, promising it, daring one to take it, and testing it. The eroticism of SM is thus intertwined (as is the eroticism of sex) with ideas about power and access. An interactionist analysis of SM play illustrates two distinct axes along which intimacy is constructed in everyday life. The first is through the transgression of moral, social, ethical, and personal boundaries. The second is the immersion in trust-risk cycles that create spaces for potential violations of trust. Outside SM, both of these are separate paths to intimate experience, for each provides access to pieces of selves that we understand to be protected from most other people. In SM, these axes intersect to construct intensely intimate experiences.

SM conflates these paths to intimate experience, creating for its participants a sense of higher, deeper, more intense intimacy. The edgework of SM is not only collaborative; it is also intimate. Intimacy in SM is not only an outcome of collaborating the edge, but *central to its appeal.* "Intimate edgework" is not merely "collaborative edgework" that results in intimate feelings; it is distinct from collaborative edgework in that it takes interpersonal access to others as its objective.

The immersion in repeated cycles of risk and trust represents the ultimate boundary, continually creating and recreating spaces of potential violation. From the top and from the bottom, whether the scene is D/s or straight SM, SM play transgresses all sorts of boundaries. These transgressions themselves construct intimacy, but the cycle of risk and trust is the ultimate edge on which all SM plays—the edge between being violated and not being violated.

SM is a site in which creative energies are directed toward all of these things—coping, reproducing, subverting, and transforming gender as a power structure. SM play as it occurs in Caeden can only occur not in a patriarchal context, but in a *changing* patriarchal power context. It is only in this context, amid these changes, and from the inside out, that we can begin to understand the resistance to reductionism that underlies the words of the members of the SM community nationwide who call SM "what it is that we do."

Concluding Notes: Erotic Subjectivity and the Construction of the Field

The postmodern view of ethnography as a jointly constructed narrative, rather than an accurate objective depiction of social reality, has gained support in recent years. Despite increasing crossover between the two, questions concerning the role of the ethnographer remain unsettled. In the field and in her writing, what the ethnographer "does" with her feelings, her presence, her narrative, her voice, her body, and her sexuality is a matter of interest for ethnographers across disciplines and intellectual inheritances. At times, the objectives of ethnography themselves are at issue. The disagreements between "realist" (Van Maanen 1988) or "academic" ethnography (Rinehart 1998) and postmodernist ethnographies that have been termed "interpretive " (Denzin 1997), "fictional" (Rinehart 1998), and "evocative" (Anderson 2006a) are not necessarily over the roles of subjectivity and introspection, but over their intentions. Advocates of subjectivity in ethnography have been accused of navel-gazing (Jarvie 1998), and indulging in "a celebration of the personality of the anthropologist" (Ryang 2000). Postmodernist ethnographers have responded with claims that realist ethnographers fail to recognize that "understanding is visceral" (Denzin 1995) and have called analytic ethnography an attempt "to contain, limit, and silence the personal, or the self, in the research context" (Burnier 2006). Some scholars subscribe to the possibility of an integrated approach (Anderson 1999, Lerum 2001) and others have ventured examples of integration, blending personal introspection with conventional analytical approaches (Ronai 1995; Frank 2002). I have endeavored to situate this book in this blended space.

Long after most of this manuscript had been written, I had a fascinating conversation with a colleague from another institution. Anna[1] had read a paper I had written, based on this chapter, in which I touted the virtues of subjective analysis (Newmahr 2008). She wanted more information about my subjective experience of SM than I had shared in that article: Did I enjoy my play? What did I like? What didn't I like? Did I find it erotic? Are these people my friends? Why didn't I stay in the community once my research was finished?

I answered only her last question: because I was finished. I wrote the dissertation, landed a job, and moved to another city. I left the other questions unanswered. I did not see (and I am not certain that I see even now) how these questions would further, enrich, or usefully complicate an understanding of the people with whom I had spent so much of my time during these years. Still, her inquiries troubled me for reasons that I view as relevant to this book, and to ethnography more generally. They underscored an important question about where to draw the line in subjective analysis and representation of the self in ethnographic work.

While divulging the researcher's emotional responses to field experiences may be valuable, it is not *necessarily* so. I agree with critics of this kind of ethnography that all too often we assume that our emotional experiences in the field are relevant and instructive to our audience. There are, though, aspects of my subjective experience in the field that are germane to how my understanding came to be what it is, rather than something else. These are important pieces of the puzzle of SM. This illustrates some of the intersections between my own subjective analysis—that is, taking myself as the subject of analysis during fieldwork—and the central arguments of this book. The following section begins with my field notes about my first SM scene, and explores the ways in which my subjective analysis informed my project.

Emotional Experiences in SM Play

I told Russ I would be ready in a minute. When I returned to the room, he wasn't there. Suddenly someone grabbed my hair from behind me and pushed me up to the cross at the wall, putting my arms above my head. My heart was pounding; I knew it was Russ, but I also knew people were watching us—watching me. He slid the blindfold over my eyes (which made me slightly less self-conscious) and gently pulled my hair out from underneath it. He lifted my shirt over my head and removed it. He cuffed my left wrist and fastened it to the bolt above. I remember feeling relieved;

I hadn't known what to do with my hands. He did the same with my right hand. I spread my feet apart a little bit, and he hit them back and forth to indicate that he wanted me to spread them further, which was, it turned out, a good idea, and I was soon glad he did it.

He trailed his fingers along my shoulders and back before beginning to flog me with a very light, barely stingy touch, which felt nice. It changed rather quickly; I don't really remember the transition; he hit me and I thought "Whoa, that was hard . . ."—but it didn't quite hurt. [. . .]

A few strokes later, I forgot entirely about the people watching me, and about how I was going to remember everything or when I was going to write it. I also forgot about Russ. In the beginning I had been picturing him back there; I could hear him breathing. But at some point I thought of nothing except the feeling . . . I don't think I've ever felt that single-minded before. The only thing on my mind was when the next blow was going to come.

It's a difficult sensation to describe. It's quite forceful; I was aware that it was somehow hard. *I knew that he was swinging it hard and I knew it was landing hard; I felt the profundity of the blows . . . but I never thought "Ow." It's not an "ow," really. It feels like the noise you make when you get into a really hot bath and it's too hot but you like it anyway . . . a sigh and a moan at the same time. No matter how hard it was, it felt like that sound—intense but ambiguous.*

He stepped up behind me three or four times, grabbing my hair and checking in on me. He asked me how I was doing. I told him I was fine.

Another time he came close and grabbed my hair. I said "Hi!" and laughed. I think he laughed a little bit . . . he said "Hi" and asked how I was doing. I felt giddy and just . . . gleeful. I felt in love—not with anyone in particular, but somehow head over heels. [. . .]

Afterward, I was most definitely a little out of it. I had a very hard time remembering that Simon—new to the scene that night—was someone I didn't already know, and I kept speaking to him with too much familiarity, asking him, "You were in here? Right there? The whole time??" I remember someone talking about the childhood rhyme Fuzzy Wuzzy, but I couldn't quite follow the conversation. I babbled about something—I don't remember what—but I caught myself at some point and thought, or maybe said aloud, "I'm not making very much sense." I was talking to Simon when Russ asked me from across the room whether I was okay. I made a thumbs-up sign and said, "I'm aces." Aces?

Before this scene occurred, I was, like most people, someone who had never done anything like it. I had never (at least not since childhood) had my hair pulled, nor been shirtless in view of a dozen other people. I had certainly never stood blindfolded and cuffed to a cross while a person I barely knew hit me repeatedly on the back with a large leather flogger. It had never occurred to me that the experience of flogging might be akin to that of a rigorous deep tissue massage, and though I was aware of the claim that SM could cause the altered state commonly referred to as "subspace," I did not quite believe it.

The boundary between freedom of movement and restraint was also new, and the fact that I was restrained in public was significant. I was aware of my ambivalence about engaging in this symbolic space. This performance of powerlessness was troublesome, and it fascinated me. The contradiction between being too tough to do this and being tough enough to do this was palpable. Finally, although I was overwhelmed by intellectual and emotional ambivalence at the beginning of the scene, the intensity of the sensory assault had facilitated in me an uncharacteristic and powerful single-mindedness by the time it ended.

My analysis of my own internal and external responses to this scene paved the way for a much broader perspective on SM. Because I did not think of myself as a person who likes pain, my understanding of the sensations I was experiencing was muddy and confusing. Preliminary research had encouraged me to think about the pain/pleasure dichotomy, but I had no lived experience on which to draw. I found myself completely unable to determine whether to categorize this flogging as painful. It felt, I later tried to explain to friends and colleagues, "like a 500-pound gorilla pounding me across the upper back with his forearm"—diffuse but very hard. Despite my best intellectual efforts, the fact that the sensation was pleasurable seemed to indicate to me that it could not (therefore) be painful. This inability to understand "pain" that did not quite "hurt" led me to explore the conceptual dissonance between eroticism and violence in the Caeden community (and beyond).

I was also very aware that I was feeling grateful to Russ, which surprised and troubled me. I expected to feel anger, catharsis, resentment, victimization, or turmoil of one sort or another, all of which I had been prepared to explore in a participant-observation study of SM. I did not expect gratitude to be a salient and profound part of my experience. My first impulse was to pathologize my response; was this something similar to "capture-bonding," the psychological explanation for Stockholm syndrome? Knowing little about Stockholm syndrome, but doubting that a forty-minute consensual flogging scene would have produced it, I moved beyond the discourse of pathology.

On the most comfortable level, my gratitude to Russ was professional. I had moved from observer to participant. For the first time I was fully convinced that I would not be able to understand SM without doing SM. Because Russ was the person who had, in a sense, facilitated what was a role shift for me, I felt grateful to him for having helped me to move my project along. But I was also compelled to confront a more personal gratitude. The intensity of the sensation had stopped the constant barrage of ever-racing thoughts, an effect that I had not anticipated and with which I was tremendously impressed. The power of this bodily experience trumped the power of my compulsion to think, and I felt grateful to Russ for what I was experiencing, paradoxically, as liberation.

I was also glad to be unharmed. By this time, I was familiar with the basics of SM safety, and I felt comfortable with Russ. However, I was aware that an accident in such a situation could have been injurious, and unlike the myriad risks in everyday life, this one was not easily justifiable for me. Ironically, I felt closer to Russ because we had entered into a situation in which the possibility of harm was higher than usual, and he had not caused me harm. My appreciation that I was not injured, then, translated into gratitude toward Russ—that he was skilled enough to avoid harming me. Put in the terms of the community discourse, Russ had "kept me safe"—even as it was at his hands that I could have been otherwise. The fact that I had fully expected this outcome did not mitigate the gratitude I felt for its arrival.

These introspections about my own play contributed to a deeper understanding of how SM works. They provided conversation topics and specific questions to ask during discussions as well as interviews. They helped me to discern which aspects of experience appeared to be mine alone, and which were shared—and by whom. The feeling of gratitude for the ability of play to "stop" a racing mind, for example, was volunteered time and again, in interviews and casual conversation. This sense of gratitude is bound up with notions of power, submission, and dominance in complex ways in SM. It is not part of the discourse, though; had I not experienced it and chosen to examine this part of my experience, I would likely not have investigated its role in SM interactions.

Finally, this was a new and profound bodily experience, and Russ was not only the person with whom I shared it, but also the person at whose hands it occurred. The movements of the body during a flogging (and during most SM play) are not the same as movements during dancing, sports, or sex. The responses that were being produced in and performed by me were unfamiliar. I did not recognize the sounds I made, and I assume that the expressions on my face would not be recognizable to people I know in other social contexts.

Boundaries—both normative and personal—were transgressed with every strike of the flogger, every bodily response, and every glance of the observers. I was aware that I was granting Russ and the onlookers access to normally hidden (and previously unfamiliar) aspects of my self. Somehow, I felt, they now "knew" me better. From the decision to be there to the actions and my responses, these boundary transgressions generated in me a greater sense of intimacy with Russ, and to a lesser extent, with all those who had witnessed it.

These aspects of the SM experience—feelings of gratitude, access, and intimacy—are not readily apparent in the discourse of the community. Some of these emotional experiences are so taken for granted that it is uninteresting to community members. Some of it is simply unexplored. My willingness to examine the very personal sense that I made of my first SM scene—and how it "made me feel"—generated questions and problems and new perspectives that I was able to explore with the people in Caeden.

Pain and Meaning-Making

When I was starting to think about leaving the field, I reflected regularly on my experiences of play as a whole. In one entry in my field journal, I tried to articulate the physical sensations I had experienced, and my responses to them, while bottoming:

> *The singletail hurts. It hurts my skin; it slices me and feels hot, sharp, mean, and sadistic. I have to work to take the singletail. It's somehow personal—much more personal than the flogger—it hurts because this person wants to hurt me. And the fact that this person can hurt me so much from so far away is trippy.*
>
> *"Hurt" isn't the right word for the way flogging feels. It knocks me around, it knocks the wind out of me, it makes me feel strong and tough, and it's an intense sensation, but unless the flogger is particularly stingy, or my back is already abraded, the pain of flogging doesn't "hurt" me. But it is pain—the too-hot-bath kind of pain. It's diffuse, it's everywhere, it makes everything stop because it's bigger than I am. But it's a pain that just feels good, that doesn't need to be recontextualized or worked through or ridden . . . the pain of massaging sore muscles. Just more intense.*
>
> *Pressure point stuff, on the other hand, hurts a lot. It hurts deep and sharp at the same time . . . it reverberates through my body and makes me feel overcome, but it's so focused, so not diffuse. It directs everything to*

that spot and the pain of that is dizzying—the physiological reactions happen pretty much immediately for me—I get light-headed and loopy and weak almost instantly. The effects disappear quickly when the sensation stops, though—I think they last longer from sustained pain like a whipping. Pressure point play makes me shake my head back and forth quickly, as if I'm trying to shake off the effect of a drug that's setting in (blades do this to me too)—the sensation is too overwhelming to handle and I don't quite know how to process it. (This also happens when there are multiple things going on at the same time; multiple pressure points make me feel like I'm going to implode—short-circuit.) More than anything else I've done, pressure point stuff seems to be much more about sensation than context—context changes it, helps it, forms it, but it isn't very relevant. Pressure points hurt so badly, so easily, and so immediately that I just stop in my tracks.

Punching is also very much about context. I think it's very personal. It's not something I can do casually, or at least it feels that way. The pain feels very deep. It's thuddy like a flogger but much less diffuse, much more focused. It's just so fucked up. To stand there and let someone punch me, over and over—without anything but his fists and an intent to hurt me . . . that's a big experience, and it can be very heady. Each time a punch lands, my entire system is shocked. Somehow, over and over I'm stunned by the punches, the physical connection of fist to muscle, the depth of the (physical) pain—it drives into me, moves my body. On a psychological/emotional level, punching assaults me, like nothing else does. I experience punching as an attack—as something is he is doing because he wants me, personally, to be hurt, by him and with his hands. The fact that I'm allowing *this makes it all the more fucked up.*

Backhanding is a similar kind of assault-feel for me, but it's wrapped up in completely different symbolism, and the pain is vastly different. There's thud with a backhand, but the predominant feeling is knuckle, and the length of the hand across the face . . . so much bone-to-bone; it's more a crunch than a thud. It's much more frightening than punching, and it can feel out-of-control in a way that punching doesn't.

Blades are another story altogether. Playing with blades can run the gamut for me—they can tickle and feel lovely, they can hurt a little, and they can hurt a lot. Even the hurt can be different. It depends a little bit on the technical aspects—where it is, how sharp, how it's being moved—but it's also very much intertwined with symbolism and emotional/psychological responses to symbolic meaning. The pain can be precise and exquisite and intense, but it can also be ticklish and giggly (and yet still be pain); that may be context also. Sometimes blades don't hurt at all, but they require such focus and restraint that the intensity of the sensation is "mistaken" for pain. When they hurt and when they don't, and whatever kind of hurt it is, they cause an instant physiological reaction in me, akin to pressure points—my heart rate increases, I pant, I shudder and tremble, all pretty quickly after the blade touches my skin. On the psychological level, blades can fuck me up. They make me feel like I'll do absolutely anything. They make me high, as instantly as pressure points but with much less pain. They make me feel reckless and risky and on the edge of everything.

My analysis of these notes led me to thoroughly explore the ways others talked about pain and sensation, in my field notes, in interview transcripts, and in conversations during my fieldwork. At that point, I had not thought very deeply or conceptually about pain itself, beyond noting who claimed to like it and who claimed to be averse to it. My writing about my own pain illustrated that for me there were different kinds of pain, different functions of pain, and different strategies in talking (and not talking) about pain. Because others had not thought about it, they were not likely to proactively list the ways in which they understood pain, or even tell me whether the pain of a singletail was qualitatively different for them than the pain of a blade. The impetus to ask these questions, and many others, came from reflecting on my personal experiences of SM.

Erotic Subjectivity

Despite an increase in the tendency toward reflexivity in ethnographic accounts, subjectivity specifically regarding sexuality in the field remains a challenge for many ethnographers. Don Kulick recounts three reasons that anthropologists have "remained very tight-lipped about their own sexuality" in the field (Kulick 1995, 3). These reasons extend to ethnography outside of the discipline also; sociology shares the inheritance of the positivist-realist tradition in social science. Until relatively recently, fieldworkers have tended to render themselves invisible in their texts across all realms. Yet even as this has changed in both disciplines, erotic subjectivity of ethnographers has only rarely made appearances in their texts.[2]

Esther Newton posits that the exploration of sex in the field, for anthropologists, explodes the question of the racialized and sexualized other; Don Kulick reminds us that "the sexual behavior of the other has been widely understood to be a point of irreconcilable difference between 'us' and 'them'" (Kulick 1995, 4). In my case, that of an American sociologist studying a mostly white, mostly Jewish community in an American city, my erotic position in the field is not so easily understood as intertwined with colonialism of the exoticized Other.

However, in the Caeden SM community, the boundary between myself and "Other" *was*, on one level, the presumably sexual behavior of SM participants. Once I engaged in many of the behaviors, the most obvious boundary between the ethnographic self and Other was much blurrier. On another level, though, it is not the behaviors themselves but the eroticization of those behaviors that constitutes SM participants as Other. Specifically erotic subjectivity, then, would have been problematic for me in this work. The members of this community, defined as Other by the *eroticization* of SM, are widely viewed as unwell, either dangerous or deeply troubled. Treating myself as an erotic subject would have left me with two choices. The confirmation that SM was *not* erotic for me would reinforce an essentialist perspective of eroticism and pathologize SM, positioning me as the "normal" researcher who engaged in SM but did not find it erotic. The alternative (the confirmation that it *was* erotic for me) would render *me* unwell; in that case, I would become either dangerous or deeply troubled (and likely, I must have been all along), and my work might be received very differently. Ultimately, then, as sympathetic as I am to the call for ethnographers to deal theoretically and methodologically with their own erotic experience in the field, I have permitted these concerns to constrain both my fieldwork and my representation.

The fact that I experienced the field as much less explicitly a sexed space than I had anticipated seemed initially to simplify matters, but this was not the case. In the first place, I needed to explore why I was finding this, why I had expected otherwise, and exactly what that meant. Second, my obligation to represent the surprising nonsexual richness in SM seemed to me to directly compete with my obligation to represent the eroticism of SM (for most people in the community). Finally—and perhaps most importantly—the extent to which I saw so much more than sex in SM, coupled with my erotic invisibility in the text, might, I feared, threaten my ethnographic authority; would the reader trust me as I tried to explain that I ultimately concluded that SM was not quite "about" sex? And if I were "erotically subjective" in my text—if I did choose one of the two decidedly unfavorable options—wouldn't that undermine this very point? My aim at present is to share the context in which I came to understand SM, including its relationship to eroticism, the way that I did.

Like all ethnographers, I made decisions in the field that led me to see the community as I did and to represent it as I have. The most significant of these was the choice not to engage in spanking. In Caeden, there is a subset of the SM scene that consists of people who *only* spank. This is not the case for other SM activities; there were no people who engaged in only whipping scenes or blade scenes. Partially for this reason, and partially because the demographic was different, people who limited their SM to spanking were generally viewed as a subset of the scene, not quite "real" members of the SM community. Very early, I viewed spankers (and there is an organization in the Caeden community devoted entirely to spanking) as categorically distinct from the larger SM scene.

As one activity in an SM repertoire, however, spanking is ubiquitous in Caeden. It is considered the least risky kind of sensation scene, and hence the one that newcomers are most likely to choose. It is also perhaps the least objectionable of all SM activities for outsiders. Most members of the community engage in spanking on occasion, even if it is not among their primary or favorite activities.

Spanking functioned not only as a scene activity, but as a greeting, as a flirtation and as an explicit invitation. Although consent is generally taken very seriously in the community, it seemed unnecessary with spanking; even among acquaintances, casual swats on the ass were rarely negotiated, and not considered particularly meaningful to anyone, it often seemed, except me. Consent seemed simply to exclude all activities directed toward the ass. In part because of this, and for closely related political and ideological reasons, I was, quite personally, averse to spanking.

My bias was rooted in my inability to separate spanking from two distinct but related sets of symbolic meanings: discipline and punishment, and the related conflation of love and violence in adult-child relationships. Members of the community did not see spanking as intrinsically interwoven with these ideas. I saw spanking as being firmly and necessarily rooted in structural and hierarchical violence and domination. Although I engaged in countless conversations with participants and friends about this, I never did arrive at an understanding of spanking outside of the context of adult-child role play.

Ultimately, though, as (I like to think) any committed ethnographer, I did try spanking (and caning). These were more challenging scenes for me than anything else I did in the field. What I viewed as "corporal play" was easier for me as a top than as a bottom, but I found it troubling regardless. I find it troubling to write this even now, much more willing to invite readers to imagine me being punched in the face than being spanked.

Of course, my inclination to bottom the way that I did could have arisen only within and because of the gender regime. I had not entirely abandoned the fierceness of my "third-wave" emotional response to what Naomi Wolf called "victim feminism" (1993). Even in SM (perhaps especially in SM), I felt, women must be viewed as at least *potentially* equal to men. In a consensual situation, a man who hits a woman is privileging her status as a decision-maker *over* her status of presumably inferior physical strength; he refuses to protect her. In the narrative that I wrote, and drew on, for, with, and through my fieldwork, my play partner hits me because I want him to, not because I am naughty or incorrigible or evil, and not because I am childlike. In that context, he may be an assailant, but I am not, hierarchically, a victim. All things being equal (though of course they are not), in a consensual situation, a man who hits me *as if I were a man* is engaging, with me, in a subversively feminist act.

My feelings about spanking, then, were inextricable not only from the masculine-feminine binary in the first place, but from the cultural-historical deployment of this conflation as a tool for the social control of women and children. Nevertheless, my decision impacted my project in several important ways.

First, because safe spanking requires much less of a learning curve than other activities, my reluctance to engage in it meant that I could safely play only with people with some experience in the scene. Playing with more experienced tops granted me access that I would not otherwise have easily obtained. Through these associations, I gained social status and a greater understanding of the political aspects of the community. More significantly, it opened different avenues in my SM play. Because I played most often with veteran tops, I played along boundaries that I would not have otherwise. Newer tops would not have been inclined to play as close to "the edge" as some of my partners were, and I would not have been as comfortable with risk as I was with experienced play partners. The elimination of spanking from my repertoire seems therefore to have functioned as a shortcut to a wider variety of high-sensation play with more experienced players, which I view as having had a significant impact on my understanding of SM itself and this community.

For the same reason, the fact that I did not play with spanking also rendered topping even less likely for me. Throughout most of my time in the field, I did not have the skills or experience to offer alternatives to spanking. It was fairly late in my fieldwork before I could even begin to acquire the skill set to top.

Third, my reluctance to spank coded me as less flexible and less easygoing than most people—particularly compared with most people who bottomed.

This continually called my identity as a bottom into question. In turn, it prompted questions for me (and, by extension, for others) about relationships between SM identifications, gender, and power in the community.

Finally, of course, my aversion to spanking precluded me from gaining an understanding of an activity that is popular in the scene; I continue to have difficulty understanding spanking from a perspective other than my own. The subset of people in Caeden who limit their activities to spanking are in many ways excluded from my analysis. This subset appeared to be uncharacteristic of the larger community in three ways: they were disproportionately men, they were older (over sixty-five), and, also in contrast to the larger community, many of them were thin. I do not know whether my analysis in this book resonates for spanking, or whether it will make sense to people whose sole or primary related interest is spanking.

In this light, of course, it is not surprising that SM seemed less about sex to me than about violence, eroticism, and intimacy. Had I endeavored to better understand spanking from the perspective of people in the community, or had I focused on those who only spanked, these activities might seem more profoundly about sex (and perhaps less about violence). Nevertheless, the range of SM activities in which I *did* engage was much broader than the range of those that I viewed as inextricably rooted in structural hierarchy. On many levels, then, I believe that these decisions ultimately served me well.

This is not to argue that violence *itself* is not also patriarchal, structural, or hierarchical. Violence, particularly against women, is all of these things. Whatever way I played, I still, as both a biological and a social category, understood myself as a woman. Therefore, violence that was explicitly sexual (that is, directed at my breasts or hips or cunt), or even inextricably gendered (as I viewed spanking to be), evoked in me a different response than violence that was not, and I began to seek the latter fairly early in my fieldwork. I sought to complicate questions of gender regimes and sexuality and power and violence, and by playing in these ways, I was better able to do so. Significantly too, these insights were remarkably late in coming; it was well over a year after I left the field before I understood my limits and approaches to play the way that I now understand them.

As is always the case in fieldwork, the choices that I made constructed the field and my writing in particular ways. It is my hope that my attention to these choices and their implications help me, and my readers, understand the limits of my analysis. However, these same choices led me to understand things I could not otherwise have. It is important also to note that I did not have to look long or far in order to find people who played in ways with which I was more comfortable. The community that I came to understand it is no less real than the one I would have understood had I made different decisions.

Ethnographic Voices

My conversation with my colleague Anna also illuminates the tension between ethnographic responsibility and the ethnographer's right to privacy. It is true that a deeper exploration of my own emotional experiences in play could provide insight into SM—but it would also provide insight, and perhaps even its deepest insight, into *me*. Anna's question forced me to consider, more consciously, what I wanted to reveal in my work about SM play about my own responses to SM play, and to what ends. This engenders a host of important questions about ethnographic representation: at what point, and in what contexts, do insights into the ethnographer's emotions become a desire or expectation on the part of the audience, and how reasonable is this expectation? What does the ethnographer "owe" her audience in her representation of a community or of her experience? The realization that readers may want more—not about the community, but about me—underscores questions about representation, privacy, distance, authority, and competing ideas about what does and what does not constitute violation.

I did not set out to ask or to answer questions such about whether SM was erotic, healthy, or anti-feminist. I wondered all of these things, but I endeavored to ask first, "What's going on here?" In exploring this question, I asked countless times what was going on with *me*. In regard to an understudied and highly stigmatized community, the questions that Anna asked me—how, qualitatively, did I find it, whether it was erotic for me, whether I "do" SM now—ask me to serve as a voice of academic legitimacy, a researcher's authoritative stamp on the questions of whether SM is acceptable or not, erotic or not, feminist or not. I did not wish to do this. I hope instead to have rendered SM more understandable (by which I mean differently and sociologically understandable), and I include my experiences and reflections as a means to this end.

There are, though, personal reflections and experiences that I do view as relevant to conversations about ethnographic methodologies. My struggle to find, or choose, an ethnographic voice is one of these. As a neophyte ethnographer, I vacillated between the voices of participant, observer, erotic subject, sexual object, bottom, feminist, sociologist, and ethnographer. When ultimately I came to realize, as Carol Ronai (1997) points out, that I cannot switch neatly back and forth, I was bothered, for if I cannot change my voice, then I cannot change the representation of my perspective. And if I cannot change my perspective, then how do I understand the differences between my fictions and my "truths"? Perhaps in part because of my discomfort with the gray spaces in between reality and fiction in which an ethnographer builds, understands, and tells stories, I reflected often on my experience on the boundary between my work and my increasingly fragmented sense of self:

> *Ethnography is a very lonely endeavor, even as it leaves me no time for my own head, my own peace of mind—even as it never leaves me quite to myself, it is lonely. The role is unique, and no one in either "world" can quite understand . . . in many ways I think this lends itself to self-obsession, though not, by necessity, absorption, since I am so fully absorbed in everyone else. As I'm absorbed in them, however, I'm obsessed with me—my role, my impact, my thoughts, my perceptions, my theories, the way I am received and treated, my perspective. . . everything is about me even as I immerse myself in them.*

Several months into my fieldwork, my identity conflict arrived at its resolution (inasmuch as it was going to) at the Playground. The night before, I had written in my journal:

> *Ethnography depends on, I think, the constant, all-encompassing endeavor to be liked. To remain conscious of being liked nearly all of the time is exhausting. The most fundamental difference between Dakota and Staci, I think, is that Dakota is nice. She may get opinionated and snippy if pushed, but ultimately, it is important to her that as many people like her as possible. When this is threatened, she has to think about it . . . how to fix it, is it worth it, should she repair this relationship, cultivate that one . . . Dakota often cannot extricate her feelings about people from what she knows they can contribute to her work, on every level, including the emotional experience of being involved with them . . . and thus is not very "true."*
>
> *I'm starting to not like Dakota very much. And I don't know what to do about that, because I can't just get rid of her. Staci would ruin my research. But it's going to be Staci who has to deal with the post-research fallout—when Dakota leaves, Staci will be left to defend herself, and Staci isn't quite sure that any of this is defensible.*

That night, at the club, I was suddenly sick of everyone around me. I was tired of the scripts I heard repeatedly, tired of having to explain why I didn't want to play with this person or that person, tired of hearing my own repetitions of who I was and why I was there. By writing in my journal, I had brought my sense of fragmentation (and hypocrisy) to the surface, and I was tired of being nice. I was tired of the social dysfunction, tired of feeling pity for people I was "studying," tired of my own relentless ethical dilemmas over authentic and inauthentic presentations, tired of trying to figure out whether I "really" liked someone or "really" wanted to play with him or her. I was sick of my own questions about whether it was imperative that I learn to top soon, imperative that I play with a woman, imperative that I engage in spanking.

Exhausted by the tension between my identity as researcher and my identity as a community member, I found a quiet corner of the club and sat on the floor. Adam found me, sat next to me, and asked me what was going on. Without hesitation, I told him everything. I hated all of these people. I hated myself. I hated him. What the hell was I doing here?

"Ah. Hello, Staci," he said. "I was wondering when you'd show up."

His use of my real name in the field crystallized for me that my problem was my own reluctance to use one voice. His implication that it was only a matter of time before I lost the ability to live dually, deceitfully (in my view), clarified for me that all of this was my hang-up, my problem. In asking his subsequent questions about whether I had to be quite so careful, Adam granted me the "permission" of the insider to just be there. This compelled me to think about what exactly I found so concerning. Where was my courage? Was I afraid that if I offended people in the scene that I would have no project? Was I afraid that my academic peers would conclude that I was (also) a pervert—and therefore not a legitimate researcher?

One of my earliest concerns, among many, about undertaking this project was the fear that it would be sensationalized. I thought I had interesting questions and I wanted the project to be taken seriously. When my work progressed and I began to present my thinking at conferences, attendees wanted so many details about SM that I rarely had a chance to engage them in theorizing play as social interaction. On the relatively rare occasions on which I divulged my topic in professional situations, people winked and giggled, wagered over whether I needed a spanking, or asked me whether the members of the community had all been abused. As I endeavored to wrap my mind around my argument that SM is not quite "sex," these exchanges grew increasingly frustrating for me. This was a specifically sexual sensationalism, and I was at the center of it. It was a titillating topic for people. I did not want it to be. Their voyeurism made me personally uncomfortable, and it offended me intellectually. I began to guard against it in casual conversation and in professional situations. Ultimately, although I have consciously struggled against it, this defensive posture made its way into my writing.

The relationship between SM and sexuality was thus the central struggle for me at every level throughout this project. The assumption that SM is always "about" sex was too often refuted by the goings-on of the community. Community discourse vacillated on the matter; eroticism and sex and heat were not quite the same thing. My own experience in the field only complicated things, constrained by my ethnographic choices, my politics, and my own erotic maps.

For most people, sex is intimate. For most people who engage in SM, play is also intimate. If intimacy is erotic, it is easy to see how people come to understand SM as erotic. These assumptions and conceptualizations need to be further problematized. The SM community is more complex than the available research suggests. It challenges us to think differently about the relationships between intimacy, eroticism, and sexuality. It provides a space for the replication, and the simulation, of patriarchal power and for the glorification of violence and cruelty, but it also demands that we look critically at the assumptions that these are all necessarily one and the same. SM provides a space—or at least Caeden did while I was there—in which people can, potentially, navigate the constraints of gender and power and violence differently than they do in their everyday lives.

Glossary

dominant/submissive (dom/sub) Noun or adjective used most commonly to connote people who play with psychological/emotional dominance; often frequently incorporates physical/sexual power exchange (femsub—female submissive, maledom—male dominant, etc.).

dungeon A type of club or play space (or sometimes merely another name for a club) that is designated for SM play.

flogger A whip, usually but not always made of leather, consisting of one handle to which multiple flat strands ("falls") are attached.

kinky Having an interest in, or relation to, sexual activity outside of mainstream, conventional conceptualizations of sexuality.

play As a verb, to engage in a scene; as a noun, the engaging in a scene or scenes, in general.

play space Any area understood to be acceptable for engaging in scenes.

quirt A short, forked whip with two falls.

safeword A signal given by the submissive or bottom to end the scene. Many people also have safewords to slow the scene down, or to stop a particular action while remaining in scene. It is also used as a verb.

scene A (usually) pre-negotiated erotic power exchange; participants agree on the type of scene and on limits before engaging in SM activity. This agreement may be explicit (even written), or implicit, in the case of long-term or previous scene partners. The word is also used to refer to the SM community in general.

singletail A long whip with one tail. As a verb, it means to whip someone using a whip with one tail.

switch As a noun, someone who tops and bottoms; as a verb, to change between topping and bottoming.

top/bottom Used in both noun and verb forms, and refers most often to physical SM activity, as opposed to dominance/submission, but, as nouns, are less identity-focused than "sadist" and "masochist."

vanilla Used most commonly to refer to activities, events, and/or people that are not SM-related. However, is sometimes less broadly applied to people/events/activities that are not "kinky," regardless of whether SM is their particular kink.

Wartenberg wheel A handheld stainless steel instrument, originally designed to test neurological responses on skin. The handle is usually approximately six inches long, and at its end sits a sharply spiked wheel (akin to a pizza cutter with longer spikes).

Notes

Introduction

1. Other organizations cropped up along the East Coast during the seventies, though none has been as successful or endured as long as TES.

2. "Play" is used as both a noun and a verb, to refer to SM interaction specifically (e.g., "Do you want to play?") and generally (e.g., "It depends on the play").

3. All proper names regarding the community I studied, including the names of people, places, and organizations, have been changed.

4. "The National Coalition for Sexual Freedom is a national organization committed to creating a political, legal, and social environment in the United States that advances equal rights of consenting adults who practice forms of alternative sexual expression." National Coalition for Sexual Freedom Mission Statement, http://www.ncsfreedom.org.

5. In the two years preceding my entry into the field, the community had been thrice burned by people who claimed to be academic researchers, but who were journalists, bloggers, or students whose work either explicitly attacked SM participants or depicted SM in a particularly unfavorable light. This happened twice again while I was there, though in one of these cases the writer claimed to be a participant and did not disclose his project.

6. The swinger scene is an alternative sexual community of mostly heterosexual couples who swap partners for otherwise conventional sexual activity.

7. As the identification labels themselves suggest, "dominant" and "submissive" are used in the community to draw on narratives of unequal power relations in SM play. They are used as both nouns and adjectives. Male dominant/female submissive were the most common identification labels in EPP by far, but there were exceptions.

8. This subset of the community differs from Horizons in significant ways, many of which manifest themselves in differences in gender relations. An exploration of these differences is beyond the scope of this work.

9. Friends from the scene tell me that they think this may, in 2010, be changing.

10. See, e.g., Abu-Lughod 1986; Bourgois 1996; Prieur 1998; Duneier 1999.

11. Interestingly, friends outside the SM community later informed me that the name I had chosen was a "stripper name." People in the scene, however, most often guessed a relationship to the Dakota, the famous building in front of which John Lennon was killed.

12. By press time, however, the word "kink" appears to have experienced a significant resurgence in the community. I am no longer sure that it is less common than either BDSM or SM.

1. Defiance

1. I was smaller than most of the members of the community, and was often referred to as "tiny" and "skinny." It is possible that respondents may have been disinclined to discuss weight issues with me. However, informal word-of-mouth investigation suggests that the desire to weigh less was not an issue with which most people in Caeden were especially concerned, at least discursively.

2. For developments of these arguments, see Messerschmidt 1999; Monaghan 2005; and Bell and McNaughton 2007.

3. See Bell and McNaughton 2007 for a thorough account of the literature.

4. See Beauvoir 1952; Connell 1987; Doane 1991; Halberstam 1998; and Hole 2003.

5. Interestingly, Jeri and Shane were the only respondents who left the community before I did.

2. Geeks and Freaks

1. See Calhoun 1980 for a notable exception.

2. See Evans 2007 for a review of research on sense of community and psychological sense of community.

3. The date has been changed.

4. In Caeden, the word "pervert" is used widely and positively, in an often conscious effort to reclaim SM from the model of pathology.

5. See Brubaker and Cooper (2000) for a compelling and thorough critique of the use of identity as a category of analysis.

3. Tipping the Scales

1. Both Hopkins and Stear are deconstructing SM as it occurs privately, rather than public SM communities.

2. "Scat" (short for scatophilia) refers to erotic play with feces.

3. In Caeden, not all leathermen are SM participants, and many characterize their activities the way that Weinberg, Williams, and Moser's leathermen did. These particular activities, though, are viewed as SM in both communities in Caeden. As I did not participate in the gay (male) leather scene, I am grateful for the insights of others who are familiar with the national leather community, most notably Boymeat.

4. The general resentment of wankers stems from their explicit and immediate "use" of other people's play for sexual gratification. Many community members express a sense that this behavior "cheapens" their play. Additionally, women in particular tended to be uncomfortable with wanking, often viewing it as symbolic or suggestive of sexual violence.

5. It should be noted that in some D/s relationships, participants do not call their scenes "play," in a deliberate construction of their activities as something more significant than a leisure pursuit.

6. Though it is common to use SM in broad reference to the community and its activities, when talking about play specifically, the term narrows considerably, referring particularly to play that involves pain and anguish in the absence of a de facto hierarchy.

7. In 2002, the film *Secretary* sparked controversy within the Caeden community, for featuring a character struggling with self-mutilation who finds fulfillment in a D/s relationship.

8. This usage refers to play, sexual and romantic engagements, or any combination thereof, with multiple partners.

9. The power of the blacklist in the SM community extends nationally; players with unsafe or otherwise significantly negative reputations can be blacklisted in SM clubs, venues, and private parties within hours.

10. There were several reasons for this. I did not know how to top and could not therefore do it safely. Also, at the beginning of this project, I was most interested in issues of interpersonal power between "submissive" women and "dominant" men. I further expected that with a dual identity as a researcher and a new top, I would have more difficulty finding play partners than as a researcher and new bottom. Significantly, I was unwilling to grapple with IRB issues if my fieldwork involved hitting people. And, finally, I was generally more comfortable ethically with bottoming than with topping.

11. Interestingly, though women are more likely in Caeden to enter the scenes as bottoms as men, they are far more likely to later identify as switches.

4. Fringe Benefits

1. I am indebted to D. J. Williams (2006) for the suggestion that SM might be understood as serious leisure.

2. See Newmahr 2010 for a more detailed analysis of SM in relation to the numerous aspects of serious leisure.

3. "Boi" in the community refers (most often) to a lesbian or an FTM transgendered person with an identity and presentation as an adolescent boy.

4. "Breath play" usually refers to anything that restricts the flow of oxygen, to either the lungs or the brain. This is most commonly accomplished by placing a hand over the bottom's mouth and nose, by applying pressure to the trachea or to the carotid artery, or by covering the bottom's head or face with non-permeable substances such as plastic.

5. Having later witnessed other such situations, I have no cause to suspect that the concern for me was heightened because of my role as a researcher. The community is similarly protective of all newcomers, particularly those who bottom.

6. The hermeneutics here are hotly contested, but I contend that submission is best understood as a particular kind of bottoming, in which the objectives of play are intertwined with experiences of power and powerlessness.

7. See Lewis and Weigert 1985; Misztal 1996; Möllering 2001.

8. Excerpt from interview with John Geirland, "Go with the Flow," *Wired*, September 1996, issue 4.09.

5. Badasses, Servants, and Martyrs

1. The exceptions to this are female dominatrixes.

2. More men top exclusively than bottom exclusively, and more women bottom exclusively than top exclusively. There are women who exclusively top, but the majority of the women I knew who did so were professional dominatrixes, who, again, I am not here considering part of the public SM scene in Caeden.

3. Often in this case, the accusation that the bottom is "topping from the bottom" comes more readily than the identification of the top as a "service top." Both are considered derogatory, but the former is an action rather than an identity and therefore the insult is less severe.

4. The exception to this is bratting, which might be viewed as badass bottoming presented in a more palatable (less overt) way, to preserve the fantasies of powerlessness.

5. I use "post-feminist" to refer to a period in which the word "feminism" and various conceptualizations of meanings of the word became part of the shared vernacular for people outside of academic and activist circles.

6. Another reason that the pro-domme/client relationship differs meaningfully from SM in Caeden is the absence of a gender-subversive space here, for topping in this context is paid service.

7. I claim this as the case overall, but there are important contradictions. For example, though it is generally accepted that tops should bottom before learning to top, this is more actively encouraged, and more actively occurs, among women who top. Men who top are more likely to only top throughout their SM careers.

6. Reconcilable Differences

1. See Dworkin 1981, 1987, and MacKinnon 1987.

2. Although players create their own safewords, the community also, on the whole, accepts a "traffic light" safeword system as a default. "Yellow" means that the scene needs to slow down; the top should check in and be prepared to stop.

7. Collaborating the Edge

1. This is reference to the 1960s sci-fi show *Lost in Space*. It is used to indicate that a person (in the show, the character Will Robinson) is about to make an irreversible mistake.

2. I witnessed this only three times during my fieldwork and was told a handful of stories about other instances in the history of the community.

3. See Kidder 2006; Lois 2001; Ferrell 1995, 2002; Laurendeau 2006; Laurendeau and Van Brunschot 2006; and Lyng 2005.

4. This is not necessarily the case, as was demonstrated in a case in Attleboro, Mass., when tops and bottoms were arrested during a raid of a private party, allegedly on the grounds that a person is not legally permitted to consent to assault.

5. Faye, introduced in chapter 4, had witnessed the death of a man via flogging.

8. "What It Is That We Do"

1. See, e.g., Hatfield 1984; Clark and Reis 1988; Baumeister and Bratslavsky 1999.

2. See Jamieson 1999; Pasko 2002.

3. See Boles and Garbin 1974; Enck and Preston 1988; Ronai and Ellis 1989; Barton 2001; Frank 1998; Pasko 2002.

4. Written by C. Edward Crowther.

5. "Barebacking" is unprotected anal sex, generally in the absence of certainty about the HIV statuses of the participants. "Bug-chasing" is the practice of attempting to become infected with HIV through unprotected sex.

6. I am referring here to murder as social interaction; this analysis is only in regard to one person killing another while both are in one another's physical company.

7. See, e.g., Russell 1982; Rian 1982. See Hopkins 1994 for a thorough summary.

8. See Brownmiller 1975; Dworkin 1981; MacKinnon and Dworkin 1997.

Concluding Notes

1. This is a pseudonym.

2. For exceptions, see Ronai 1998, and the collection of works in Kulick and Wilson, eds., 1995.

Bibliography

Abu-Lughod, Lila. 1986. *Veiled Sentiments: Honor and Poetry in a Bedouin Society.* Berkeley and Los Angeles: University of California Press.

Aldrich, Sarah, and C. Eccleston. 2000. Making Sense of Everyday Pain. *Social Science and Medicine* 50(11): 1631–41.

Anderson, Leon. 1999. The Open Road to Ethnography's Future. *Journal of Contemporary Ethnography* 28(5): 451–59.

———. 2006a. Analytic Autoethnography. *Journal of Contemporary Ethnography* 35(4): 373–95.

———. 2006b. On Apples, Oranges and Autopsies: A Response to Commentators. *Journal of Contemporary Ethnography* 35(4): 450–65.

Athens, Lonnie. 1992. The Creation of Dangerous Violent Criminals. Urbana: University of Illinois Press.

———. 2005. Violent Encounters—Violent Engagements, Skirmishes, and Tiffs. *Journal of Contemporary Ethnography* 34(6): 631–78.

Barton, Bernadette. 2001. Queer Desire in the Sex Industry. *Sexuality and Culture* 5: 3–27.

Baumeister, Roy F. 1988. Masochism as Escape from Self. *Journal of Sex Research* 25(1): 28–59.

Baumeister, Roy F., and E. Bratslavsky. 1999. Passion, Intimacy, and Time: Passionate Love as a Function of Change in Intimacy. *Personality and Social Psychology Review* 3(1): 49–67.

Beauvoir, Simone de. 1952. *The Second Sex.* [1st American ed.] New York: Knopf.

Beck, Ulrich. 1992. *Risk Society: Towards a New Modernity.* Trans. Mark Ritter. London: Sage.

Becker, Howard. 1963. *Outsiders; Studies in the Sociology of Deviance.* London: Free Press of Glencoe.

Bell, K., and D. McNaughton. 2007. Feminism and the Invisible Fat Man. *Body and Society* 13(1): 107.

Berger, Leah. 2001. Inside Out: Narrative Autoethnography as a Path Toward Rapport. *Qualitative Inquiry* 7(4): 504–18.

Berger, Roni. 2000. Gay Stepfamilies: A Triple-Stigmatized Group. *Families in Society—The Journal of Contemporary Human Services* 81(5): 504–16.

Boles, Jacqueline, and A. P. Garbin. 1974. Strip Club and Stripper-Customer Patterns of Interaction. *Sociology and Social Research* 58(2): 136–44.

Bourgois, Philippe I. 1996. *In Search of Respect: Selling Crack in El Barrio.* Cambridge: Cambridge University Press.

Brame, Gloria, W. D. Brame, and J. Jacobs. 1993. *Different Loving: An Exploration of the World of Sexual Dominance and Submission.* 1st ed. New York: Villard Books.

Brekhus, Wayne. 1996. Social Marking and the Mental Coloring of Identity: Sexual Identity Construction and Maintenance in the United States. *Sociological Forum* 11(3): 497–522.

Brownmiller, Susan. 1975. *Against Our Will: Men, Women, and Rape.* New York: Simon and Schuster.

Brubaker, Rogers, and F. Cooper. 2000. Beyond "Identity." *Theory and Society* 29(1): 1–47.

Burnier, DeLysa. 2006. Encounters With the Self in Social Science Research: A Political Scientist Looks at Autoethnography. *Journal of Contemporary Ethnography* 35: 410–18.

Butler, Judith. 1990. *Gender Trouble: Feminism and the Subversion of Identity.* New York: Routledge.

———. 1993. *Bodies That Matter: On the Discursive Limits of Sex.* New York: Routledge.

———. 2004. *Undoing Gender.* New York: Routledge.

Calhoun, Craig. 1980. Community: Toward a Variable Conceptualization for Comparative Research. *Social History* 5: 105–29.

Califia, Pat. 1981. A Personal View of the History of the Lesbian S/M Community and Movement in San Francisco. In *Coming to Power: Writings and Graphics on Lesbian S/M: S/M, a Form of Eroticism Based on a Consensual Exchange of Power.* 3rd U.S. ed., 245–83. Boston: Alyson Publications.

———. 1994. *Public Sex: The Culture of Radical Sex.* 1st ed. Pittsburgh, Pa.: Cleis Press.

———. 2001. *Sensuous Magic: A Guide to S/M for Adventurous Couples.* 2nd ed. San Francisco: Cleis Press.

Chan, Wendy, and G. S. Rigakos. 2002. Risk, Crime and Gender. *British Journal of Criminology* 42(4): 743–61.

Clark, Margaret S., and H. T. Reis. 1988. Interpersonal Processes in Close Relationships. *Annual Review of Psychology* 39: 609–72.

Cohen, Anthony P. 1985. *The Symbolic Construction of Community, Key Ideas.* Chichester: E. Horwood.

Collins, Randall. 2009. *Violence: A Micro-sociological Theory.* Princeton, N.J.: Princeton University Press.

Connell, R.W. 1987. *Gender and Power: Society, the Person, and Sexual Politics.* Cambridge: Polity Press in association with B. Blackwell.

———. 1995. *Masculinities.* Berkeley and Los Angeles: University of California Press.

———. 2002. *Gender: Short Introductions.* Cambridge: Polity.

Connell, R. W., and J. W. Messerschmidt. 2005. Hegemonic Masculinity—Rethinking the Concept. *Gender and Society* 19(6): 829–59.

Cross, Patricia, and K. Matheson. 2006. Understanding Sadomasochism: An Empirical Examination of Four Perspectives. *Journal of Homosexuality* 50(2): 133–66.

Csíkszentmihályi, Mihály. 1991. *Flow: The Psychology of Optimal Experience.* New York: Harper Collins.

Dancer, Peter, P. Kleinplatz, and C. Moser. 2006. 24/7 SM Slavery. *Journal of Homosexuality* 50(2/3): 81–101.

Dean, Tim. 2009. *Unlimited Intimacy: Reflections on the Subculture of Barebacking.* Chicago: University of Chicago Press.

Denzin, Norman. 1989. *Interpretative Interactionism.* London, Sage.

———. 1995. The Experiential Text and the Limits of Visual Understanding. *Educational Theory* 45(1): 7–18.

———. 1997. *Interpretative Ethnography: Ethnographic Practices for the 21st Century.* Thousand Oaks, Calif.: Sage.

———. 2006. Analytic Autoethnography, or Deja Vu All Over Again. *Journal of Contemporary Ethnography* 35(4): 419–28.

Doane, Mary Ann. 1991. *Femmes fatales: Feminism, Film Theory, Psychoanalysis.* New York: Routledge.

Donnelly, D., and J. Fraser. 1998. Gender Differences in Sado-masochistic Arousal among College Students. *Sex Roles* 39(5–6): 391–407.

Donnelly, Peter. 2004. Sport and Risk Culture. In K. Young, ed., *Sporting Bodies, Damaged Selves: Sociological Studies of Sports-Related Injury.* London: Elsevier.

Dorst, John D. 1989. *The Written Suburb: An American Site, an Ethnographic Dilemma, Contemporary Ethnography Series.* Philadelphia: University of Pennsylvania Press.

Downey, Greg. 2007. Producing Pain: Techniques and Technologies in No-Holds-Barred Fighting. *Social Studies of Science* 37(2): 201–26.

Duneier, Mitchell. 1999. *Sidewalk.* 1st ed. New York: Farrar, Straus and Giroux.

Dworkin, Andrea. 1981. *Pornography: Men Possessing Women.* New York: Perigee Books.

———. 1997. *Intercourse.* New York: Simon and Schuster.

Ellis, Carolyn. 1998. *Review of Interpretive Ethnography: Ethnographic Practices for the Twenty-first Century,* by Norman K. Denzin. *Contemporary Sociology* 27(4): 422–24.

———. 2004. *The Ethnographic I: A Methodological Novel about Autoethnography.* Ethnographic Alternatives Book Series 13. Walnut Creek, Calif.: AltaMira Press.

Ellis, Havelock. 1927. *Studies in the Psychology of Sex.* Vol. 3 (of 6). Philadelphia: F. A. Davis.

Enck, Graves E., and J. D. Preston. 1988. Counterfeit Intimacy—a Dramaturgical Analysis of an Erotic Performance. *Deviant Behavior* 9(4): 369–81.

Erikson, Erik H. 1950. *Childhood and Society.* [1st ed.] New York: Norton.

Evans, Scott D. 2007. Youth Sense of Community: Voice and Power in Community Contexts. *Journal of Community Psychology* 35(6): 693–709.

Ferrell, Jeff. 1995. Urban Graffiti—Crime, Control, and Resistance. *Youth and Society* 27(1): 73–92.

———. 1996. *Crimes of Style: Urban Graffiti and the Politics of Criminality.* Boston: Northeastern University Press

———. 2002. *Tearing Down the Streets.* New York: Palgrave/St. Martin's/MacMillan.

———. 2005. The Only Possible Adventure: Edgework and Anarchy. In *Edgework: The Sociology of Risk Taking,* ed. S. Lyng, 75–88. New York: Routledge.

Ferrell, Jeff, D. Milovanovic, and S. Lyng. 2001. Edgework, Media Practices, and the Elongation of Meaning: A Theoretical Ethnography of the Bridge Day Event. *Theoretical Criminology* 5(2): 177–202.

Fine, Gary A. 1983. *Shared Fantasy: Role-Playing Games as Social Worlds.* Chicago: University of Chicago Press.

Foote, Nelson, N. 1954. Sex as Play. *Social Problems* 1(4): 159–63.

Foucault, Michel. 1978. *The History of Sexuality.* 1st American ed. New York: Pantheon Books.

Frank, Katherine. 1998. The Production of Identity and the Negotiation of Intimacy in a "Gentleman's Club." *Sexualities* 1(2): 175–201.

———. 2000. The Management of Hunger: Using Fiction in Writing Anthropology. *Qualitative Inquiry* 6(4): 474–88.

———. 2002. *G-Strings and Sympathy: Strip Club Regulars and Male Desire.* Durham, N.C.: Duke University Press.

———. 2007. Thinking Critically about Strip Club Research. *Sexualities* 10(4): 501–17.

Freud, Sigmund. 1953 [1905. *Three Essays on the Theory of Sexuality.* Standard ed. Vol. 7. Trans. J. Strachey. Reprint, London: Hogarth.

———. 1938. Sadism and Masochism. In *Basic Writings of Sigmund Freud,* ed. A. A. Brill. New York: Modern Library.

Gailey, Jeannine. 2009. Starving Is the Most Fun a Girl Can Have: The Pro-Ana Subculture as Edgework. *Critical Criminology* 17(2): 93–108.

Gans, Herbert. 1999. Participant Observation in the Era of "Ethnography." *Journal of Contemporary Ethnography* 28(5): 540–48.

Garfinkel, Harold. 1967. *Studies in Ethnomethodology.* Englewood Cliffs, N.J.: Prentice-Hall.

Geertz, Clifford. 1973. *The Interpretation of Cultures.* New York: Basic Books.

Geirland, J. 1996. Go with the Flow. *Wired,* September, issue 4.09.

Giddens, Anthony. 1992. *The Transformation of Intimacy: Sexuality, Love, and Eroticism in Modern Societies.* Stanford, Calif.: Stanford University Press.

Goffman, Erving. 1959a. The Moral Career of the Mental Patient. *Psychiatry: Journal for Studies of Interpersonal Processes* 23: 123–35.

———. 1959b. *The Presentation of Self in Everyday Life.* Garden City, N.Y.: Doubleday.

———. 1963. *Stigma: Notes on the Management of Spoiled Identity.* Englewood Cliffs, N.J.: Prentice-Hall.

———. 1967. *Interaction Ritual; Essays on Face-to-Face Behavior.* [1st ed.] Garden City, N.Y.: Anchor Books.

———. 1974. *Frame Analysis: An Essay on the Organization of Experience.* New York: Harper and Row.

———. 1976. Gender Advertisements. *Studies in the Anthropology of Visual Communication* 3(2): 64–154.

———. 1977. Arrangement between Sexes. *Theory and Society* 4(3): 301–31.

Halberstam, Judith. 1998. *Female Masculinity.* Durham, N.C.: Duke University Press.

Hatfield, Elaine. 1984. The Dangers of Intimacy. In *Communication, Intimacy and Close Relationships*, ed. V. Derlaga, 207–20. New York: Praeger.

Hardy, Simon. 2000. Feminist Iconoclasm and the Problem of Eroticism. *Sexualities* 3(1): 77–96.

Hayano, David M. 1979. Auto-Ethnography—Paradigms, Problems, and Prospects. *Human Organization* 38(1): 99–104.

Hole, Anne. 2003. Performing Identity: Dawn French and the Funny Fat Female Body. *Feminist Media Studies* 3(3): 315–28.

Honigmann, John J. 1954. An Anthropological Approach to Sex. *Social Problems* 2(1): 7–16.

Hopkins, Patrick D. 1994. Rethinking Sadomasochism: Feminism, Interpretation, and Simulation. *Hypatia* 9(1): 116–41.

Jackman, Mary R. 2002. Violence in Social Life. *Annual Review of Sociology* 28: 387–415.

Jamieson, Lynn. 1999. Intimacy Transformed? A Critical Look at the "Pure Relationship." *Sociology—The Journal of the British Sociological Association* 33(3): 477–94.

Jarvie, Ian Charles. 1988. Comment on Sangren's "Rhetoric and the Authority of Ethnography." *Current Anthropology* 29: 427–29.

Kamel, G. W. L. 1980. Leather-Sex—Meaningful Aspects of Gay Sadomasochism. *Deviant Behavior* 1(2): 171–91.

Katz, Jack. 1988. *Seductions of Crime: Moral and Sensual Attractions in Doing Evil.* New York: Basic Books.

Kidder, J. L. 2006. It's the Job That I Love: Bike Messengers and Edgework. *Sociological Forum* 21(1): 31–54.

Klein, Marty, and C. Moser. 2006. SM (Sadomasochistic) Interests as an Issue in a Child Custody Proceeding. *Journal of Homosexuality* 50(2): 233–42.

Kleinplatz, Peggy J. 2006. Learning from Extraordinary Lovers: Lessons from the Edge. *Journal of Homosexuality* 50(2–3): 325–48.

Krafft-Ebbing, R. 1965 [1886]. *Psychopathia Sexualis.* Ed. F. S. Klaf. Reprint, London: Staples Press.

Kulick, Don. 1995. The Sexual Life of Anthropologists: Erotic Subjectivity and Ethnographic Work. In *Taboo: Sex, Identity and Erotic Subjectivity in Anthropological Fieldwork,* ed. D. Kulick and M. Willson. London: Routledge.

Kulick, Don, and M. Wilson, eds. 1995. *Taboo: Sex, Identity and Erotic Subjectivity in Anthropological Fieldwork.* London: Routledge.

Langdridge, Darren. 2005. The Erotic Construction of Power Exchange. *Journal of Constructivist Psychology* 18: 65–73.

———. 2006. Voices from the Margins: Sadomasochism and Sexual Citizenship. *Citizenship Studies* 10(4): 373–89.

Langdridge, Darren, and Trevor Butt. 2004. A Hermeneutic Phenomenological Investigation of the Construction of Sadomasochistic Identities. *Sexualities* 7(1): 31–53.

Laurendeau, Jason. 2006. He Didn't Go in Doing a Skydive: Sustaining the Illusion of Control in an Edgework Activity. *Sociological Perspectives* 49(4): 583–605.

———. 2008. Gendered Risk Regimes: A Theoretical Consideration of Edgework and Gender. *Sociology of Sport Journal* 25(3): 293–309.

Laurendeau, Jason, and E. G. Van Brunschot. 2006. Policing the Edge: Risk and Social Control in Skydiving. *Deviant Behavior* 27(2): 173–201.

Lerum, Kari. 2001. Subjects of Desire: Academic Armor, Intimate Ethnography, and the Production of Critical Knowledge. *Qualitative Inquiry* 7(4): 466–83.

Lewis, J. David, and A. Weigert. 1985. Trust as a Social-Reality. *Social Forces* 63(4): 967–85.

Linden, Robin R. 1982. *Against Sadomasochism: A Radical Feminist Analysis.* East Palo Alto, Calif.: Frog in the Well.

Lois, Jennifer. 2001. Managing Emotions, Intimacy, and Relationships in a Volunteer Search and Rescue Group. *Journal of Contemporary Ethnography* 30(2): 131–79.

———. 2003. *Heroic Efforts: The Emotional Culture of Search and Rescue Volunteers.* New York: New York University Press.

Luhmann, Niklas. 1979. *Trust and Power.* London: Pitman.

———. 1993. *Risk: A Sociological Theory, Communication and Social Order.* New York: A. de Gruyter.

Lupton, Deborah. 1999. *Risk, Key Ideas.* London: Routledge.

Lyng, Stephen. 1990. Edgework: A Social Psychological Analysis of Voluntary Risk-Taking. *American Journal of Sociology* 95(4): 851–86.

———. 1991. Edgework Revisited: Reply. *American Journal of Sociology* 96(6): 1534–39.

———. 1993. Dysfunctional Risk Taking: Criminal Behavior as Edgework. In *Adolescent Risk Taking,* ed. N. Bell and R. Bell, 107–30. Newbury Park: Sage.

———. 2004. Crime, Edgework and Corporeal Transaction. *Theoretical Criminology* 8(3): 359–75.

———. 2005. *Edgework: The Sociology of Risk Taking.* New York: Routledge.

MacKinnon, Catharine. 1987. *Feminism Unmodified: Discourses on Life and Law.* Cambridge, Mass.: Harvard University Press.

———. 1989. Sexuality, Pornography and Method: Pleasure under Patriarchy. *Ethics* 99 (January): 314–46.

MacKinnon, Catharine, and A. Dworkin. 1997. *In Harm's Way: The Pornography Civil Rights Hearings.* Cambridge, Mass.: Harvard University Press.

Manzo, John. 2004. On the Sociology and Social Organization of Stigma: Some Ethnomethodological Insights. *Human Studies* 27: 401–16.

Masfield, Nick. 1997. *Masochism: The Art of Power.* Westport, Conn.: Praeger.

McMillan, D. W., and D. M. Chavis. 1986. Sense of Community: A Definition and Theory. *Journal of Community Psychology* 14(1): 6–23.

Messerschmidt, James W. 1999. Making Bodies Matter: Adolescent Masculinities, the Body, and Varieties of Violence. *Theoretical Criminology* 3(2): 197–220.

———. 2000. *Nine Lives: Adolescent Masculinities, the Body and Violence.* Boulder, Colo.: Westview.

———. 2004. *Flesh and Blood: Adolescent Gender Diversity and Violence.* Lanham, Md.: Rowman and Littlefield.

Miller, Eleanor M. 1991. Edgework Revisited. *American Journal of Sociology* 96(6): 1534–39.

Miller, W. J. 2005. Adolescents on the Edge: The Sensual Side of Delinquency. In *Edgework: The Sociology of Risk-Taking,* ed. S. Lyng, 153–72. New York: Routledge.

Misztal, Barbara A. 1996. *Trust in Modern Societies: The Search for the Bases of Social Order.* Cambridge: Polity.

Möllering, Guido. 2001. The Nature of Trust: From Georg Simmel to a Theory of Expectation, Interpretation and Suspension. *Sociology.* 35(2): 403–20.

Monaghan, Lee F. 2005. Risk and Everyday Life. *Health Risk and Society* 7(4): 413–14.

Moser, Charles. 1998. S/M (Sadomasochistic) Interactions in Semi-public Settings. *Journal of Homosexuality* 36(2): 19–29.

Murray, Samantha. 2004. Locating Aesthetics: Sexing the Fat Woman. *Social Semiotics* 14(3): 237–47.

———. 2005. (Un/Be)Coming Out? Rethinking Fat Politics. *Social Semiotics* 15: 153–63.

Newmahr, Staci. 2008. Becoming a Sadomasochist: Integrating Self and Other in Ethnographic Analysis. *Journal of Contemporary Ethnography* 37(5): 619–43.

———. 2010. Rethinking Kink: Sadomasochism as Serious Leisure. *Qualitative Sociology* 33(3): 313–31.

———. 2010. Power Struggles: Pain and Authenticity in SM. *Symbolic Interaction* 33(3), 389–411.

Newton, Esther. 1993. "My Best Informant's Dress: The Erotic Equation in Fieldwork" *Cultural Anthropology* 8:1, 3–23

Nichols, Jeanette, D. Pagano, and M. Rossoff. 1982. Is Sadomasochism Feminist? A Critique of the Samois Position. In *Against Sadomasochism,* ed. R. R. Linden et al., 137–45. Palo Alto: Frog in the Well.

Nordling, Niklas, et al. 2006. Differences and Similarities between Gay and Straight Individuals Involved in the Sadomasochistic Subculture. *Journal of Homosexuality* 50(2–3): 41–57.

O'Donnell, Ian. 2003. A New Paradigm for Understanding Violence? Testing the Limits of Lonnie Athens's Theory. *British Journal of Criminology* 43(4): 750–71.

Pasko, Lisa. 2002. Naked Power: The Practice of Stripping as a Confidence Game. *Sexualities* 5(1): 49–66.

Plummer, Kenneth. 1995. *Telling Sexual Stories: Power, Change, and Social Worlds.* London: Routledge.

Prieur, Annick. 1998. *Mema's House, Mexico City: On Transvestites, Queens, and Machos.* Chicago: University of Chicago Press.

Rajah, V. 2006. Respecting Boundaries: The Symbolic and Material Concerns of Drug-Involved Women Employing Violence against Violent Male Partners. *British Journal of Criminology* 46(5): 837–58.

Register, Lisa M., and T. B. Henley. 1992. The Phenomenology of Intimacy. *Journal of Social and Personal Relationships* 9(4): 467–81.

Rian, Karen. 1982. Sadomasochism and the Social Construction of Desire. In *Against Sadomasochism,* ed. R. R. Linden et al., 45–49. Palo Alto: Frog in the Well.

Rice, Carla. 2007. Becoming "the Fat Girl": Acquisition of an Unfit Identity. *Women's Studies International Forum* 30(2): 158–74.

Rinehart, Robert. 1998. Fictional Methods in Ethnography: Believability, Specks of Glass and Chekhov. *Qualitative Inquiry* 47(2): 200–224.

Ronai, Carol. 1995. Multiple Reflections of Child Sex Abuse. *Journal of Contemporary Ethnography* 23(4): 395–426.

———. 1997. On Loving and Hating My Mentally Retarded Mother. *Mental Retardation* 35(6): 417–32.

———. 1998. Sketching with Derrida: An Ethnography of a Researcher/Erotic Dancer. *Qualitative Inquiry* 4(3): 405–20.

Ronai, Carol R., and R. Cross. 1998. Dancing with Identity: Narrative Resistance in the Discourse of Male and Female Striptease Dancers. *Deviant Behavior* 18(2): 99–119.

Ronai, Carol R., and C. Ellis. 1989. Turn-Ons for Money—Interactional Strategies of the Table Dancer. *Journal of Contemporary Ethnography* 18(3): 271–98.

Russell, Diane E. H. 1982. Sadomasochism: A Contra-feminist Activity. In *Against Sadomasochism: A Radical Feminist Analysis,* ed. R. R. Linden: 176–80. San Francisco: Frog in the Well.

Ryang, Sonia. 2000. "Ethnography or Self-cultural Anthropology?: Reflections on Writing About Ourselves." *Dialectical Anthropology* 25: 297–320.

Sacher-Masoch, Leopold. 2000 [1870]. *Venus in Furs.* Trans. Joachim Neugroschel. New York: Penguin, 2000.

Sade, Donatien-Alphonse Francois. 1965. *The Complete Justine, Philosophy in the Bedroom and Other Writings.* New York: Grove.

———. 1966. *The One Hundred and Twenty Days of Sodom and Other Writings.* Trans. A. Wainhouse and R. Seaver. New York: Grove.

SAMOIS (Organization). 1981. *Coming to Power: Writings and Graphics on Lesbian S/M: S/M, a Form of Eroticism Based on a Consensual Exchange of Power.* 3rd U.S. ed. Boston: Alyson Publications.

Sandnabba, N. Kenneth., P. Santtila, and N. Nordling. 1999. Sexual Behavior and Social Adaptation among Sadomasochistically-Oriented Males. *Journal of Sex Research* 36(3): 273–82.

Sandnabba, N. Kenneth., et al. 2002. Characteristics of a Sample of Sadomasochistically-Oriented Males with Recent Experience of Sexual Contact with Animals. *Deviant Behavior* 23(6): 511–29.

Scarry, Elaine. 1985. *The Body in Pain: The Making and Unmaking of the World.* New York: Oxford University Press.

Scott, Gini Graham. 1983. *Dominant Women Submissive Men: An Exploration in Erotic Dominance and Submission.* New York: Praeger.

Seham, A. E. 2001. *Whose Improv Is It Anyway: Beyond Second City.* Jackson: University Press of Mississippi.

Shaw, Andrea E. 2006. *The Embodiment of Disobedience: Fat Black Women's Unruly Political Bodies.* Lanham, Md.: Lexington Books.

Simmel, Georg. 1907. *The Philosophy of Money.* Ed. D. Frisby. 2nd enl. ed. London: Routledge.

———. 1950. *The Sociology of Georg Simmel.* Ed. K. H. Wolff. Glencoe, Ill.: Free Press.

Sisson, Kathy, and C. Moser. 2005. Women Who Engage in S/M Interactions for Money: A Descriptive Study. *Lesbian and Gay Psychology Review* 6(3): 209–26.

Stanko, Elizabeth A. 1985. *Intimate Intrusions: Women's Experience of Male Violence.* London: Routledge and Kegan Paul.

———. 1987. Typical Violence, Normal Precaution: Men, Women and Interpersonal Violence in England, Wales, Scotland and the USA. In *Women, Violence and Social Control,* ed. J. Hanmer and M. Maynard, 121–34. London: Macmillan.

———. 1990. *Everyday Violence.* London: Pandora Press.

———. 1993. Women, Violence and Social-Change. *British Journal of Criminology* 33(3): 449–50.

———. 1995. Women, Crime, and Fear. *Annals of the American Academy of Political and Social Science* 539: 46–58.

———. 1997. Safety Talk: Conceptualizing Women's Risk Assessment as a "Technology of the Soul." *Theoretical Criminology* 1: 479–99.

Stear, Nils-Hennes. 2009. Sadomasochism as "Make-Believe." *Hypatia* 24(2): 21–38.

Stebbins, Robert A. 1982. Serious Leisure: A Conceptual Statement. *Pacific Sociological Review* 25(2): 251–72.

———. 1992. *Amateurs, Professionals, and Serious Leisure.* Montreal: McGill-Queen's University Press.

———. 1997. Exploratory Research as an Antidote to Theoretical Stagnation in Leisure Studies. *Loisir and Societe—Society and Leisure* 20(2): 421–34.

———. 2005. Choice and Experiential Definitions of Leisure. *Leisure Sciences* 27(4): 349–52.

———. 2007. *Serious Leisure: A Perspective for Our Time.* New Brunswick, N.J.: Transaction Publishers.

———. 2008. Right Leisure: Serious, Casual, or Project-Based? *Neurorehabilitation* 23(4): 335–41.

Stoltenberg, John. 1982. Sadomasochism: Eroticized Violence, Eroticized Powerlessness. In *Against Sadomasochism,* ed. R. R. Linden et al., 124–30. Palo Alto: Frog in the Well.

Strathern, Marilyn. 1987. The Limits of Auto-Anthropology. In *Anthropology at Home,* ed. Anthony Jackson, 16–37. ASA Monographs 25. London: Tavistock.

Taylor, G. W. 1997. The Discursive Construction and Regulation of Dissident Sexualities: The Case of SM. In *Body Talk: The Material and Discursive Regulation of Sexuality, Madness and Reproduction,* ed. J. M. Ussher, 106–30. London: Routledge.

Taylor, G. W., and J. M. Ussher. 2001. Making Sense of S&M: A Discourse Analytic Account. *Sexualities* 4(3): 293–314.

Tedlock, Barbara. 1991. From Participant Observation to the Observation of Participation: The Emergence of Narrative Ethnography. *Journal of Anthropological Research* 47(1): 69–94.

———. 2004. Narrative Ethnography as Social Science Discourse. *Studies in Symbolic Interaction* 27: 23–31.

Thorne, Barrie. 1993. *Gender Play: Girls and Boys in School.* New Brunswick, N.J.: Rutgers University Press.

Truscott, Carol. 1991. S/M: Some Questions and a Few Answers. In *Leatherfolk: Radical Sex, People, Politics, and Practice,* ed. M. Thompson, 15–37. Los Angeles: Daedalus.

Van Maanen, John. 1988. *Tales of the Field: On Writing Ethnography.* Chicago: University of Chicago Press.

———. 1995. *Representation in Ethnography.* Thousand Oaks, Calif.: Sage.

Wacquant, Loic. 2004. *Body and Soul: Notebooks of an Apprentice Boxer.* Oxford: Oxford University Press.

Wagner, Sally Roesch. 1982. Pornography and the Sexual Revolution: The Backlash of Sadomasochism. In *Against Sadomasochism,* ed. R. R. Linden et al., 23–40. Palo Alto: Frog in the Well.

Walklate, Sandra. 1997. Risk and Criminal Victimization—a Modernist Dilemma? *British Journal of Criminology* 37(1): 35–45.

Weinberg, Martin S., C. J. Williams, and C. Moser. 1984. The Social Constituents of Sadomasochism. *Social Problems* 31(4): 379–89.

Weinberg, Thomas S. 1978. Sadism and Masochism: Sociological Perspectives. *Bulletin of the American Academy of Psychiatry and the Law* 6: 284–95.

———. 1995. *S & M: Studies in Dominance and Submission.* [Rev. ed.] Amherst, N.Y.: Prometheus Book.

———. 2006. Sadomasochism and the Social Sciences: A Review of the Sociological and Social Psychological Literature. *Journal of Homosexuality* 50(2): 17–40.

Weinberg, Thomas, and G. Falk. 1980. The Social Organisation of Sadism and Masochism. *Deviant Behavior* 1: 379–93.

Weinberg, Thomas, and M. Magill. 1995. Sadomasochistic Themes in Mainstream Culture. In *S&M: Studies in Dominance and Submission,* ed. T. Weinberg, 223–30. New York: Prometheus.

Weiss, Margot. 2006a. Mainstreaming Kink: The Politics of BDSM Representation in U.S. Popular Media. *Journal of Homosexuality* 50(2/3).

———. 2006b. Working at Play: BDSM Sexuality in the San Francisco Bay Area. *Anthropologica* 8: 229–45.

West, Candace, and D. H. Zimmerman. 1987. Doing Gender. *Gender and Society* 1(2): 125–51.

Wilkins, Amy C. 2008. *Wannabes, Goths, and Christians: The Boundaries of Sex, Style, and Status.* Chicago: University of Chicago Press.

Williams, D. J. 2006. Different (Painful) Strokes for Different Folks: A General Overview of Sexual Sadomasochism (SM) and Its Diversity. *Sexual Addiction and Compulsivity* 13(4): 333–46.

———. 2009. Deviant Leisure: Rethinking the Good, the Bad, and the Ugly. *Leisure Sciences* 31(2): 207–13.

Wiseman, Jay. 1998. *SM 101: A Realistic Introduction.* San Francisco: Greenery Press.

Wolf, Naomi. 1993. *Fire with Fire: The New Female Power and How It Will Change the 21st Century.* New York: Random House.

Zborowski, M. 1969. *People in Pain.* [1st ed.] San Francisco: Jossey-Bass.

Zussman, Robert. 2004. People in Places. *Qualitative Sociology* 27(4): 351–63.

Index

Staci Newmahr is an ethnographer. Her work plays with intersections of risk, eroticism, and gender. She is currently Assistant Professor of Sociology at Buffalo State College.